W9-AFW-835

The Body in Question

Why is there currently such strong academic and popular interest in 'the body' in contemporary societies? What factors shape our conceptions of the body, its naturalness, health and normality? What is the mind-body dualism and why should it matter?

This book examines these and other body questions from a critical socio-cultural perspective. In particular, it shows how conceptions of the body are affected by processes of individualisation, medicalisation, and commodification. Chapters discuss the impact of new biomedical technologies on the notion of the natural body, efforts to reshape and perfect the body, the role of the media in 'framing' body issues, processes of body classification, the impact of consumerism on concepts of health, healing and self-care, and the implications of theoretical and practical efforts to 'integrate' mind and body.

The book will be an invaluable introduction for those seeking to understand the social, cultural and political significance of 'the body' in contemporary society.

Alan Petersen is Professor of Sociology, and Research Coordinator, in the School of Law and Social Sciences, The University of Plymouth.

The Body in Question
A Socio-Cultural Approach

Alan Petersen

Routledge
Taylor & Francis Group

LONDON AND NEW YORK

First published 2007
by Routledge
2 Park Square, Milton Park, Abingdon, Oxon, OX14 4RN

Simultaneously published in the USA and Canada
by Routledge
270 Madison Ave, New York, NY 10016

Transferred to Digital Printing in 2008

Routledge is an imprint of the Taylor & Francis Group

© 2007 Alan Petersen

Typeset in Sabon
by Keystroke, 28 High Street, Tettenhall, Wolverhampton
Printed and bound in Great Britain
by Antony Rowe Ltd, Chippenham, Wiltshire

All rights reserved. No part of this book may be reprinted or
reproduced or utilised in any form or by any electronic, mechanical,
or other means, now known or hereafter invented, including
photocopying and recording, or in any information storage or
retrieval system, without permission in writing from the publishers.

British Library Cataloguing in Publication Data
A catalogue record for this book is available from the British Library

Library of Congress Cataloging in Publication Data
Petersen, Alan, 1953–
The body in question : a socio-cultural approach / Alan Petersen.
p. cm.
Includes bibliographical references and index.
ISBN 0–415–32161–1 (hardcover) – ISBN 0–415–32162–X (soft cover)
1. Body, Human–Social aspects. 2. Body, Human (Philosophy) I. Title
HM636.P47 2007
306.4–dc22   2006021514

ISBN10: 0–415–32161–1 (hbk)
ISBN10: 0–415–32162–X (pbk)

ISBN13: 978–0–415–32161–7 (hbk)
ISBN13: 978–0–415–32162–4 (pbk)

Contents

Acknowledgements

I would like to thank my colleagues at the University of Plymouth who have helped create a congenial context for research and writing. I thank Iain Wilkinson for his lively discussions and generosity in sharing ideas, and Constance Sutherland at Routledge for her patience. I am grateful to Richard Pannell for his stimulating conversations and for allowing me to borrow his books. As always, I am indebted to Ros Porter for her love and support.

1 The body in question
An introduction

Computerising the body: Microsoft wins patent to exploit network potential of skin

Fact or fiction – carrying a keyboard on your arm

Call it the ultimate wireless network. From the ends of your fingers to the tips of your toes, the human body is a moving, throbbing collection of tubes and tunnels, filled with salty water and all capable of transmitting the lifeblood of the 21st century: information.

In what may seem a move too far to some, the computer software giant Microsoft has been granted exclusive rights to this ability of the body to act as a computer network. Two weeks ago the company was awarded US Patent 6,754,472, which bears the title: Method and apparatus for transmitting power and data using the human body.

Microsoft envisages using the human skin's conductive properties to link a host of electronic devices around the body, from pagers and personal data assistants (PDA) to mobile phones, although the company is uncharacteristically coy about exactly what it may have in mind.

(Adam 2004: 3)

Top athletes seek gene therapy boost

Sports stars could use cutting-edge technology developed to help patients as an 'undetectable' doping method

Several international-level athletes have approached leading American scientists and asked them to modify their bodies genetically to turn them into unbeatable sportsmen.

The revelation has stunned sporting organisations, for it shows sportsmen are already trying to use ground-breaking genetic techniques – aimed at saving patients' lives by altering the make-up of their DNA – to boost physique and stamina.

Olympic authorities said yesterday that they feared genetically-enhanced sprinters, swimmers and other contestants will become

commonplace. There is even a risk that a few may compete – undetected
– at next month's Olympic Games in Athens.

(Campbell and McKie 2004: 5)

Uproar over IVF woman expecting a baby at 63

A psychiatrist who is due to become Britain's oldest mother at the age
of 63, was criticised last night by IVF groups, sociologists and even a
family member.

Despite insisting that 'a great deal of thought' had gone into her
decision to have a baby, Dr Patricia Rashbrook was described as 'mad'
and selfish for wanting to become a mother again at such a com-
paratively advanced age.

(Sapsted 2006: 1)

These excerpts from stories appearing in British national newspapers in
recent years provide some insight into the substantial interest in issues
pertaining to the human body in many contemporary societies. They serve
to highlight a number of themes that frequently run through discussions
about the body, regardless of the specific topic under consideration. These
include the question of the 'naturalness' and modifiability of the body
particularly in light of recent developments in biomedicine and biotechnology; changing conceptions of the human; expectations about science and its
power to alter or control the natural; the mediation of the body in popular
culture (e.g. news stories such as the above); the blurring of fact and fiction
in portrayals of the body; the relationship between the mind and the body;
and the significance of the economic, political and social contexts shaping
body classification, regulation and modification. Perhaps more fundamentally, such stories raise the question, why has 'the body' come to achieve
such prominence in everyday life and what can we learn from this about the
structure and dynamics of contemporary society? This book explores these
and a number of other themes and discusses their implications, drawing on
ideas from diverse fields of study and using a range of empirical examples.
To begin, this chapter discusses the context and rationale for this book,
outlines the assumptions and perspectives which guide my argument, and
then finishes with an outline of the chapters that follow.

Contemporary interest in 'the body'

The late 1980s and early 1990s saw a burgeoning number of discussions
about and events focusing on 'the body' which have continued into the
twenty-first century. New books and journals have been published and new
courses have explored various aspects of the body in its social contexts.
Theoretical contributions in this area have been substantial (e.g. Crossley
2001; Falk 1994; Featherstone *et al.* 1991; Mellor and Shilling 1997; Shilling

1993; Turner 1992, 1996; Williams and Bendelow 1998). Some areas of academic scholarship, such as feminism and sexuality studies, brought 'the body' into the core of their analyses and scholars began to assert the importance of developing 'embodied' theories. In 1995, a specialist journal in the field, *Body and Society*, edited by Mike Featherstone and Bryan Turner, was launched, and a number of specialist centres of study on the body and society were established. The body has figured prominently in the performing and visual arts, with exhibitions and performances exploring the body in its many dimensions – representational, expressive, and sensorial. Most spectacularly, the work of performance artists such as Stellarc, Orlan, and Von Hagens explored the manipulation, modification, and portrayal of the body enabled by new technologies and the surgical techniques of biomedicine. In the UK, in recent years, a growing number of television programmes, including *Anatomy for Beginners*, *Body Shock*, *Ten Years Younger*, *You Are What You Eat*, and *Extreme Makeover*, have been broadcast, underlining the apparently endless fascination with matters to do with the body, its representation, structure and functioning.

While there have been many useful contributions from different fields, the range of questions asked about 'the body' has been limited by a series of widely shared assumptions and approaches to emergent issues. The academic disciplines and perspectives applied to this field thus far have been considerable. Sociology, anthropology, psychology, feminism, history, politics, cultural studies, media studies, and performance studies are among contributing disciplines or fields of study, illuminating questions about the meanings and significance of the body in contemporary society. However, in my view, much of this recent work fails to engage with a number of significant body-related matters, especially the impact of new perspectives on the nature and workings of the body and of the growing use of new technologies of the body on how health, illness and normality are understood. There is a need for a thorough analysis of the economic, political, social, and justice implications of the increasing deployment of new biomedical procedures and biotechnologies for modifying and regulating bodies. This should include investigation of the diverse responses to the implications of current ways of understanding, intervening into and changing bodies. The pervasiveness of biological – particularly genetic – explanations of health and behaviour, promulgated via the media and other avenues, is arguably having a far-reaching impact on how people perceive processes of life and the possibilities for prevention, treatment or cure. Widespread fears about the consequences of 'tampering with nature', for example, are reflected in news and other popular cultural depictions of new biotechnology developments and in surveys designed to elicit public opinions on new developments. In recent years, the neurosciences have attracted growing interest, with media reports suggesting that new technologies will allow experts to 'read minds', explain differences (e.g. between men and women) and offer new treatments (see Chapter 2). Further, many commentators anticipate a range of nanotechnology innovations in medicine in the future which, according to proponents, will change the way we think about mechanisms of body repair and drug delivery. Insofar as the normative and justice implications of new biomedical and biotechnology developments and their portrayal are considered at all, discussion tends to be restricted by the frameworks of biomedicine, bioethics, and philosophy. Bioethics, which has achieved increasing influence in deliberations on the impacts of biomedicine and biotechnologies, has been dominated by certain prevalent assumptions and questions which serve to 'narrow' debate about the substantive questions raised by developments such as those described (see, e.g. Evans 2002; Lopez 2004; Corrigan 2003; Petersen 2005a). As Duster notes, ethicists have a 'trained incapacity' to see the social, cultural and political contexts that shape developments (2003: 156–157). The far-reaching personal and social implications of the tendency to treat the body as a commodity and as modifiable through medical interventions, though widely acknowledged in the literature, need exploration. The question of how publics may engage in debates about developments that arguably significantly affect everyone has been largely ignored. Unfortunately, in studies, 'the body' is often abstracted from everyday contexts and people's everyday concerns and experiences. Indeed, to talk about 'the body' at all in isolation from the person and from social, political, historical and global contexts invites such reification, objectification and abstraction – a point to which I will return at various times in the book.

Of course, there are notable exceptions to what I have described. Over the years, the socio-political and justice implications of particular theories of bodily difference and of efforts to regulate the bodies of certain groups – women, gay and lesbians, racial and ethnic minorities, and disabled people – through biomedical, psychological and other expertise and systems of classification have figured prominently in the writings of feminist scholars, sexuality scholars, 'race' and ethnicity scholars, and disability scholars. Those contributing to these fields are concerned with the implications of particular ways of understanding and intervening into bodies and with connecting theory and practice with the aim of bringing about change. For example, historical investigation has been undertaken by scholars who aim to disrupt and challenge the self-evidence of our current ways of thinking about 'the body' and its regulations by showing that they are neither inevitable nor fixed. Some of these contributions will be referred to below and in the chapters that follow. However, much social science work on 'the body' fails to articulate a view on history, the workings of politics and power and the normative and justice implications of body-related developments. I would argue that recent shifts in politics combined with innovations in biomedicine, biotechnology and information and communication technologies (ICTs), profoundly challenge established ways of thinking about the body, its workings and capacity, and call for new approaches and questions in this area.

The politicisation of 'the body'

Recent developments such as those outlined above highlight the increasing *politicisation* of 'the body' in everyday life. By this I mean that there is growing debate and contestation in relation to the nature and representation of 'the body' in culture as well as a growing concern with the regulation and control of bodies among diverse authorities. Social science work on the media and consumerism, as well as feminist work, has highlighted the meanings that attach to bodies and their performance and portrayals. With the growing emphasis on consumption rather than production as the basis for group affiliation and personal identity in contemporary societies, the question of how the body is portrayed and who controls and promotes these portrayals has become increasingly contentious. In a highly mediated and consumer-oriented context, images as much as material entities and services become the currency of exchange and consumption. The significance of the body as a consumer object was highlighted by Jean Baudrillard in his influential text *The Consumer Society: Myths and Structures* (Baudrillard 1998: Chapter 8) which was originally published in 1970. This book seems to have anticipated the growing significance of the body in consumer culture and its treatment as a commodified object. As Baudrillard argued, after centuries of denial of the body and efforts to persuade people that they had no bodies, in consumer culture 'there is a relentless effort to *convince them of their bodies*' (1998: 129; emphasis in original). Whereas once salvation was to be achieved by a focus on the soul and the denial of bodily desires and pleasures, 'the body today has become an *object of salvation*' (1998: 129; emphasis in original). People have become consumers of their own bodies. Baudrillard noted the prominence of the body in advertising, fashion and mass culture and the obsession with health, diet, therapy, youth, virility, treatments, and so on. In his view, the body has been reduced to an aesthic/erotic exchange value, which affects both the male and the female, although in somewhat different ways and to different degrees (1998: 136). Health and fitness become not so much biological imperatives, but rather social imperatives linked to status, while medicine becomes a means to 'narcissistic investment and prestige display' (1998: 138–139). Slimness has also become an obses-sion, and the means to achieve slimness – diet, exercise regimes – provide the basis for a range of new consumer goods and services. (For a discussion on the contemporary obsession with body shape and size, including the 'obesity epidemic', see Chapter 3.) Baudrillard viewed sex as a central element of this new consumer culture, thus anticipating the view of other, later writers such as Michel Foucault. As he noted, 'sex sells', as seen most explicitly in pornography, but also in the symbols and fantasies of advertising which are ubiquitous and help to sell even the most mundane items (1998: 143–150).

From the late 1960s, feminists began to draw attention to the tendency to objectify and commodify *women's* bodies. 'Second-wave' feminists of the

1960s and early 1970s challenged the notion of biology-is-destiny; that differences between men and women were natural or 'hard-wired' and thus by implication, beyond power and change. A distinction was made between 'gender' – which pertains to a socially constructed identity label – and 'sex', which refers to biological difference. Starting from this premise, writers such as Susie Orbach (1989), Elizabeth Grosz (1994), and Susan Bordo (1993) placed the female body at the centre of their analyses, showing how women's bodies and lives have been regulated by the cultural ideals of slenderness, beauty, and femininity. Beauty, fat, and diet became feminist issues, along with the environment, war, childcare, inequality in employment, organisational culture, and the gender pay gap. More recently, writers such as Judith Butler (1993) have emphasised that 'sex' does not exist outside gender relations: what is taken to be the material or biological body is always already shaped by assumptions about gender and how it should be enacted or 'performed'. Historical work has lent support to the notion that 'sex' is a 'social construction' and a relatively recent one at that. The idea of two different but complementary sexes, it is suggested, dates only from the late seventeenth and eighteenth centuries, having supplanted the earlier 'one-sex model' whereby women's bodies were seen as the inferior version of the male body (Laqueur 1990). Feminist scholarship has shown that since the eighteenth century the biomedical sciences have contributed to the construction of difference, in studies of gross anatomy (e.g. Schiebinger 1989, 1993), theories of hormones (Oudshoorn 1994) and, more recently, genetics (Fausto-Stirling 1992).

Although arguably not accorded as much prominence as feminism in public debates, the work of those working in the fields of gay and lesbian studies, disability studies, and 'race' and ethnicity studies have also helped politicise 'the body'. Scholars have emphasised how a politics of the body – involving the categorisation, labelling, and regulation of particular bodies – has operated so as to mark as different and marginalise different groups. Recent scholarship has revealed that, in the area of sexuality, sexual science has focused considerably on the homosexual body, which has been subject to scientific and medical interventions with the view to its 'treatment' and 'normalisation'. A range of scientific theories has been developed to explain homosexuality, with contributions from genetics, endocrinology, cognitive psychology, and neuroscience. The question of whether homosexuality is 'hard-wired' in the body, or is a product of social environments, has preoccupied scholars during the modern period (see, e.g. LeVay 1996). Homosexuality has been defined as a form of sexual deviance and in the late nineteenth century homosexuals were described as a 'third sex' (van der Meer 1994). This politics of categorisation and labelling has been highlighted by a developing history of gay struggles (e.g. Weeks 1977) and of sexology (Bland and Doan 1998a, 1998b), and by enquiries into the politics of 'coming out' (Sedgwick 1994). Disability scholars have drawn attention to the marginalisation of 'non-normal' bodies and challenged the medical model of disability which focuses on the impairment to the exclusion of the person. As work from this field emphasises, biomedical technologies, such as genetic technologies, by focusing on 'fixing' 'damaged' bodies or preventing future disabled bodies, may serve to devalue the lives of those who already have disabilities (Bailey 1996). Because they tend to live longer than men and suffer a disproportionate burden of poverty, disabled women may be especially vulnerable to discrimination (Kallianes and Rubenfeld 1997; Rock 1996). 'Race' and ethnicity scholarship is diverse, but this work has also served to bring the issue of body classification and regulation to the forefront of research and to highlight the taken-for-granted character of the white European male standpoint. 'Whiteness' as much as 'blackness' became an issue for theorisation in 'race' and ethnicity research, with some writers drawing attention to the frequent tendency to conflate ethnicity and 'race' in discussions and thereby inadvertently to reinforce racist assumptions (e.g. Ahmad and Jones 1998). Self-identified 'black' and developing world feminist scholars also challenged Western feminists' assumptions about a universal sisterhood, pointing out that racial or ethnic identification sometimes overrides gender identity in some contexts; that women were often united with their men in overcoming colonial or neo-colonial oppression (Spivak 1993; see also Grant 1993).

Michel Foucault   social theorist

One writer who has been especially influential in the developing field of body scholarship has been the French historian and philosopher, Michel Foucault. Foucault asked radically new and interesting kinds of questions about familiar issues and problems, such as medicine and health, sexuality, and criminality. His work found resonance among many critical scholars who were dissatisfied with current theories of knowledge and strategies of change. He always located issues within a historical context, although he proposed a distinct kind of historical enquiry that sought to unsettle the present by drawing attention to the 'conditions of possibility' for the studied phenomenon. His approach is thus critical, and radical, though in a different way to, say, Marxism or earlier strands of feminism. His work is a major although not the sole influence on this book – both in terms of the areas chosen for analysis and the kinds of questions posed – and his ideas are referred to explicitly at various points in the discussion.

In a series of publications and lectures, Foucault drew attention to the emergence of new forms of power and knowledge in the modern period (beginning late eighteenth century), which focused on life processes and the regulation of the body as a biological entity. In his early work in areas such as criminal justice, medicine, mental illness, and sexuality, Foucault explored how new domains of knowledge and practice served to 'fabricate' and regulate the body, to make it docile, useful and productive. In his view, control over biological processes – 'bio-power' – was integral to the development of modern societies which were becoming more urbanised as capitalism progressed. As Foucault argued, '"bio-power" was without question an indispensable element in the development of capitalism; the latter would not have been possible without the controlled insertion of bodies into the machinery of production and the adjustment of the phenomena of population to economic processes' (Foucault 1980: 140–141). At the same time, power was becoming more diffuse and evident at every level of the social body and in a diverse array of institutions (for example, in the family, in schools, in the military, in penal institutions, and in medicine), and worked through systems of classification and surveillance. In Foucault's view, Jeremy Bentham's panopticon characterised the modern form of disciplinary power. This works not so much through external forms of monitoring, but rather through self-surveillance. Since people are never certain whether or not they were under observation, they constantly scrutinise and discipline their own behaviour. This 'disciplinary' power is the most effective form of power, Foucault argued, and differed from earlier forms of power, and most particularly 'sovereign' power, which was demonstrated in a more overt and violent manner, most visibly through the public execution (see Foucault 1977).

Some feminist scholars have drawn on Foucault's ideas to offer insightful analyses of the dynamics of power as it operates on women's bodies and lives (e.g. Ramazanoglu 1993; Sawicki 1991). One area of feminist interest where Foucault's ideas have been fruitfully applied has been the politics of reproduction. Jana Sawicki, for instance, has examined the positive and productive power of new reproductive technologies, showing how they serve as disciplining devices and create new categories of human subject and new experiences; for example the infertile, genetically impaired mothers, mothers whose bodies are not fit for pregnancy, mothers who are psychologically unfit for fertility treatments, and so on (1991: 83–85). As this work emphasises, the way in which categories are constructed profoundly affects the possibilities for personhood. There is a mutual relationship between how we distinguish between people (and, one might add, between people and other animals or the physical or natural environment) and how individuals think and act, whether as a 'homosexual'/'gay' person, a woman or man, a disabled person, a person of a certain 'race' or ethnicity, and so on (see Hacking 1986). Foucault has offered feminists a more sophisticated view of power than that proposed by some earlier feminists who very often portrayed women as passive victims of an all-dominating 'patriarchal' system. Such a view of power, of course, affects how one views the opportunities and strategies for change. Seeing power as residing in categories and distinctions focuses attention on knowledge and those who produce knowledge and leads to caution in relation to grand and simplistic political strategies that aim to confront 'class rule', 'patriarchy', and so on.

In his final work, his later two volumes of the history of sexuality, Foucault (1985, 1986) tried to redress some of the shortcomings of his earlier work, which he came to recognise over-emphasised processes of domination, by giving more attention to individual agency and to 'practices of the self' whereby individuals constituted themselves as particular kinds of subject (e.g. as ethical, law-abiding, healthy, responsible citizens) and *subjected themselves* to power. Although Foucault's work was incomplete at the time of his death (1984), his concept of governmentality (or rationality of government), introduced mainly via a series of lectures, and developed subsequently by others such as Nicholas Rose (1999), Pat O'Malley (2004), and Mitchell Dean (1999) sought to give prominence to the interconnection between 'top-down' power (technologies of domination) and 'bottom-up' power ('technologies of the self'). In other words, Foucault seems to have been thinking through the issue of the relationship between structure and agency that has long occupied sociologists and other social scientists and inevitably makes its appearance in discussions around 'the body' and other areas of social enquiry.

While Foucault's work has been influential in thinking about 'the body', much writing has focused on the earlier rather than the later work of Foucault and has tended to overlook the significance of the work of Foucaultian scholars who have employed the notion of 'governmentality' to investigate various domains of social life. Described by Rose as a 'style of analysis', and as being concerned with a kind of empirical investigation of 'what is said and how it is said' and the conditions which make this intelligible, governmentality scholarship offers a new approach and explores a novel set of questions for understanding politics and power (see Rose 1999: 3, 57). Using the metaphor of diagnosis, governmentality scholars do not seek explanation for phenomenon – as though there were a final cause for what is being explained but rather, like the role ascribed by Nietzsche to artists and philosophers, to view phenomena as 'signs or symptoms of a certain play of forces' (Rose 1999: 57–58). Through a certain style of historical investigation ('genealogy' or 'history of the present'), governmentality scholars seek to unsettle the self-evidence of current ways of thinking and acting, by showing them to be historically contingent and open to challenge and change. In contrast to forms of historical analysis which take the present as self-evident and focus on the continuities that inevitably led to the present, genealogy directs attention to discontinuities (or ruptures) in history and seeks to 'make the present strange' and to ask why the present came to appear as natural. Thus, policies, programmes, and strategies that may appear to be progressive, such as penal, health and welfare reform, are revealed to have regulatory effects. The question of how particular categories of human being came to be 'made up' and how certain groups, such as the sick, the insane and the mad came to be seen as problematic are made central to the analysis.

Recent governmentality scholarship has drawn attention to the significance of 'freedom' and 'choice' to the contemporary workings of power, specifically in societies with liberal and neo-liberal forms of rule. Increasingly, individuals are called upon to live life in an entrepreneurial way – to view day-to-day decisions in terms of assessments of costs and benefits, and to consider the investment potential of choices and relationships. Decisions in all aspects of life – including in relation to health and the presentation, care and use of our bodies – are subject to the rationality of the market. Private goals and desires increasingly are linked to public goals. To be a 'good citizen' one should play one's part in managing one's risk, promoting one's health or preventing illness, regulating one's diet, and so on. Although Foucault's ideas are invaluable for those seeking to make sense of these trends, one needs to complement this work with that of scholars working from different perspectives in a range of disciplines if one is to adequately grasp the various implications of the burgeoning number of body-related developments.

Guiding themes

As noted, news stories which speak about new technologies of the body, such as those referred to at the beginning of this chapter, highlight a number of recurrent themes in discussions about 'the body'. In this book, I will draw extensively on news stories about body-related issues along with other material, since they offer a rich source for exploring changing conceptions of the body and visions of how the body may be changed, controlled, treated, or improved. Since the chapters of this book will repeatedly return to certain key themes, elaboration on these at this point is necessary to help set the scene for what follows.

The 'naturalness' and modifiability of the body: the significance of new technologies

The first two excerpts presented at the beginning of this chapter illustrate visions of how the body may be used or enhanced in its performance or operations through its interface with or modification by technologies; in these instances, as a transmitter of information and to make one an 'unbeatable sportsmen', respectively. Although both the articles are about developments which are imagined rather than already existing, the potential modification of the body suggested by these scenarios brings into question the idea of the natural body. Within the broader culture, there has been a tendency to view technologies and bodies as separate and separable. The former are seen as 'man-made' (i.e. socially produced) practical applications of science (implements, devices, gadgets, etc.) that exist separate from the body which is viewed as pre-social. In this view, technologies may be applied to bodies (e.g. lotions, surgical instruments, x-rays, pills) or used by bodies to allow them to do things they would otherwise be unable to do (e.g. cars, mobile phones, computers). However, developments such as those described in the news items would seem to unsettle the distinction between technologies and bodies. Gene therapies are proposed for treating genetic-related diseases, for example, by replacing a mutated gene with a 'healthy' one. The idea of using the body's conducting properties to create a computer network would seem to be a means of utilising a 'natural' property of the body – its conductance – so as to better integrate it with mobile phones, pagers and as yet unimagined other devices, presumably to make it more useful, or a 'better machine'. (The questions of more useful *to whom* and with *what implications*, are worth asking and will be discussed later.) The idea of genetically modifying athletes to enhance their performance is already embedded in popular discourse and is the focus of some bioethical concern (Miah 2004). New technologies such as genetic technologies raise the question of where to draw the line between 'nature' and 'culture' and what, if any, limits exist or should exist in modifying the body. Some writers have spoken of the collapse of the nature/culture dualism, so that social identities increasingly are based on biological categories (Rheinberger 1995). More and more, people begin to define themselves and organise collectively on the basis of biological, particularly genetic, criteria (e.g. Rabinow 1992). It would seem that the notion of social solidarity, developed during the period of the rise of the welfare state has been replaced at least to some extent by solidarity based on biological criteria; hence Adriana Petryna's (2002) term 'biological citizenship'. The increasing pervasiveness of genetic explanations for behaviour and identity and the search for genetic interventions and modifications raise profound questions for what it means to be human.

Changing conceptions of the human

The development of new technologies of the body has led some writers to speculate that societies are moving towards a 'post-human' future (e.g. Haraway 1991; Waldby 2000). The idea that the body may be altered and perfected by technologies in the ways described, however, is hardly novel. It has long been the focus for speculation and fascination in Western societies, as is reflected in numerous science fiction writings (on which more will be said, below). The vision of human perfectibility and of being able to overcome apparent corporeal weaknesses and limitations has been a recurring theme in the modern period, but can be traced back to at least the origins of scientific thought if not the beginnings of human history. For example Leonardo da Vinci's flying machine revealed the fantasy of overcoming human constraints on aerial mobility. Recent developments in biomedicine and biotechnology and information and communication technologies (ICTs), though promising to push the boundaries of human limitations beyond current imaginings, can be seen as part of a long history of efforts to develop technologies to such ends. The increasingly routine use of biomedicine to alter the body, to improve its functioning (e.g. hip replacements, knee reconstructions, coronary bypass operations) or enhance its appearance (reconstructive or cosmetic surgery) would suggest, however, that such technologies are becoming 'normalised' within medicine and the broader society. That doctors are evidently open to using such technologies on a routine basis and that many people expect that they will have access to them would seem to indicate changing views about the 'natural' lifespan of the body and the inevitability of its decline and decay. This, together with other developments, such as the use of reproductive technologies, for example to enable older women to have a baby, reported in the third article above, challenge established concepts of the 'normal, healthy' body and the natural human reproductive cycle. Although, at the time of writing, genetic therapies do not exist, they are widely expected to be part of the future repertoire of new body technologies that will transform medicine as well as practices of self-care. As the second article suggests, indeed, some sections of the public believe that such technologies already exist and can be utilised to improve their performance. Recently, nanotechnologies have also been the subject of scientific discussion and popular representation (e.g. Michael Crichton's *Prey*), with suggestions that a newer range of technologies of the body is on the horizon. Some cosmetics, including sunscreens, already include nanotech-nologies which, some scientists argue, pose 'dangers linked to the ability of nanoparticles to cross into areas of the body that larger particulates cannot reach' (Fleming 2006). New biotechnologies are the topic of both fascination and fear, with utopian visions of their applications vying with dystopian visions of 'nature biting back', as seen for example in the recurrent popular cultural imagery of Aldous Huxley's *Brave New World* and Mary Shelley's *Frankenstein*. Have we entered, or are we about to enter a post-human future of cyborgs (cybernetic organisms), that is, hybrid human-machines? And, if so, should this be celebrated or feared? These are questions which body scholars are grappling with and they will be explored later in the book.

Expectations about science and its powers

We live in a period dominated by scientific expertise and belief in scientific 'fixes'. Science has to a large extent supplanted religion as the basis for authority on and explanation of our natural and social worlds. This is not to say that religious authority is insignificant. Religion, in its diverse forms, continues to exert a considerable influence either directly (through formal codes, dictates, observances) or indirectly (through civic rituals such as marriage, guiding ideals, legislation, etc.) over much of the world's population. As Bryan Turner notes, religion has been centrally concerned with the disciplining and control of the body, hence religious proscrip-tions about sexuality, diet, restraint, and so on. As he notes, religion can be regarded as 'a system of bonding and binding through which human bodies are controlled and disciplined' (1991: 118). Religious frameworks and language inform contemporary practices of the confession and the incitation to 'bear witness' to one's suffering and illness – evident, for example, in some forms of narrative analysis (see Chapter 5). However, increasingly, science rather than religion provides the source of authority in explaining the natural and social worlds and in solving personal, social and environmental problems. All three news articles presented at the beginning of this chapter reflect *belief* in science and its power to alter or regulate a supposedly natural (i.e. pre-social) body, in these cases purportedly for beneficial ends. As reflected in the second and third articles, science is seen to hold the key to solving limitations presented by 'nature', particularly in relation to bodily performance and reproductive capacity. 'Nature' is viewed as subject to control or regulation by rational science and technology; i.e. 'culture'. According to some strands of feminist thought, the assumption that science can control nature reflects a masculine bias in science's knowledge, since science is associated with rational thought, which in modern Western societies is coded masculine, while 'nature' is closely associated with femininity (Warren 1994). The aim of science, it is argued, is to dominate culture. This is most evident in technologies of reproduction which, in effect, entail efforts by men to control the bodies of women (Corea 1985).

Belief in the power of science to control and alter the natural is perhaps nowhere more evident than in the field of human genetics. Techniques for identifying DNA materials, and genetic testing in the clinic, are seen to be two useful applications of the so-called genetics revolution. Many countries have developed, or are developing, national DNA databases, which are seen to greatly assist criminal investigators in solving crimes. The concept of DNA 'fingerprinting', used in the context of criminal investigation, indicates that our genetic material is personal to us, presenting an apparently 'foolproof' means of detecting the guilty (Nelkin and Andrews 1999: 191). Population-based genetic databases ('biobanks') are also being developed in many countries for research into the genetic, lifestyle, and environmental contributions to disease (Gottweis and Petersen in press). Such databases offer the promise of enhanced classification of bodies and diseases, and thus help create order from the apparent disorder of 'nature'. Genetic testing is often undertaken with pregnant mothers, to test for genetic-related diseases, such as Down's Syndrome so that there is the option of terminating the pregnancy if desired. Increasingly, such tests are used to screen for other conditions, such as breast and ovarian cancer, which is also seen to lead to improved choices in health and lifestyle. Proponents of such tests argue that the individual will be able to better plan their life rather than simply 'leave things to chance'. It has been suggested that, in the future, testing will be available for many conditions, including so-called 'late-onset' conditions, which is presumed to benefit both affected individuals and society as a whole. While science is widely seen as having considerable *beneficial* powers, one also needs to recognise widespread concerns about the dangers of the efforts of science to control 'nature'. These include increased surveillance and control over people's bodies and lives, the commodification of life, 'playing God', the intrusion on people's 'right not to know' and loss of genetic privacy, the potential for discrimination on the basis of genetic difference, and growing economic and social inequalities arising from unequal access to the benefits of resulting technologies. In the field of genetics, for example, some writers see the potential for the emergence of a 'genetic underclass' comprising those who have unequal access to new genetic tests, treatments and enhancement technologies (Kelly 2005: 137). Feminist scholars point out that new genetics-based reproductive technologies are far from neutral in that they have different impacts on women's and men's bodies and lives (e.g. Ettorre 2002; Steinberg 1997). As became apparent during the consultations for Britain's national genetic database, UK Biobank, some groups are concerned that samples collected for genetic databases may be used for purposes other than those stated, for example for cloning, for commercial profiteering, for determining insurance premiums and employability, and so on (Petersen 2005a: 282). A strong science-based culture presupposes that research is seen by publics as legitimate and will meet publics' consent, especially if their participation in research projects is called for. However, legitimacy and consent, it would appear, can no longer be taken for granted. It has been suggested that publics are increasingly distrustful of scientists and other authorities, especially in the wake of a number of widely publicised medical scandals involving misuse of human tissue remains, as occurred in Alder Hey Hospital in Liverpool and the Bristol Royal Infirmary. Regardless of the validity of this claim, which is difficult to substantiate, there is at least a widespread *perception* of such mistrust among scientists and policy makers and recognition that scientists need to establish legitimacy and consent for their work if it is to be funded and to find useful application. Even when legitimacy and consent are established, there is still no guarantee that scientific research will not have discriminatory or other deleterious outcomes. For example, research that leads to new genetic tests which are seen to offer people greater choice may have unintended eugenic effects (Petersen In press). The merging of technologies, such as genetics and computing, which is seen to bring improvements in healthcare, may facilitate new forms of simulated surveillance (control before the event) (Bogard 1996), even though this may never have been the intention of those who developed the technologies. Science always has social effects, whether intended or not, and is always embedded within relations of power.

The mediation of the body in popular culture

The above articles also highlight the significance of the media as a source of information about science and events that shape public knowledge about the body and issues pertaining to the body; for example medical and other science 'breakthroughs' (see Chapter 2). Although I have chosen examples from print news media, we should not lose sight of the fact that the contemporary media is highly diverse and pervasive: including, apart from the press, the internet (websites, email), television, radio, magazines, mobile phones, pamphlets, and billboard advertising. In media studies, there is considerable debate about the influence of the media on publics' views and about the most appropriate model for understanding the mediation process. It is difficult to ascertain media influences in any straightforward way; however, given its pervasiveness, the potential of the media to shape public knowledge and policies would appear to be substantial. Earlier media effects models, which suggest that the media directly influence relatively passive audiences through the messages they convey, have been replaced by more sophisticated models. These models focus on the ways media frame events and acknowledge that audiences 'actively interpret' and subvert media messages. In the emphasising of the latter, however, there is the danger of overlooking the potentially profound ways in which media may shape public discourse and policies pertaining to bodies and body issues. It is difficult not to ascribe some role to the media in the formation of public knowledge about issues such as body weight, body shape, over-eating, and anorexia, for example. The potentially powerful role of the media in modern societies has long been recognised by social scientists and commentators such as Marshall McLuhan and Quentin Fiore (2001; orig. 1967) and Baudrillard (1998) (see Chapter 6). Feminists, such as Susan Bordo (1993), have also attributed an important role to the media in objectifying women's bodies and in contributing to body image problems and eating disorders.

In relation to the reporting of science and technology issues, recent evidence highlights the complexity of the news mediation process. In the UK, in recent years, the science community's responses to news reporting of issues such as GM crops, and research into embryonic stem cells, cloning, and nanotechnology show concern about the potential of the media to shape public responses to these technologies. Scientists frequently complain that the newspaper press 'misrepresents' or 'distorts' science fact, or fictionalises or sensationalises issues. This suggests that scientists are uninvolved in news production, which is contrary to recent evidence on the role of scientists in shaping stories. Scientists may achieve a degree of control over the content and portrayal of coverage through various means, such as the use of news releases (which may be embargoed until what is judged to be the most propitious time), staged news events, and the use of particular language and metaphors when they are cited or quoted (Alison *et al.* 2005; Petersen 2001). The scientists who announced the cloning of Dolly the sheep, for example, employed a combination of such strategies in their efforts to maintain control over the story and the images (Petersen 2002). Scientists are the frequently quoted or cited sources in news stories on genetics, which allows them to shape how stories are 'framed' (Conrad 1999; Petersen 2001). They are keen to portray science in a positive way to maintain public support for their work, which is necessary to ensure the continuity of research funding (Nelkin 1987).Editorials in science journals, which are a forum for the expression of widely shared elite views in science, have been found to have great expecta-tions of human genetics and of developments in the understanding and management of disease (Miller *et al.* 2005). These expectations of benefits are likely to follow through into news media coverage of genetic medicine. The tendency for news media to focus on research on single-gene disorders, for example (see, e.g. Petersen 2001), is arguably due, in part, to scientists' efforts through news releases and other public forums to emphasise the potential short-term implications of research on single gene disorders (e.g. new genetic tests for particular diseases) so as to engender public support for their research. A more complex picture of genetic contributions, suggested for example by gene–gene and gene–environment interactions, would be more difficult to 'sell' to publics and funders of research, particularly since this implies much longer timeframes and uncertain research outcomes. The necessity for scientists to simplify their work and to use the media to emphasise its potential benefits has become crucial with rapid developments in the biosciences and the pervasiveness of different forms of media. Such evidence suggests that simplistic models of mediation need to be replaced by more sophisticated models that acknowledge how claims-makers may seek to gain legitimacy for their views by privileging certain facts and portrayals and ignoring others. This would lead one to ask questions about the *media politics of body representation*. Such questions may include: why do certain portrayals of the body achieve prominence in the media in the first place? Who are the sources for stories and how may this influence the nature of the portrayals? How do particular groups use or seek to use the media in their efforts to influence public knowledge and policies? Why are certain perspectives, portrayals and voices absent? And, how may the framing of body-related issues potentially shape public knowledge and policies?

The blurring of fact and fiction in portrayals of the body

The question of what is fact and what is fiction in portrayals of the body, in news items such as the above and other media, arguably has become increasingly difficult for publics to discern with rapid developments in technologies and the pervasiveness of media at all levels. Frequent conflicting expert opinion about new technologies and their implications and risks, such as genetics and nanotechnologies, cannot easily be assessed in the absence of alternative, non-media-based sources of information, which are rare in modern complex societies. For example, what should one make of periodic claims that certain doctors or groups, such as the Raelians, are about to clone a baby, a prospect which some see as being within the realms of 'science fiction'? Where should one begin to look for evidence that would enable one to confidently assess such claims? Is there and can there ever be an unmediated, disinterested source of knowledge that would assist one in making an assessment? Commercial and other imperatives of day-to-day news reporting and other media production (e.g. wide-circulation magazines, television), which lead to an emphasis on the 'breakthrough' story, controversy, and personalities, undoubtedly contribute to a certain bias in the kinds of issues that get reported and how they are reported.

A study of articles reporting research on genetic-based differences of sex and sexuality that appeared in a range of widely circulated science journals, such as *Science, New Scientist,* and *Scientific American,* revealed that scientists draw on popular cultural imagery and metaphors in describing their work, some of which may be described as 'fictional' (Petersen 1999). Popular cultural imagery and metaphors, including those that appear in the genre of fictional literature, are shared by a broad section of the population, including scientists, and so provide the basis for a common language that must be relied upon if communication is to occur at all. In discussions about the fictionalisation of 'science fact', the role of fictional imagery in the construction and representation of fact tends to be overlooked. Fictional narratives often foreshadow actual developments ('facts'), which then in turn inspire literary and other cultural forms. The fictional writer, Margaret Atwood, has talked about the influence of news events on her own work (e.g. *Oryx and Crake*), which she describes as 'speculative fiction' rather than science fiction, since it draws its inspiration from developments already under way rather than simply imagined ones (Petersen *et al.* 2005). I would argue that the fact/fiction dichotomy needs to be examined critically in relation to arguments about media portrayals of the body. There is need for appreciation of how this dichotomy may serve to bolster the power of scientists, by ascribing them authority to define the boundaries of science, and how it may limit understanding of the role of 'fiction' in the representation of 'fact'.

The relationship between the mind and the body

The question of the relationship of the body to the mind has been an enduring one in Western thought. The idea that the mind is separable from the body is often attributed to René Descartes, who was writing in the seventeenth century, although the idea can be traced back much earlier in Western thought (Rozemond 1998). Scholars in the social sciences and humanities have drawn attention to how this dualism (sometimes referred to as Cartesian dualism) has been maintained and have explored its social implications. Biomedicine in particular has been criticised for treating patients as bodies rather than as persons with experiences, views, and feelings. It has been argued that since the rise of scientific medicine the body has been treated like a machine, which needs 'fixing', generally through highly invasive means (e.g. drugs, surgery) (Capra 1983). The first two articles at the beginning of this chapter convey a view of the body as an objectified, de-personalised, passive entity. It is difficult to say with certainty that medicine has ever been 'holistic' in the way portrayed by some writers, such as Capra. However, according to many scholars, pre-scientific medicine was both art and science and did not involve the objectification of the body or at least not to the same extent evident today. Such objectification often is seen to lead to the 'de-humanisation' of medical practice. The growing popularity (particularly among women) of complementary and alternative medicines

(CAMs) (the choice of words reflects one's perspective on their compatibility with biomedicine) has been interpreted as an indication of widespread dissatisfaction with biomedicine as currently practised and recognition of its limits in treating problems of a complex nature.

Like 'nature' which has been viewed as subject to domination by 'culture', in modern Western culture, increasingly 'the body' is seen as subject to control by 'the mind'. Being overweight, unfit, poorly dressed, and so on, is seen as indicative of a lack of self-discipline or control by the mind. As Foucault noted, in modern societies, the disciplining of minds and bodies goes hand in hand. Control of the psyche has figured prominently in various regimes of body management, in health promotion, illness prevention and fitness management, at work, and in military training and the theatres of combat. Consumerism presupposes a certain kind of mental disposition or 'mind control'. The seemingly endless information communicated via the media and through various expert sources about the importance of body maintenance and of 'looking good', 'young', 'sexy', and so on, and how to achieve the 'ideal' body, underlines the contemporary emphasis given to 'mind over body' and the body as a project to be worked on. As with the control of 'nature' by 'culture', there is a gender dimension to this emphasis on body discipline and regulation. Women are seen to be more 'in touch' with their bodies, and the desire to project a sexy body is strongly associated with femininity. Observed differences in men's and women's health-related behaviours and regimes of body maintenance, such as women's apparent greater willingness to seek health advice and to submit themselves to various bodily 'improvements' (cosmetic surgery, facials, leg waxes, etc.) has been attributed in part to these cultural associations (see Chapter 3). To overcome the problems brought about by this mind–body separation, some writers have argued for greater attention to the emotions in social enquiries and to the use of patient's narratives in treatments. Further, CAMs have been increasingly incorporated into healthcare (see Chapter 5). However, as I will argue, there are various unrecognised implications of these efforts to 'integrate' body and mind.

The economic, political and social contexts shaping body classification, regulation and modification

As I have argued, much recent work on 'the body' fails to grapple with the profound economic, political, social, and justice implications of recent efforts to modify and regulate bodies, particularly via the growing use of biomedical technologies. The extreme individualism and consumerism evident in many contemporary practices of the body arguably reflects the influence of neo-liberal politics and policies on thinking and action (Dean 1999; Rose 1999). Individualism manifests in the strong emphasis on care of the self and the self-management of risk, while consumerism can be seen in the focus on freedom through choice in the market-place. The body has become a site for the expression of *vulnerability* arising from uncertainties about the implications of incursions into 'nature' (e.g. infections from antibiotic-resistant bacteria, cancers arising from toxic environments) and loss of control over bodily processes or presentation (e.g. disease, 'obesity', ageing). Many recent body-related developments promise enhanced individual control or management of risk or minimisation of uncertainty. The growing use of screening for risk (e.g. for obesity, genetic disease) and emphasis on illness prevention (e.g. weight loss, regular exercise) reflect the pervasive rationality of risk within contemporary societies (e.g. Beck 1992; Giddens 1991; O'Malley 2004). Risk can be viewed as part of the technology of neo-liberal governance that operates by encouraging individuals to govern themselves (Petersen 1996). Knowing one's risk (e.g. as revealed through a health check or a genetic test), it is argued, provides the basis for 'freedom of choice' in health decision-making and life planning. Recent heightened fears about the risks posed by food contamination, the use of biomedical and biotechnological innovations, and human interventions into the environment arguably have served to justify increased surveillance and monitoring of and intervention into the bodies and lives of individuals and particular groups. New technologies deriving from genetics, the neurosciences, and nanoscience, referred to above, when combined with digital technologies, promise new forms of risk profiling and simulated surveillance (Bogard 1996). The growing availability of new biomedical technologies which are promoted through 'direct-to-consumer' advertising', including means for modifying one's body and enhancing one's appearance, take 'responsibility' to a new level (see Chapters 3 and 4). As in other areas of life, responsibility in healthcare and in body maintenance and enhancement is demonstrated through the purchase of products and services available in the market-place. The manifestations and implications of this individualism and consumerism, for example in practices of body modification and beautification and enhancement, are recurring themes in the chapters of this book.

Outline of the remaining chapters

Chapter 2 interrogates the concept of the natural body. As noted, recent developments in biomedicine and biotechnology unsettle assumptions about the naturalness of the biophysical body. The nature–culture (or nature–nurture) debate is long-standing and in order to make sense of the phenomenon of 'the body' it is important to place the discussion in a broad historical and social context. The chapter examines the enduring influence of Darwinism and some recent views on the relationship between 'nature' and 'culture'. I examine the role of the news media in 'framing' science and technology issues, focusing on two areas of research and development that have been portrayed as having the potential to radically change the way we think about the natural body; namely neuroscience and embryonic stem cell research. I draw attention to some issues which are *not* covered in news stories. As

I argue, one needs to get behind the news to examine the processes of science and news production in order properly to assess claims about new body technologies and their impacts. As I conclude, while the expectations attached to such developments may help shape future actions and policies it is by no means certain that technologies will materialise in ways depicted.

Chapter 3 investigates efforts to reshape and perfect the body. It explores a number of questions about the sources, operations and implications of body modification and management practices, beginning with discussion about contemporary concerns around body shape and weight. The idea of 'normal' body size and shape is questioned by recent social science research showing the considerable historical and cross-cultural variability of ideals of body shape, size and appearance. This work emphasises that the contemporary Western 'ideal', thin body is not only historically recent but globally something of an anomaly. The chapter highlights the gender biases of this ideal. As argued, over the last few decades there has been a growing divergence between the ideal female body and average body weights. The chapter examines the basis of current concerns about 'the problem of obesity', the cultural significance of 'fatness', and some implications of the 'fight against fat'. It assesses the relevance of Pierre Bourdieu's work in understanding the socio-cultural significance of bodily difference, and then discusses the character, power and influence of 'the body shape industry' in contemporary society. It examines the selling of the beauty ideal and feminist perspectives on the role of the beauty industry. Finally, the chapter identifies some new questions that are prompted by observations on the rapidly changing norms and practices of body modification and management and the global dispersion of Western ideals of perfection or 'beauty'.

Chapter 4 explores the mechanisms and socio-political dimensions of body classification in the contemporary West, particularly in the context of growing consumerism in healthcare and more generally. It also explores some concerns about classification that have arisen in response. The chapter begins by placing classification in a broad context, exploring the variability of classifications across cultures and through time. The significance of the distinction between the normal and the pathological and of biomedical classificatory systems is discussed. The chapter then investigates the impact of the workings and rationality of the market on the changing classifications of health and illness, especially the shift in emphasis from 'health' to 'enhancement' in the marketing of products and services. The example of Viagra is used to illustrate the blurring of this distinction and to highlight some implications for healthcare and notions of normality and identity. Next, the chapter examines the role of the body and bodily difference in the changing classifications of identity and how this reflects and is reflected in contemporary politics. The discussion explores these themes with reference to recent changing views on age and ageing. Finally, the chapter finishes with some speculations on the future of classification in light of recent trends in politics and technological developments.

Chapter 5 examines some dimensions and implications of the contemporary focus on 'powers of the mind', with specific reference to the arenas of health and healing and self-care. In many contemporary societies there is growing dissatisfaction with the tendency within medicine and more generally to focus on the body to the exclusion of the mind. This chapter discusses this development and critically examines some responses. It begins by examining the enduring influence of Cartesian dualism then evaluates some recent theoretical and practical efforts to 'reconnect' or 'integrate' the mind and the body. Again, the profound influence of individualism and consumerism on thinking and practices is noted, particularly in the field of complementary and alternative medicines (CAMs). Philosophies and practices oriented to the 'whole person' have helped to sustain an ever-growing array of products and services which are promoted on the promise of 'empowering' the individual and creating 'healthier', more 'balanced' lives. As argued, well-intended efforts to 'empower' people may serve to reinforce individualism and consumerism in healthcare.

Finally, Chapter 6 summarises the main themes and arguments of the book and identifies a number of questions for further investigation. These relate in particular to challenges posed by newly emergent technologies of the body arising from genetics, nanoscience and neuroscience, and their convergence and routine use for body enhancement under the pressure of market forces. It is argued that the questions of whether these technologies will substantially improve bodies and lives and whether they should be supported need to be debated with input from many different constituencies, including lay publics, disability groups and patient groups, natural scientists, social scientists, healthcare professionals, educationalists, NGOs, business interests, and policy makers. This implies the democratisation of science and technology and culture and the posing of new kinds of questions. The importance of gaining a better understanding of the workings of the media and of political economy in particular is emphasised. Recent developments related to consumerism, such as growing biomedical tourism, I argue, raise significant normative and justice issues that should be part of critical studies of 'the body'.

2   What is a natural body?

One of the recurrent themes in the social science literature on the body has been the 'naturalness' of the body. Is there a biophysical or corporeal body unaffected by social processes and power relations? To what extent is 'nature' subject to control by 'culture'? And, what are the political and practical implications of efforts to achieve such control? I suggested in Chapter 1 that technological developments have unsettled the *idea* of a clear separation between 'nature' and 'culture' and hence of the existence of a natural or pre-social body. According to the tenets of evolutionary theory, the body is subject to change and adaptation over a very long period of time as a result of environmental pressures. It could be argued then that technology as a cultural artefact simply accelerates and directs processes of change and adaptation that would inevitably occur due to environmental pressures. Thus, genetic modifications affected through screening or new therapies may be seen to advance the process of making people more adaptive to their ever-changing environments. Some scientists indeed argue this in relation to so-called germ-line genetic engineering, which they see as having the potential to eliminate disease from the human gene pool (see Stock and Campbell 2000). As I also mentioned in Chapter 1, the idea of changing or perfecting the body is by no means novel. However, recent developments, or at least their portrayal, suggest that control of 'nature' through technological intervention is now realisable and imminent. Science derives much of its legitimacy from the claim that it can control and alter 'nature' in ways that will benefit people and there are great expectations within many contemporary societies that it *will* deliver what is promised. This impression is reinforced especially by media reporting which offers almost daily news stories of technological 'breakthroughs'. In this chapter, I critically examine the nature–culture debate with reference to two fields of research that recently have been in the news and which are portrayed as having the potential to substantially change the way we think about and treat the body, namely neuroscience and embryonic stem cell research. Both areas are contentious precisely because they are seen to allow control over fundamental processes of life and to have the potential to radically transform human lives in the future. This chapter examines how these developments are represented and in particular the expectations attached to them. Given the long history of interest in changing the body, it is useful to begin however by locating the nature–culture debate in a historical and social context.

The nature–culture debate in a historical and social context

Social science has long grappled with the issue of 'nature versus culture', or as it is sometimes formulated 'nature versus nurture', especially in discussions about the formation of human subjectivity. As Diane Paul (1998) notes, the nature–nurture controversy was debated in the early twentieth century and 'by the 1920s it had become conventional to deny the opposition of nature and nurture, assert that science and common sense had converged on a reasonable middle position, and declare the issue dead' (1998: 82). However, as she notes, it is 'a debate that refuses to die' because 'there are politics everywhere in the nature–nurture debate' (Paul 1998: 90). Clearly, much is at stake for both social science and for social policy and practices of how this issue is seen to be resolved. If it is believed that humans are defined by their biology and that human differences are 'hard-wired' (e.g. in genetic make-up or brain functioning), and implicitly unalterable, then this has substantial implications for how people are likely to view and relate to others, for what are seen to be the prospects for individual and social change, and for what are believed to be the most desirable social arrangements. Intelligence tests, school grading, career guidance advice, and much social policy (e.g. retirement and unemployment provisions) carry underlying assumptions about natural differences in human abilities, capacities and/or make-up and, through their deployment, serve to confirm that there are indeed such differences. In much social science and in public debate there is rarely reflection upon the social and historical variability in ideas about nature and culture and their relationship. It is widely assumed that the contributions of 'nature' and 'culture' to the shaping of human subjectivity and action can be resolved 'once and for all' through rational argument and/or scientific evidence. The discipline of psychology is perhaps least critical of this assumption, and yet is probably most influential among the social science disciplines in shaping public knowledge about human beings, their behaviour and differences. Psychology textbook discussions about aggression, for example, present theories in terms of what is known about the contributions of 'nature' and 'nurture' as though science will eventually reveal 'the truth' (Petersen and Davies 1997). This denies how psychology's discourses and practices create the reality of the phenomenon that is studied.

Since the late nineteenth century, the ideas of Darwin and his followers have had a profound influence on views of both 'nature' and 'culture' and on systems of classification (see Chapter 4). Darwinism, the doctrine that human and other life forms evolve through a process of 'natural selection', whereby behaviours and attributes that have 'adaptive' value survive, whereas those that do not, disappear, has provided the model for thinking and the language and metaphors for talking about the natural and social world. Darwin, of course, presents *one* theory of evolution and others before and since Darwin have proposed other theories. Although often discussed in terms of its value in scientific interpretation ('descent with modification'), the establishment of evolution as 'fact' has shaped our view of the world and our place in it (Dupré 2003: 12, 40). Darwin's views became predominant because they were consistent with an emerging discourse on the origins of species, and helped to explain and justify the hierarchical and unequal society associated with industrial capitalism. Darwin's famous phrase 'struggle for existence' is a metaphor which found resonance in the emerging capitalist order and has influenced thinking about the social world as well as the physical world (Maasen and Weingart 2000: 41–62). The influence of Darwinian ideas on social thought and social action (e.g. Social Darwinism) shows how ideas may flow between the natural sciences and the social sciences. Marx's historical materialism, for example, presents an evolutionary view of social development: feudal society gave rise to capitalist society, which in time, through 'natural' laws of development (contradictions and resulting social tensions and class struggles) led inexorably to the emergence of a communist utopia. As with Marxism, at least in its classic formulation, evolutionary ideas often appear to be radical and liberating. That is, the 'freedom' from material constraint (oppressive living and working conditions, in the case of Marxism) and from disease, early death, disability, and mental and physical pain (in the case of natural sciences, particularly the biomedical sciences) are widely believed to be outcomes of the evolutionary development of ideas and practices. Evolutionary theory suggests that conditions, policies and practices are in a process of constant change and improvement.

Sometimes explicitly, though perhaps more often implicitly, Darwinism has informed discussions about new technologies of the body, such as new drugs, genetic therapies, prenatal tests, reconstructive surgery, and implants of various kinds. That is, scientific research of 'natural' processes is seen to 'progress' and to 'improve' bodies and lives. What is often not acknowledged is that the evolutionary theory of Darwin can be and has been used to justify all kinds of inequalities and injustices, including racial discrimination, eugenics, and sex discrimination and exploitation. The deployment of a crude dictum 'survival of the fittest' has been used to justify ruthless competitivism in the workplace and to explain why some people succeed in life and become wealthy and why others fail and remain poor. Darwinism has lent legitimacy to colonial regimes and to the exploitation of indigenous peoples and populations of the developing world. Rich, developed, nations are seen to have succeeded because they have superior civilisations. Recently, proponents of evolutionary psychology have suggested that rape and other kinds of exploitative behaviours can be explained by genes, and hence are 'natural', the implication being that it is inevitable (see, e.g. Thornhill and Palmer 2000). Darwin's theory of evolution has persistently provoked debate. For example in some states of the USA, the idea of gradual changes through evolution which result in variations among populations and species has been vigorously contested, principally on the grounds that it is seen to conflict with creationism or the idea that humans were directly created by God. The notion of 'intelligent design' is proposed by those who believe that certain features of the universe and living things are best explained by an intelligent force rather than by an undirected process such as natural selection.[1] In some states, schools have attempted to remove references to evolution from the biology curriculum or to stick labels on textbooks stating 'Evolution is a theory, not a fact', as occurred in Georgia's Cobb County.[2]

Social constructionism has been presented as offering something of an antidote to the biological or naturalistic view of the body and its development promoted in particular by Darwinism. The basic premise of social constructionism, namely that 'nature' is 'constructed' rather than constituting a pre-social physical reality ('biology') on the face of it seems radical and potentially liberating; however, as Ian Hacking (1999) points out, the overuse of the construction metaphor has undermined the radical potential of this approach to knowledge. In addition, constructionist analyses are often confusing in that writers often talk about X, Y or Z being constructed when in fact they are referring to the *idea* of X, Y or Z being constructed. Further, as Bruno Latour has noted, constructionists' reference to the 'social representations' of 'nature' assumes an oppositional 'real nature'. The construction of knowledge about 'nature' creates two domains: 'nature as it is, and the variable representations we make of it' (Latour 2004: 35). As Latour argues, 'nature' itself is an artefact of modern Western thought and culture: it does not exist as a category in non-Western cultures since 'they have never found a use for it' (2004: 43). Consequently, he proposes that 'nature' is best viewed as a political idea rather than as occupying a domain of reality separate from 'society' or 'culture'. Kate Soper (1995) has also drawn attention to *the politics of the idea of nature*, showing how it has been both defended and contested by social movements in the recent past. She has identified 'nature-endorsing' and 'nature-sceptical' arguments without claiming that these correspond in any simple way with different political positions. Like Latour, Soper contends that discourses about the human–nature relationship are pre-figured by a distinction between 'ourselves' and the world of nature. As she notes, it is not possible to speak about nature without at the same time speaking about ourselves (Soper 1995: 73). Thus dominant cultural views about sex, sexuality, 'race', and so on, are reflected in conceptions of and discussions about 'nature'; for example, references to 'mother nature'.

Social constructionists tend to reject any reference to nature or biology in explaining behaviours or differences for fear that this will reinforce biological determinism and associated political ideologies. However, as Soper notes, to disallow any appeal to natural differences, needs, instincts, pleasures and pains, can lead to a new form of determinism – social determinism – and to deny the benefits or powers that may derive from an appeal to 'nature' (Soper 1995: 138–139). An appeal to 'natural' rights, for example, can be used to defend groups' access to resources or freedom of movement or freedom from oppressive practices. Contrary to what is implied by many constructivist arguments, it is not always the case that that which is culturally instituted is always more temporary and readily amenable to change than the givens of biology. For instance, it may be easier to alter the body to bring it into conformity with cultural ideals of gender appearance than to change the norms themselves (Soper 1995: 140). According to Hans-Jörg Rheinberger (1995), the modern sciences, including the biomedical sciences, have fabricated an idea of nature that suggests that social development involves liberation from the constraints of nature. However, an acceleration of changes in life processes (e.g. alteration of the earth's surface and atmosphere, genetic modification), has meant that 'a fundamental alteration in the representation of nature is taking place, which we are still barely realizing' (Rheinberger 1995: 260). In Rheinberger's view, the ideal of science as 'uncontaminated by social constraints, politics, power, and destruction', which inspired many scientists at the end of the Second World War, has been eroded. As he notes, 'Today, biology has lost its innocence. It is no longer about discovering facts, it is about inventing facts' (1995: 257). According to Alan Irwin and Mike Michael (2003), the erosion of the status of science in many contemporary ('postmodern') societies can be linked to the increasing interpenetration of science with other spheres of society. In their view, modern societies have been characterised by a process of differentiation, whereby there is an 'increasingly refined separation of various spheres of human activity from one another' (Irwin and Michael 2003: 70). Expert institutions and scientific disciplines have proliferated as more and more aspects of the natural and the social world have been subject to calculation and control. Such control has been equated with the idea of modern progress. Increasingly, however, the differentiation between science and society has become less clear as a result of a number of forces. These include the growth of uncertainty, new forms of economic rationality, the transformation of time and space, and the growing reflexivity of both science and society (Irwin and Michael 2003: 71–72, citing Nowotny *et al.* 2001).

The politicisation of 'nature'

The politicisation of the idea of nature is seen in recent debates on body-related issues, including health scares, concerns about penicillin-resistant 'super-bugs', and discussions about the impacts of the 'new' genetics, nanotechnologies, and other biomedical technologies. That is, claims about nature being open to modification in the ways and extent envisaged and about the beneficial implications of the use of technologies for the individuals or groups whose bodies are subject to intervention or change, and for society in general, have been both vigorously promoted and contested. On the one hand, research undertaken in a number of fields is premised upon a vision of the alterability and perfectibility of the body. The argument of biomedical researchers and their supporters is that the supposedly objective knowledge derived from science will provide the foundation for technologies that will allow the body to be repaired, or made more resistant to disease or pain, or more able to perform certain functions, or better integrated with technologies or the external environment. Wrinkles can be made to disappear, blocked arteries can be cleared, and failed hearing can be restored. It is argued that individuals will be presented with options that will allow them more choice in their health-related decisions and lifestyles. New developments are often supported by patients and their families. Many people affected by diseases and disabilities are desperate for cures and often organise through patient groups to lobby for more research funding or for changes in legislation to support particular kinds of research. On the other hand, some groups have expressed concerns about the consequences of altering 'nature'. Anxieties about the deleterious consequences of scientists 'going too far' through inadvertently producing mutant or self-replicating life forms, for example, are common. The fear of 'nature biting back' can be seen in the recurrent images of Frankenstein and Brave New World, found not only in science fiction genre, but also in news and other media (Alison *et al.* 2005; Petersen 2001). Opposition groups, such as UK's GeneWatch[3] and Greenpeace[4] periodically warn of the 'slippery slope' that lies ahead if scientists tamper with nature. These include not only health problems and hazardous by-products, but also the infringement of rights in the workplace, in insurance, and against particular groups; for example, indigenous peoples, and disabled peoples.

Recently, a number of previously self-evident assumptions about science, nature, and the body have been questioned by a growing number of critical scholars and activists working in a range of different fields. As noted in Chapter 1, great expectations are attached to science and its powers to control and alter nature and to thereby 'serve society'. Some writers have drawn attention to how the creation of expectations about pharmacogenetics and other biomedical technologies may help shape the future of medicine (e.g. the creation of 'personalised' drugs) (see Hedgecoe 2004), even if not in ways imagined. Statements of expectation perform a strong rhetorical function, in attempting to persuade publics of the inevitability and desirability of the portrayed future. If enough people, particularly those in a position to influence policy believe that certain types of research and application will occur and are likely to be useful then resources are likely to be mobilised to advance that research and its applications. Scientists and sponsors, particularly corporate sponsors, whose profits depend hugely on the rise and fall of stocks and shares, are acutely aware of how publics' perceptions can influence the fate of new research. As indicated in Chapter 1, scientists have sought to control the content and portrayal of science news, and are keen to emphasise the benefits of their research and to show that they pursue 'responsible' research, so as to establish public confidence in their work (Nelkin 1985). A considerable amount of research in the field of science and technology studies has drawn attention to how science is socially accomplished (through day-to-day routine practices in the laboratory and other settings, the mobilisation of professional networks, the translation of raw data into publications, and so on) and to the cultural values and biases which underlie its practices (e.g. Latour and Woolgar 1986; Latour 1987). Science is heavily dependent on research funding, and increasingly corporate sponsorship, which influences both the lines of research undertaken and how research is portrayed in the public domain. The links between scientists and their corporate sponsors are often strong, and there is considerable blurring between public and private interest. For example, research on population-based human genetic databases ('biobanks') (referred to in Chapter 1) which involves the long-term storage of DNA, personal medical and genealogical data, for example, although sponsored by governments and promoted for 'the public benefit', frequently depends on the financial support of the corporate sector, either through direct ownership of the data (e.g. Iceland's Health Sector DataBase) or by purchasing access rights to data (e.g. UK Biobank). This is likely to mean that there is a focus on diseases which are common and hence 'profitable' rather than on 'unprofitable' diseases which, although serious, affect only a relatively small proportion of the population (Foster and Sharp 2005).

The example of biobanks and other recent biotechnology research also emphasises that the question of what counts as beneficial in science and technology is open to debate, and varies through time, across contexts, and according to the standpoint of the speaker/s. Technologies deemed beneficial at one time or in one context or by one group, may be deemed hazardous at another time or in another context or by another group. As the notion of science as self-evidently objective and separate from society has been eroded, lay publics seem more prepared to question the usefulness of particular technologies and, in some cases, to reject technologies. The proliferation of consumer and environmental activist groups would appear to offer evidence of this. In the UK, the USA, Western Europe, Scandinavia, and elsewhere, many authorities are embracing a new conception of 'the public' in relation to science and technology. A long-standing emphasis on the 'public understanding of science', which assumed that the task for scientists and authorities was to educate publics who are assumed to lack knowledge (i.e. the so-called 'deficit model') is being replaced more and more by the notions of 'public dialogue' and 'public engagement', which suggest a more democratic relationship between experts and lay people (Irwin and Michael 2003: 19–64). At least in official rhetoric, lay knowledge and contextual information is accorded value in the development of new technologies, partly it would seem in response to growing realisation that science and technology that does not meet broad public consent and is not perceived as relevant to local contexts is likely to be resisted. In the UK, for example, the emphasis on 'public engagement' followed in the wake of public rejection of GM crops and in a context of a perception of a decline of public trust in science in general (see Chapter 6).

At the time of writing, what 'public engagement' means *in practice* and its implications for scientific authority is far from clear. Whether it is possible to achieve the degree of openness, transparency, and two-way communication suggested by the democratic perspective, especially given existing structures and disparities in power and knowledge is questionable. Official reports on 'science and society' published in the late twentieth and early twenty-first centuries reveal a tension concerning the relationship between science and its publics: 'a general emphasis on inclusion, openness and public values' vies with a 'tendency to retreat to more technocratic and "top-down" models' (Irwin and Michael 2003: 55). However, the importance of greater transparency and openness is at least widely acknowledged and 'dialogue' has become a central concept within policy initiatives (Irwin and Michael 2003: 63). At the same time, there is steadily growing recognition of the unequal impacts of the uptake of new technologies of the body: while some groups may benefit, others may be disadvantaged. New gene tests may allow some individuals who want the information to know for certain (or at least entertain the illusion of certainty) that their health condition has a genetic basis. However, others may feel under pressure to take the tests because they exist and may be concerned about the consequences of being tested, and fear (justifiably or not) discrimination at work or in insurance. Similarly, body modification practices such as cosmetic surgery and implants may improve the self-conception of a relatively small number of individuals, but leave unquestioned the sources of the pressures which lead to such modification, such as the widespread portrayal of particular body ideals, and may cause many more others to feel discontent with their bodies. An over-emphasis on individual treatments and enhancements diverts attention and resources away from strategies and programmes that may benefit whole populations. It should be noted that it is a relatively small segment of the population, mostly in the rich developed world, which tends to have access to the above technologies and that these are being developed at a time when there are growing global disparities in wealth and health.

The view that science has the potential to alter nature in ways claimed by scientists with benefits for 'the public' underlies arguments for bioscience research and its applications as well as diverse policies and practices affecting the treatment, enhancement and management of the body. In order that scientific activity can be undertaken, it is essential that publics believe that scientific enquiry is disinterested (i.e. unaffected by politics and power) and that its outcomes are essentially beneficent (e.g. new drugs, reduced healthcare costs) and that any implications and problems can be adequately regulated. This belief also tends to be shared by governments who invest substantial amounts of public funds on innovations arising from new fields of biomedical and biotechnology research and development, and create a regulatory environment supportive of research and development. For many, if not most fields of biotech/biomedical research, scientists, representatives of the pharmaceutical and biotechnology industry sector, and policy makers tend to share the view that, first, the benefits of new biotech/biomedical developments *on balance* outweigh their risks and that, second, risks/ problems associated with biotech/biomedical developments are mostly amenable to control and that, third, adopted regulatory mechanisms are free of adverse, unanticipated consequences. Publics ('the consumers'), on the other hand, are assumed to be willing recipients of science's products, who, it is claimed or assumed, will be 'empowered' through developments. These portrayals of science and its publics are promoted by diverse media, including the news press, advertising, health advice, the Internet, and other forums. More and more, new biotech/biomedical developments are promoted on the basis that they will improve bodies and lives, particularly through creating more options ('choice'), and hence enhanced 'freedom of choice' for individuals. The following paragraphs critically examine these arguments and claims in detail, including the notion that altering the natural body in prescribed ways necessarily 'empowers' individuals, drawing on some recent newspaper reports on developments in the fields of neuroscience and embryonic stem cell research.

The role of the media

As indicated in Chapter 1, the news media are a rich source for stories on body-related issues in many contemporary societies. News reports provide a 'window' for examining changing constructions of the body as well as expectations about how science may change the natural body so as to restore or improve its health, appearance, and functioning. They are worthy of investigation because they are pervasive and provide a common reference point in public discussions about new technological developments. They offer a useful starting point for examining the mediation and the politics of the representation of science and technology, nature, and the body. I would argue that understanding the operations of the media in general, and of the news media in particular, is crucial to an understanding of how science is *accomplished*. Recent press reports of a number of biomedical and bio-technology developments lend the impression that science is able to change the natural body in ways unimaginable in the past. Stories often include claims about the potential of particular lines of research and convey the impression that 'breakthroughs' and applications are imminent. They reflect belief in the power of science and portray visions of utopian and dystopian futures associated with its applications. This portrayal is assisted by the use of particular language, metaphors, literary devices, and accompanying illustrative material. It is therefore important to closely examine how the portrayal of science and technology issues in the news may shape expectations, policies and personal behaviours.

Despite the undoubted significance of the media in the formation of public discourse, as argued in Chapter 1 it would be wrong to assume that the media directly influence the views of readers or audiences, 'causing' them to think and act in line with messages, as seems to be suggested by 'media effects' research. Media influence is difficult to demonstrate, since publics are likely to engage with media in highly diverse ways, and there are potentially a considerable number of factors affecting views and actions. However, the way stories are 'framed' is likely to shape expectations which influence actions and policies. By giving prominence to certain claims, facts, themes or images and ignoring others, news media are likely to confirm beliefs and heighten fears about possible futures. Stories about particular issues have the potential substantially to shape the terms in which issues are considered, especially if alternative or critical viewpoints are absent. Articles are generally written with an assumed public in mind: different sectors of the media are pitched at particular 'reader profiles', and use language, metaphors, and references with which readers are likely to be already familiar. Stories are chosen by journalists and editors with a view to their potential relevance and interest to particular publics, and a connection to readers is established through various means, including use of catchy headlines, humour, personal stories, expert quotes and reference to unusual or controversial issues or events. News reports about all kinds of issues, such as MMR vaccinations, MRSA ('superbugs') the SARS virus and BSE, have very likely contributed to widespread fears about risks to health. There is good reason to believe that news framing of issues about biomedical technologies may similarly shape expectations about their implications, both their benefits and risks. There is some evidence of this in relation to the reporting of stem cell treatments, with people seeking treatments in the wake of news coverage of promising new developments in this field (see, e.g. Boseley 2006a, 2006b).

Rather than viewing news items on body-related issues as a journalistic translation of science fact, which is suggested by the so-called science popularisation model of science news reporting (Logan 1991), they can be viewed as a product of complex interactions between scientists, other stakeholders in science developments (e.g. patient groups, NGOs, religious groups), journalists and editors who vie for control over the public definition of science and its implications. In a context of clashing images and metaphors, it has arguably become increasingly difficult for publics to make sense of developments and to know how to distinguish between 'science fact' and 'science fiction' (Petersen 2005b). (See Chapter 1.) The blurring of 'fact' and 'fiction' in portrayals of science is clearly evident in recent news reporting on 'breakthroughs' in neuroscience and embryonic stem cell research. These fields have attracted wide interest because of their potential to change the way we view humans and to solve problems long seen as rooted in 'nature' and thus immutable. They therefore call strongly upon the imagination as to how they are likely to develop in the future. Close examination of recent news coverage of neuroscience and stem cell research 'breakthroughs' reveal a mostly positive vision of science and its potential to control 'nature' for beneficial ends. Such news stories arguably contribute to the shaping of the future by generating expectations about imminent applications. While the news articles are interesting for how they portray issues, as I note, they are perhaps more interesting for what they do not tell us. One really needs to 'get behind the news', to examine processes of science and news production to really make sense of the representation of issues. This calls for exploration of what happens in the laboratories and in the professional networks and in the process of communicating findings (the massaging of results, the downplaying of negative findings, the issuing of carefully worded press releases, the negotiations between scientists and journalists, and so on) (e.g. Latour 1987; Latour and Woolgar 1986). While it is not possible to get a 'complete picture' of science production and communication, an understanding of these processes is necessary if one is to appreciate why certain issues achieve coverage while others are ignored and also why issues are portrayed as they are.

Reading and shaping minds: neuroscience research

A number of press reports on developments in 'mind reading' and the potential to shape minds through pharmaceutical and other means appeared in the UK newspapers in the early 2000s. Such stories have a long history in Western popular culture. George Orwell's (1949) *1984* and the movie *Brainstorm* (1983), for example, foretold a future of thought and emotional control through technological developments. These particular stories tell of the more sinister implications of such developments. Recent press reports, however, suggest that science developments are rapidly closing the gap between 'fact' and 'fiction', presenting 'useful' applications as well as dangers.

> Scientists predict brave new world of brain pills.
> > (*The Guardian*, 14 July 2005)

> Where belief is born: Scientists have begun to look in a different way at how the brain creates the convictions that mould our relationships and inform our behaviour.
> > (*The Guardian*, 30 June 2005)

> Read the book, see the movie? Now smell it too.
> > (*The Guardian*, 7 April 2005)

> Meet the mind readers: Paralysed people can now control artificial limbs by thought alone.
> > (*The Guardian*, 31 March 2005

> Scans that read your mind fuel ethical worries.
> > (*The Observer*, 20 March 2005)

The last article, which I examine here in some detail reports research on brain scans which promises to have applications beyond the clinic. As the article reports:

> This growing prowess [in scanning the brain] is part of a revolution now sweeping medicine. Doctors are using scanners to study brain activity and develop techniques that could soon make breakthroughs in treating patients with depression, schizophrenia and other mental illnesses. But these scanners – called positron emission tomographs, functional magnetic-resonance imagers and near infra-red spectroscopes – are also starting to play a role in everyday life, researchers have realised. Soon they could be used to tell if a person is lying, to predict that a violent criminal could soon attack again or that they are not really in constant pain as they claim.
>
> (McKie 2005: 13)

The article notes that the UK scientist who is undertaking the research has attracted a 'steady flow of lawyers' to her laboratory who wish to know whether she can 'show that litigants suing employers over industrial injuries are lying when they say that they are in constant pain'. The scientist is quoted, saying that although her team is presently not prepared to carry out such tests, 'in a couple of years we will be ready to answer those questions'. The article also reports that there has been increasing interest among 'people in commercial and government circles' who wish to 'harness' such research. It goes on to say that 'brain scans could soon be used by schools admissions staff, employers or law enforcement agencies when recruiting. Pilots, detectives and doctors could all be rated by scanners for their pessimism or risk aversion'. And, it cites a neuroscientist who 'has warned that such assessments could be performed while carrying out tests for other purposes. The subject would be unaware why they were being tested'. The article also reports that 'President Bush's Council on Bioethics is to examine the legal, political and social implications of neuro-imaging' and that 'It has decided that opening the minds of individuals to public scrutiny is an unsettling issue, a point backed by academics and lawyers on both sides of the Atlantic'. It cites the work of a researcher at another, US, university who is undertaking research on the brain activity of whites 'who held strongly negative views about individuals with dark or black skins'. This researcher is quoted: 'I don't think we have got to the point where we can say anything about how people will act in the future, but I think we will – it's a matter of time'. The article is accompanied by what appears to be an image of a brain scan, with the accompanying description: 'Brain scans could soon be used to tell if people are lying about work injuries or to vet job applicants'.

A number of observations can be made about how this story is 'framed'. First, like many science news stories, it is a story which tells of the power of science to 'unlock the secrets of nature'. It is interesting to note the considerable references to the views of science experts, a number of whom are quoted, thus conveying the impression that the work is unmediated (straight from the experts), and thus credible. As noted in Chapter 1, the use of quotes or citations from scientists is common in news stories on bio-technology or biomedical issues and allows scientists scope to frame stories in a way that favours science – in terms of its truth or falsity, and its powers and implications. The article refers to a number of applications in medical treatment, 'for patients with depression, schizophrenia and other mental illnesses', though only well into the article (the fifth paragraph). The scien-tist who has undertaken the study is quoted, making some reference to the implications of the project for 'rating' pain, but offers no comment on the implications for health or healthcare more generally. The main focus is on the power of the new technology and the imminence of its applications. The use of phrases like 'in a couple of years we will be ready to answer those questions' (a quote from the scientist whose work is being reported), 'the growing prowess is part of a revolution now sweeping medicine', 'soon they could be used to tell if a person is lying', and 'it's a matter of time' (a quote from a second scientist), and so on, create a sense of anticipation about developments in the field. The subtext is that the progress of science is inevitable and that science will eventually force nature to 'give up its secrets'. Indeed, 'success' appears to be 'just around the corner' – a portrayal which mirrors that found in an earlier study of news reporting on medical genetic developments (Petersen 2001). Also consistent with many news stories on medical genetics and with earlier fictional portrayals of 'mind reading', such as those described above, the article reveals a dystopian vision of developments, as seen in the discussion of the 'ethical' concerns raised. There is no comment on the validity or overall value of the research, whether the technology has the powers described, whether the 'mind' can be adequately understood in biophysical terms, exactly who will benefit and how, whether the benefits of the research outweigh the potential risks and whether this kind of research should be supported and conducted.

The reference to 'reading minds' in the above article is interesting, suggesting that the mind is like a book, waiting to be deciphered by the scientist. One can see parallels with the Human Genome Project in the use of the book metaphor. That is, in discussions about the Project, the human genome was described as 'the book of life' or 'blue-print', and scientists talked of 'editing', 'de-coding' or 'mapping' the human genome (see, e.g. Condit 1999: 159–177). In the above portrayal, there is no discussion of the utility of the book metaphor and its particular value and limits for under-standing mental processes. The science itself remains unquestioned and appears unquestionable. Further, there is no mention of who is funding the research and what they hope to achieve or who owns the knowledge or who is most likely to benefit from the research. Nor are the views of potential 'users' (e.g. patient groups) or critics of neuro-imaging research presented. Insofar as 'ethical' issues are raised, these focus narrowly on particular applications of the technology *once it is developed*. Broader social, political, and policy implications (e.g. increased surveillance and social control, the generation of social inequalities, diversion of resources from other fields of research with perhaps more socially useful applications) receive no mention. In the absence of critical comment on the research and of other contextual information that would assist readers to assess its value and impacts (e.g. about history of the research, who is funding it, who will own the knowledge, who will benefit, and so on), it would be difficult for most to judge the validity of the claims and the potential value and implications of the research. How would readers know what to believe; how to distinguish 'fact' from 'fiction'? The article makes no reference to alternative sources of information which might help readers to reach an informed view. The interested reader could, perhaps, undertake a search of 'Google' and track the researcher's website. The cited researcher's University's website (not referred to in the article) indeed outlines the nature of the research, explaining that 'Our research aims have been to utilise FMRI [functional magnetic resonance imaging] to determine which brain regions are responsible for the different aspects of pain perception and then selectively modulate these regions via pharmacological or behavioural means'. Other information on the website confirms that the research's focus is on the clinical significance of understanding and measuring pain:

> Despite many advances in our understanding of the basic mechanisms underlying the major clinical pain states, effective therapies are still lacking. This is largely because development of novel drugs and a clearer understanding of pain processing in humans are hampered by a lack of objective measures of human pain. Our research focuses specifically on this issue by utilising a novel imaging approach to obtain objective information non-invasively from human subjects experiencing pain.[5]

This website, however, makes no mention of the potential applications of the research in the areas indicated in the news article, such as assessing whether people are lying when suing employers over industrial injuries, or use by schools' admission staff or law enforcement agencies when recruiting. If the quote in the news article does accurately reflect the researcher's views, it would appear that they have no objection to the research being used for other, non-medical uses. That is, they are quoted as saying that evidence deriving from brain scans could be used in court, once the technique is perfected. However, there is nothing on the website to indicate that they see their work as supporting these other potential applications of the research. Further, the website makes no reference to the ownership of the data, patenting issues, or reference to patient groups' views on the research, which would be useful for the 'informed consumer'. The definition of the issue remains firmly within the biomedical domain, while the question of who owns the data resulting from research is not discussed. The research presents a biological reductionist view of pain in that no acknowledgement is made of the complexity of the phenomenon of pain, including its socio-cultural, psychological and physiological aspects. Its assumption that pain is a sensation located in the physical body and can be understood without reference to the emotional responses and experiences of the person is deeply rooted in Western thinking and can be traced back at least as far as Descartes. (See Chapter 5.) It suggests that suffering can and should be relieved through biomedical intervention (the quick 'fix'), rather than through a multi-faceted approach involving a range of strategies, including attention to the emotional state of the person and the social context which affects the definition, experience and expression of pain. Significantly, as the website indicates, the research is funded by biomedical research bodies or companies: Dr Hadwen Trust; GlaxoSmithKline; Erasmus Wilson Dermatological Research Fund; Wellcome Trust; Pharmacia; National Institutes of Health. While a number of these bodies are independent medical research trusts, some are among the world's largest multinational pharmaceutical companies (GSK and Pharmacia (acquired by Pfizer in 2003)), who will no doubt want a relatively quick return on their research investment by way of patents for new diagnostics and drugs. Pharmaceutical companies have become increasingly interested in the use of drugs for treating depression and other mental conditions and support research in a number of fields of neuroscience which show promise, including that which has implications for the treatment of pain.

I am not suggesting that these funders directly influence the research and its reporting. However, a framing of the research which emphasises the powers of the neuro-imaging technology and its imminent applications would obviously be to the benefit of researchers who work in the field and who rely on public support which is necessary to secure ongoing funding for their work. It is hardly surprising that scientists who undertake research in this field will emphasise the benefits and outcomes of their work. Although there is never a guarantee that funding support for any research project will continue into the future (numerous factors, including movements in the stock market and changes in government regulations, will shape funders' investment decisions), projects which are expected to deliver outcomes in the near future are more likely to receive funding than projects whose outcomes are longer term or unknown. Investors want quick returns, and research with perceived immediate practical applications in the market-place or public bureaucracies is seen to have the potential to offer those returns. I have discussed this case in some detail because it so neatly illustrates how a particular framing of biomedical/biotech issues may help create a climate of expectations about research which shapes the future, both the nature of the research that is undertaken and also likely responses to evolving applications. In the framing of stories, not only is the question of what is reported and how it is reported important, but also what particular issues, themes, and viewpoints are neglected and hence not established as subject to decision-making. For publics who are heavily reliant on news media it is difficult to know what is absent in news reporting, although the issues at stake for groups who are most likely to be directly affected, such as people suffering from particular conditions or disabilities, can be significant.

An article, 'Chip reads mind of paralysed man', which appeared on the front page of *The Guardian*, also in early 2005, would seem to illustrate well the difficulty for readers of knowing what is absent in the story. According to the article, 'A severely paralysed man has become the first person to be fitted with a brain implant that allows him to control everyday objects by thought alone' (Sample 2005a: 1). The man, who had been left paralysed after a knife attack and is now wheelchair-bound and 'unable to breathe without a respirator' and has 'no chance of regaining the use of his limbs', 'has become the first patient in a controversial trial of brain implants which could help disabled people to be more independent by tapping into their brain waves'. As the article explains:

> During the three-hour operation, electrodes were attached to the surface of Mr Nagel's [the patient's] brain. They were positioned just above the sensory motor cortex, where the neural signals for controlling arm and hand movements are produced. Surgeons completed the operation by fitting a metal socket to Mr Nagel's head so he could be hooked up to a computer.
>
> (Sample 2005a: 1)

The article notes that the scientists, 'led by Professor John Donoghue, a world expert in neurotechnology at Brown University in Rhode Island', 'used a computer to decipher the brain waves picked up by the implant'.

This story is a typical good news science story, with science appearing to offer a practical application that could potentially benefit people who are severely physically disabled. The research is portrayed as being socially useful, in presenting the opportunity for severely disabled people to gain or regain control of their body functions and to live relatively 'normal lives'. Readers are informed that 'In early trials, Mr Nagel learned to move a cursor around a computer screen simply by imagining moving his arm' and that 'By using software linked to devices around the room [he] has since been able to think his TV on and off, change channel and alter the volume'. In the article, the scientist is quoted: 'Eventually, we want him to use it [the software] to control the lights, his phone and other devices . . .'. The article also notes that:

> In the most recent tests . . . Mr Nagel was able to use thought to open and close an artificial prosthetic hand and move a robotic arm to grab sweets from one person's hand and drop them in another. He has also sharpened his skills at computer games by playing the old arcade game Pong.

In other words, the subtext is that the technology has assisted this disabled man and potentially other disabled people to undertake 'normal' human activities. The article finishes with a prediction from the scientist that 'the implant . . . will ultimately allow paraplegics to regain the use of their limbs'. However, although 'We're very encouraged by Matthew . . . we're cautious. It's just one person. There's further to go, but we're absolutely on the way' (Sample 2005a: 1).

On the face of it, there may seem to be nothing contentious about this story of science 'breakthrough' and promise. Like the first story, it suggests that the breakdown in a natural function can be remedied and suffering alleviated through biomedical intervention. The technological 'fix' appears close at hand. However, again, there is little contextual information that would allow publics to assess the claims that are made, including critical commentary and information on funding sources. Significantly, readers are offered no perspective from representatives of disability groups as to whether they support the research and judge it to be potentially useful in terms of significantly improving the lives of people with disabilities. The ethics of such research is not discussed, though there is passing reference to 'a controversial trial', which suggests that there has been some contention about the research; however, no details of the controversy are provided. Some disability scholars and activists are critical of the use of such technological innovations in the absence of changes in social views on disabled people and alterations to the physical environment in order to facilitate mobility. Technological innovations are often developed from the abled person's view of a 'normal' body and life rather than reflecting any real understanding of what disabled people want and need. Such stories may lead to unrealistic expectations among disabled people and their families that there is hope for their predicament when, in fact, as the scientists' concluding comments indicate, the research is based on a trial involving one person and is not conclusive. One can imagine other, perhaps more questionable uses of such research, such as mind control, as outlined in the earlier news article. Interestingly, a search of the researcher's lab website (Donohue Lab) reveals that among funders of this research are The Defense Advanced Research Projects Agency (DARPA).[6] This Agency, which its own website explains is 'the central research and development organization for the Department of Defense (DoD)', 'manages and directs selected basic and applied research and development projects for DoD, and pursues research and technology where risk and payoff are both very high and where success may provide dramatic advances for traditional military roles and missions'.[7] The researcher's website provides no details of how this research may advance the DoD's objectives. Again, although I am not suggesting that the research or its reporting is directly influenced by the funders, a 'framing' of new stories about the research which suggests that outcomes are imminent and potentially beneficial is favourable to the research in that it is more likely to receive support than research where outcomes are longer-term and of uncertain value.

That some companies believe in the potential of science to shape the mind in ways described above is reflected in a news story which reports that Sony Electronics 'has patented a device to evoke smells, flavours and even a sense of touch in audiences brains, in the hope of enhancing the movie-watching experience' (Sample 2005b). As the article explains: 'According to the [patent] documents, pulses of ultrasound would be fired at the audience's heads to alter the normal neural activity in key parts of the brain'. The article refers to the patents which describe how 'carefully directed ultrasound beams could evoke different sensations in people's brains, including tastes, smells and touch'. It goes on to say, 'One of the advantages is that no invasive surgery is needed to assist a person, such as a blind person, to view live/recorded images'. A spokeswoman for the company is quoted as saying in *New Scientist* magazine, 'This particular patent is a prophetic invention. . . . It was based on inspiration that this may someday be the direction that technology will take us'. Despite questionable assumptions behind the use of the technology, such as whether it is valid to influence people's senses through such means, whether publics will want to be influenced in this way and whether people will have similar responses to particular sensations (a problem raised by one cited commentator, in the last paragraph of the article), it would seem that corporate decisions have been made on the premise that the technological altering of minds through the means described can work and that it will find useful commercial application. The article seems to suggest that because the technology involves no 'invasive surgery' for those who need 'assistance' to view live/recorded images it is unlikely to be seen as objectionable. Assumptions are made about what human subjects ('consumers') desire from movies, while human feeling is reduced to neurological functioning. This case illustrates well how an expectation about science and about its ability to shape nature may have real material affects, by way of influencing corporate behaviour and potentially research funding decisions.

Regenerating the body: stem cell research

Recent news reporting and policy discussion on stem cell research, particularly embryonic stem cell research, also reveals considerable expectations of science; namely that diseased and damaged bodies may soon by regenerated through the development of stem cell treatments. These news articles suggest that science is rapidly releasing humans from the constraints of nature, in effect allowing them to replicate cells and rebuild themselves anew through use of therapeutic cloning technologies. A number of highly publicised cases in the UK news media, including the Hashmi couple's plight to use the techniques of pre-implantation genetic diagnosis (PGD) and tissue typing to select a 'perfectly matched' sibling who would provide the donor cells in order to help save their son who is suffering from the blood disorder beta thalassaemia, and Christopher Reeves' championing of stem cell research in the USA, has brought this issue to public prominence (see Petersen *et al.* 2005). Research involving the use of human embryonic stem cells has been the focus of considerable controversy in recent years in large part because it is seen to involve the discarding of embryos (unused from IVF treatments, or made specifically for research) which have the potential to develop into human beings. The sanctity of life or 'right to life', when life begins, commodifying life (the creation of 'designer babies'), using one life to save another and the psychological effects on recipients of treatments (which surfaced in the Hashmi case) have been issues at the centre of debates. While, according to proponents of stem cell research, 'the public' stands to benefit from attendant medical applications, there have been diverse assessments of the value and implications of research. Some groups, including certain religious groups and right to life groups, have made considerable efforts to stop research through legislative and other means. Many scientists and policy makers, however, see great potential in the medical applications of stem cell research, and believe it could provide the basis for a flourishing biotech industry.

Different countries have developed different regulatory policies in response to local political, cultural, religious, and other factors, with the USA, for instance, taking a more restrictive policy at the national level than the UK, which has granted licences to some science groups to undertake research, which is seen by some to provide an economic advantage in the biotech 'race'. Although not often part of the news headlines and public discourse on stem cell research, the economic expectations for the field are considerable, with policies pertaining to stem cells (and other biotechnology developments, e.g. human genetic databases) in different countries often embroiled in projects of nation-building (Jasanoff 2005: 7–9). In late 2004, the UK and California (after the passing of Proposition 71 in November of that year which legalised stem cell research) were heralded by some commentators as 'leading the world in stem cell research', due to the propitious legal and institutional contexts for such research (*Medical News Today*, 8 December 2004) (http://www.medicalnewstoday.com/medicalnews.php?newsid=17472) (Accessed 12 May 2005) A subsequent news item suggested that China was also 'set to become the leader in the field of stem cell research' (Tomlinson and Adam 2005). Developments in South Korea and publicity about the fraudulent research of Woo Suk Hwang, however, served to highlight the significance of economic interests and national identity in research decisions in this field (Gottweis and Triendl 2006). The issues surrounding stem cell harvesting and research and the factors affecting different policy responses are highly complex and I can do no more than touch on just a few of them here. In particular, I wish to focus on the guiding visions of the field of research in relation to the regeneration of the body, for overcoming disease, disability, and dysfunction, again, emphasising how the portrayal of research in news media may help shape future actions through the heightening of expectations. The case of stem cell research provides illustration of the playing out of the politics of the idea of nature: claims that science has the ability to control nature for beneficial purposes are strongly promoted or contested by a range of groups on religious, human rights, health and other grounds. As with the news reporting of neuroscience research, referred to earlier, it is interesting to note the exclusion of certain issues from coverage and thus potentially public debate.

Recent news items reveal the perceived regenerative potential of stem cell treatments. Some of these include:

Pioneering stem cell surgery restores sight
TimesOnline[8]

Eggs taken from stem cells may delay menopause
The Guardian, 5 May 2005

Stem cells could improve hearing
BBC News UK Edition, 22 November 2004[9]

Cystic fibrosis stem cells made
BBC News UK Edition, 9 September 2004[10]

Stem cells promise stroke therapy
BBC News, UK Edition, 26 July 2004[11]

Cell transplant for NZ woman
tvnz.co.nz, 24 March 2005[12]

Such stories of promising lines of stem cell research suggest that defects or failures of the body can be corrected or limitations overcome through treatments. Words such as 'restore', 'delay', and 'improve', used in the title of the above stories, immediately signal the nature of the promises attached to stem cell research. These are stories of hope, sometimes involving the miraculous recovery of damaged organs and transformed lives. As with stories on neuroscience research, discussed earlier, scientists are frequently quoted, pointing out the significance and potential applications of research. It is worth examining some of these in some detail, since they illustrate well the expectations for the field.

The first story, 'Pioneering stem cell surgery restores sight' tells of 'more than a dozen' patients who have had their damaged eyesight restored through a form of surgery involving the transplantation of stem cells cultured in a laboratory into their eyes. An ophthalmic surgeon who had developed the technique is quoted, saying that doctors were 'astonished at how the cells appeared to trigger the eye's natural regeneration of its damaged surface'. The article notes, 'Tests on the patients after a year revealed no trace of the DNA of the stem-cell donor, meaning that the repair was carried out by the eye's own cells – a permanent healing process that does not require long-term use of powerful drugs to suppress the patient's immune system'. A patient who lost his sight through an industrial accident involving caustic acid is also quoted, saying how the operation had 'transformed his life'. The second story, 'Eggs taken from stem cells may delay menopause', announces that 'Scientists have used stem cells to grow healthy human eggs for the first time, a development they believe will usher in new fertility treatments and enable women to delay menopause by a decade'. The article draws attention to the shortage of donors of eggs which are 'desperately needed by fertility clinics to help women trying for babies through IVF'. It notes, 'The research suggests that a near limitless supply of eggs could be produced by taking a woman's own stem cells and growing them into eggs in the lab'. The researcher 'who led the work' explains that 'women are capable of producing new eggs later in life, rather than being limited to the quota they are born with'. The article also notes that 'his work could lead to advances in fertility treatment that would allow women to grow and store their own viable eggs, so they can delay having a family until an older age'. And, finally: 'The stem cells could also be used to rejuvenate ageing ovaries, with the potential of delaying menopause for 10 to 12 years'. (As noted in Chapter 1, if recent news stories are to be believed, the prospect of older women giving birth is now feasible.) The third story, 'Stem cells could improve hearing', reports that research on stem cells could be used for the treatment of people with certain types of hearing loss. Again, a scientist is quoted, saying how he is attempting to convert embryonic stem cells into cells for the human ear. Although he says the research is in the 'very early stages', 'this sort of treatment could eventually help people who've lost their hearing as a result of degeneration of the cochlear, those who've lost hair cells because of loud noise or drug treatments, and people with certain genetic conditions'.

These accounts present a view of science as a progressive force, as involving the gradual accumulation of knowledge leading to the 'unlocking of nature's secrets' to allow control over life itself. Scientists appear as heroic figures devoted to advancing the health of the public. Limitations on bodily functions and lifestyles brought about by disease, debilitating events and ageing that in the past may have been seen as God-given, natural or simply due to 'bad luck' are seen as subject to remedial action through biomedical intervention. Stem cell research is portrayed as saving or empowering lives and as thus oriented to the benefit of 'the public'. The inclusion of personal narratives of transformed lives assists in this positive portrayal of research. The subtext is that it is unarguable that research which can restore lost faculties or functioning, such as loss of sight or hearing or inability to reproduce, should be supported. Such positive stories of biomedical developments have been found to be common in the news on health and medicine (Karpf 1988). Appeals to health have strong rhetorical power, especially since, increasingly, as individuals we are called upon, as a duty of citizenship, to play our part in advancing health (Petersen and Lupton 1996). It cannot be doubted that many people's lives are detrimentally affected by such losses or declines in function and to many people it would seem reasonable that anything that can be done to improve the health and well-being of people should be supported. It is assumed that it is something that 'we', the news-reading public, can all agree on. Indeed, why would one object to research which has the potential to restore health and well-being? However, as in the news stories on neuroscience developments, mentioned earlier, there is an absence of reference to contextual information or alternative, more critical views which may potentially affect how one assesses the claims and the significance of the research. The style of news portrayal, which tends to focus on a single narrative theme (e.g. the 'breakthrough', the good news story) works against the presentation of complexity, ambiguity and inclusion of multiple voices. What such stories mostly *do not* portray are the behind-the-scenes struggles of scientists in competition with other scientists to achieve the 'breakthrough' which can lead to incredible pressures on researchers and, in some cases (as with the Hwang episode) fraudulent practices (the creation of fake stem cell lines). The Hwang episode revealed the failures of governance in biotechnology research, the economic and political pressures to achieve success, and the unrealistic expectations for the field (Gottwies and Triendl 2006).

It is interesting that not long after the Hwang case was reported, another news item revealed that a top UK stem cell researcher had left the UK to take up a research position in Spain (Barnett 2006: 13). In the article, the scientist argued that he was concerned about how stem cell research was relayed to the media in Britain. It was reported that he was unhappy because his university had organised a press conference to announce that the university had cloned a human embryo. This conference was to coincide with the publication of Hwang's research in *Science*. The scientist expressed concern about promises made when acute diseases may be cured, which he considered to be 'not responsible', given that there are 'plenty of desperate patients out there'. As he went on to say:

> People have to stop promising things. We know nothing about how we will cure these acute diseases, especially using stem cells, and we must not support the concept that stem cells are the holy grail and will cure all diseases. They will definitely cure some diseases but not all.
>
> (Barnett 2006: 13)

As noted, embryonic stem cell research has been highly contentious for a number of reasons and has become the subject of considerable debate. The nature of the issues discussed and the policy responses often vary considerably between jurisdictions, reflecting the dynamics of local socio-cultural and politico-economic contexts (see Jasanoff 2005: 192–202). However, different positions tend to polarise around very different visions of science and its power to alter nature. In the USA, for example, influential 'pro-life' groups and a number of consumer groups have vied with scientists and health policy makers in their efforts to establish a preferred definition of the issue. US President Bush's decision in 2001 to limit federal funding of stem cell research to a small group of stem cell lines already available on or before 9 August of that year was criticised in early 2005 by many scientists and 'several directors' within the US's National Institutes of Health (NIH) who in speaking out against the policy 'br[oke] with a tradition of deference to top administration officials'.[13] Government debates about proposed changes in legislation to allow access to new stem cell lines revealed the nature of some fears about this field of research, in particular the equating of embryonic stem cell research with eugenics or efforts to engineer the human germ line. In April 2005, one US newspaper announced that the vote on a bill (subsequently rejected) that would allow embryonic stem (ES) cell research to take place on human embryos left over from fertility treatments and donated for research was delayed for a second time by the Senate of the state of Washington, 'after an "emotional" debate in which one state Senator, Republican Alex Deccio, compared ES cell research to the Holocaust and genocide in Africa'.[14]

Despite great sensitivities surrounding such research and legislative restrictions in some jurisdictions, many countries see great promise in the field, both in medical and economic terms, and a growing number are investing in embryonic stem cell research projects. For example, in April 2005, of 25 EU member states 'more than a dozen allow at least some forms of embryonic stem cell research' (Stafford 2005: 419). A number of Asian countries are also investing in embryonic stem cell research, including China, Singapore and, as noted, until recently South Korea (Tomlinson and Adam 2005). According to a report in the *Wall Street Journal*, published in April 2005, 'several large US companies – including Johnson & Johnson, General Electric, BD, Invitrogen and the US-based research unit of Novartis – have begun "stepping gingerly" into the "politically charged arena" of human embryonic stem cell research'.[15]

> Although large companies previously had been 'notably absent' from the debate over the scientific and moral implications of the research, their recent involvement indicates 'how the scientific – and commercial – appeal' of the research is 'luring some companies into at least exploratory work', according to the *Journal*. Their involvement – ranging from using the cells to test new drugs to developing new transplant treatments – also might 'spur spending and help win wider acceptance' for the research, the *Journal* reports. However, some companies are attempting to keep a 'low profile' over their involvement with embryonic stem cells, according to the *Journal*. A *Journal* survey of the 12 largest drug firms by sales showed several previously undisclosed research projects involving embryonic stem cells, although many firms denied involvement with stem cells and had policies against such research.[16]

In a field which involves such obvious sensitivities, it is hardly surprising that companies have sought to keep a 'low profile' and, in some cases, not disclose research projects involving embryonic stem cells. As recent events show, the stakes in the representation of this field are high. In August 2006, researchers claimed to have 'creat[ed]' human embryonic stem cells without destroying the embryo itself' (Abbott, 2006), thus removing a major ethical hurdle confronting scientists working in this field. As an online *Nature* article noted, the paper outlining the research 'attracted worldwide media excitement' while 'Shares in Lanza's [the researcher's] company, Advanced Cell Technology 'leapt five-fold in price in just 10 hours.' However, 'this was quickly followed by a backlash as it became clear that all 16 of the embryos used in the research had been destroyed.' Many scientists in the field were reported to have objected to the paper's 'overall packaging' (Abbott, 2006). It is difficult for publics to know whether research that is reported in the news is representative of all work in the field and is accurately portrayed. Concerns among companies to maintain confidentiality to protect promising new fields of research in a highly competitive market-place and among scientists to emphasize the novelty and value of their research may curtail opportunities for publics to learn about new work and to have access to the kinds of information that would allow them to assess the claims being made. Fears in the commercial sector that public reactions may lead to a backlash against promising new research is likely to reinforce secrecy and reliance on 'commercial confidentiality' in negotiations in this field. The behind-the-scenes interactions between commercial interests and policy makers, and other influential stakeholders have an undoubted influence on the policies that affect what research gets funded and gets reported in the news as 'breakthrough'. As in other emergent fields of biotechnology establishing public trust is crucial to technological development, and a positive portrayal of new research in the news media undoubtedly assists in this regard. The exclusion of the majority of 'the public' from decision-making about stem cell research is antithetical to the ideal of 'public engagement' which, as noted earlier, increasingly has been espoused by governments and other authorities in recent years. (See Chapter 6.)

Concluding comments

Debates about the relative contributions of 'nature' and 'culture' to conceptions of the human and about the potential of technologies to alter the natural body through technologies such as those described above will no doubt continue into the future. As I indicated, there is much at stake for both social science and for social policy and social practices concerning how such issues are portrayed. With the development of a growing number of new technologies of the body, as a result of research in biomedicine and biotechnology, expectations about the potential to change nature in particular ways for the benefit of 'the public' are likely to increase in the future. There seems little doubt that the idea of the natural body, if not overturned, has at least been substantially unsettled by recent biomedical and biotechnology developments. I have focused on the above examples of news stories in some detail because they illustrate well the beliefs that surround science and its powers to intervene into and change the natural body. As I argued, news media portrayals are worthy of close examination by those interested in the constructions of the body because they are a major source of knowledge on new body technology 'breakthroughs' for many people and reflect broader visions about how science and technology may change bodies and lives, for better or worse. The above stories suggest considerable promise about the potential of science to alter nature, to offer more control over biophysical processes, to help overcome human suffering, and to create healthier, happier lives for individuals. A strong theme in these stories is the potential of the applications of research to 'empower' users of technologies, through offering them more choice in healthcare and, in some instances, in other areas of their lives. The way these stories are 'framed' may contribute to the heightening of expectations about their development and thereby help shape actions and policies. In the absence of readily accessible alternative sources of information on developments and knowledge of contextual issues shaping them, it would be difficult for publics (including policy makers) to assess the nature of the claims that are made. There are powerful interests at work in the development of body technologies and in promoting the view that science can alter and 'tame' nature in the ways depicted. However, although such depictions may help shape expectations and hence possible futures, there is no certainty that scientific developments will materialise in the ways depicted.

This chapter has focused on body technologies *in development or promised* rather than already widely used and the expectations associated with them. In the next chapter, I examine people's engagements with technologies of the body *already widely marketed and in use*. Specifically, I examine technologies and practices for reshaping and perfecting the body. In the process, I hope to reveal the active ways in which individuals and groups may engage with body ideals, to both reinforce and disrupt views on what constitutes a 'normal, healthy' body.

3 Re-shaping and perfecting bodies

In recent years, within the media and more generally there has been a burgeoning interest in various forms of body modification and management. Advertisements and television programmes about obesity, face lifts, breast implants, penile enlargements and other cosmetic surgery, sexual enhancement technologies (e.g. Viagra), anti-ageing creams, treatments for short stature, body decoration and body piercing, body building, and the like, lend the impression of a veritable market-place of ways to re-shape, improve or perfect the body. Biomedical treatments, including laser and new surgical techniques, which allow doctors to nip, tuck, and suck away unwanted fat and iron out wrinkles and accentuate parts of anatomy (e.g. silicone breast implants) have arguably contributed to an increasingly consumerist orientation to the body and health and to changing perceptions of the natural body. The body shape and beauty industries involving biomedical and pharmaceutical companies which have a global reach, governments, medical and public health authorities, and other groups, have no doubt fuelled much of this interest, with promises of creating more desirable bodies and transforming lives. While there is nothing especially new about some of the claims – advertisements for cosmetic surgery, including face lifts, nose reconstructions, tummy tucks, liposuction and hair transplants were widely requested by the end of the 1980s (Balsamo 1996: 63) – in the early twenty-first century they have become all pervasive. A growing number of television programmes, magazine articles and Internet sites on body modification, involving 'real stories' of success (and sometimes failure), have helped to make widely accessible knowledge of such technologies and promote the view that potentially everyone can benefit.

In this chapter, I explore a number of questions about the sources, operations and implications of body modification and management practices, beginning with concerns around body shape and weight. Specifically, I examine the socio-political context shaping the drive to achieve the ideal 'perfect' body size, shape and appearance and highlight the significance for conceptions of the normal healthy person. I contend that 'perfection' is a dangerous illusion: an unrealisable ideal whose pursuit can predispose to extreme forms of body modification and personal harm, and reinforce inequalities. However, as some recent social science work reveals, people's engagements with body modification and management practices are complex and do not always accord with the portrayals presented by some commentators and sections of the media. In the chapter, I focus attention on the make-up and operations of the body shape/size and beauty industries and the body experts and authorities themselves – particularly biomedical scientists, public health bodies, doctors, psychologists, and psychotherapists – and the claims they make about the body and its treatment. And, I focus on the 'consumers' and question some common assumptions about their engagements with beauty and body modification practices. And, finally, in light of recent developments in this field and shifts in power and politics, I conclude the chapter by pointing to some new questions and areas in need of investigation and discussion. I begin, however, by examining some social science contributions to understanding issues of body shape or size and appearance to date, which underline the variability in notions of normality and beauty.

The social science literature on body shape/size and appearance

There has been a great deal of social science research exploring the cross-cultural and historical variability in ideals of body shape, size and appearance and what they signify for identity, health and well-being. However, generalisation from existing work can be hazardous. Cross-cultural comparisons can prove especially difficult when based on data from studies employing different definitions, methodologies and samples and undertaken at different points in time. In some cases, apparent relativity in ideals and practices may be more temporal than cultural (Nasser 1997: 16). Further, the cross-cultural salience of some categories can be questioned. Categories such as 'obese' and 'fat', which have biomedical and negative connotations, may have little salience in non-Western societies or cultures (Popenoe 2004: 4). Discussions about body weight in particular are replete with normative assumptions (e.g. about 'normal, healthy' body shape, size and weight and the relationship between body weight and health) and are restricted by the use of biomedical, psychological, psychiatric and psychoanalytic frameworks and categories. Historical research also suffers from limitations in being limited largely to Western societies. However, notwithstanding these caveats, there is evidence enough to challenge the notion that there is a universal and fixed 'normal' or 'healthy' or 'beautiful' body. The ideals of body shape and size and beauty and what they signify for identity, health and vitality, vary *across* societies and change through time *within* societies (see e.g. Grogan 1999: 133–137). In the West, for example, as recently as the 1950s, the ideal 'healthy' body was much fuller than that valued in the early twenty-first century – the often-cited example of that period being Marilyn Monroe (Bordo 1993: 141). Views about beauty and how to make oneself 'beautiful' have changed considerably in the West since the nineteenth century, when more and more women began to regularly use make-up. In Victorian times, suspicion surrounded women's use of cosmetics to enhance appearance, for a variety of reasons. For men, cosmetics were seen as potentially disguising disfigurement from disease or rejuvenating the appearance of older women and thus providing an 'unfair weapon in the armoury of unscrupulous women' (Gimlin 2002: 23). It was also associated with prostitution and stage makeup used by actresses (2002: 23). Indeed, debate about women's use of 'paint' continued up until the First World War. Growing interest among women in the use of beauty products in general from the mid-nineteenth century has been linked to women's new sense of identity as consumers and increased advertising of brand-name products and 'feminine' products (Peiss 1998: 50, citing Gimlin 2002: 27). I examine feminist views on the beauty industry and beauty practices in more detail later in the chapter.

Popenoe makes the broad observation that in the vast majority of human societies body ideals tend towards a larger body size, especially for women, which is associated with health rather than illness, while in the contemporary affluent West, tall streamlined thin bodies are most highly valued and are seen as signifying health, success and happiness (Popenoe 2004: 4). Over the last few decades, in the USA at least (which would seem to replicate the situation in the UK and many other Western countries), there has been a growing divergence between the ideal female body and average weights. While fashion models have been growing thinner, the average size of women has been growing larger (Gimlin 2002: 5). It would appear that Western ideals of body shape and size are becoming more and more pervasive at the global level and that this is at least partly responsible for growing concern in non-Western societies about body size/weight, which would seem to contribute to the growth of clinical cases of eating disorders or body dissatisfaction in these societies. In her book *Culture and Weight Consciousness*, Mervat Nasser comments that 'eating pathology, a condition thought to be unique to white Western cultures is now emerging in societies/races/cultures that were for a long time presumed immune to this pathology, and possibly occurs with similar or even higher rates of those reported in the West' (1997: 46). Drawing on data from studies among populations in non-Western societies and among ethnic minority groups in Britain, North America and elsewhere, Nasser believes that exposure to Western society and its norms of weight and shape preferences has led to increased concerns with weight and disordered eating patterns (1997: 46). Further, findings of body dissatisfaction among women from Hispanic, Asian and Zulu communities which did not traditionally experience such problems have been reported by Grogan (1999: 136–137) and Seed *et al*. (undated), respectively.

One theme in the social science literature in this field has been the culturally variable conceptions of self or identity associated with particular body sizes, shapes and appearances. Different societies ascribe the self with different degrees of autonomy and agency reflecting different relations between the individual and the community or society. Whereas in the contemporary West body shape or size is formulated as a project of the self, with 'fatness' seen as indicative of lack of self-control, laziness, ill-health, and low status and as therefore carrying a social stigma, in some other societies (e.g. Fiji, Jamaicans), it may signify one's connectedness to the community, happiness, vitality, beauty, or sex appeal (Popenoe 2004: 5). The links between identity and embodiment, however, are more explicit for women than for men. As some feminists have argued, for women, the body is a primary signifier of the self to the outside world – a point which is exploited by the beauty industry in its efforts to urge women to use its products and services (Gimlin 2002: 4–5). The identities that attach to bodies of people of different ages may also vary across cultures and societies. Whereas in many societies ageing is valued and equated with the accumulation of wisdom and older people are accorded considerable status in the community, in the contemporary West, ageing is negatively connoted and seen as indicative of a deterioration of mental and physical capacities, which is reflected in body management practices and products oriented to achieving a 'younger look' and reversing 'the ravages of time' (e.g. use of anti-ageing creams, face lifts). Bodies tend to be classified according to their worth within the capitalist market-place. In the contemporary West, older bodies are seen as having little economic value, which is mirrored in employment and social policies that discriminate against the elderly through their implicit assumptions about people's abilities to contribute at different ages. (See Chapter 4.) However, the images and stereotypes of ageing that shape everyday practice may bear little relation to the trajectory of people's lives and subjective experiences (Featherstone and Hepworth 1991). Bourdieu (1986) contends that in contemporary society, aesthetic judgements in relation to bodies – their appearance (including thinness and fatness), gesture, posture and behaviour – involve class distinctions. Bodies carry different physical signs of their status within the class system. They have varying symbolic or 'cultural capital' and are seen as having different potential for generating economic capital. As Bourdieu argues, the body is viewed as the only tangible manifestation of the 'person' and 'the most natural expression of innermost nature'. Physical facial signs, expressions, bearings, gestures, and so on, can be 'read' as signs of one's degree of distance from nature (Bourdieu 1986: 192–193). (On 'reading faces' see Chapter 5.)

In Bourdieu's view, body management preferences and practices carry the signs of class. The capacity to differentiate between and appreciate these preferences and practices (what Bourdieu refers to as 'habitus') is internalised by individuals and becomes the basis for defining one's class and distinguishing it from other classes. Thus, one's 'social identity is defined and asserted through difference' (1986: 170–171). Tastes in food, and views on how best to nourish the body and on the effects of food on its strength, health and beauty and the categories that are used to assess its affects, are marked by class.

Taste, a class culture turned into nature, that is, *embodied*, helps to shape the class body. It is an incorporated principle of classification which governs all forms of incorporation, choosing and modifying everything that the body ingests and digests and assimilates, physiologically and psychologically. It follows that the body is the most indisputable materialization of class taste, which it manifests in several ways. It does this first in the seemingly most natural features of the body, the dimensions (volume, height, weight) and shapes (round or square, stiff or supple, straight or curved) or its physical forms, which express in countless ways a whole relation to the body, i.e., a way of treating it, caring for it, feeding it, maintaining it, which reveals the deepest dispositions of the habitus.

(Bourdieu 1986: 190)

As Bourdieu explains, biological differences may be emphasised and symbolically accentuated by differences in bearing, gesture, posture and behaviour, as well as modifications of appearance through cosmetic changes (hairstyle, make-up, beard, moustache, etc.) and other means (1986: 192). (One can add here the increasing focus on extreme forms of body modification or cosmetic surgery – see below.) The idea that the body can be 'read' as an indicator of one's moral and social status is hardly novel. In the nineteenth century, physiognomy was based on the premise that one could develop a classification of character types based on the observation of physical body types. Thus, criminals could be readily identified through certain physical defects, as seen in the work of the Italian criminologist, Cesare Lombroso (1835–1909). (See also Chapter 5.) The novelty of Bourdieu's work is in drawing attention to the profound significance of body classifications for both contemporary social class differentiations *and* for self-identity and everyday practices such as food preferences, fashion choices, and so on.

Though his work is insightful and influential, Bourdieu's schema can be criticised for presenting an over-determined view of subjectivity (awareness of self) and agency, and arguably over-emphasises the significance of class, which in contemporary society has become less important for identity and action. That is, individuals are presented as unreflectively internalising the hierarchical, class-based system of classification and the valuing of bodies within capitalist society, suggesting little scope for subversion or contestation of that hierarchy (see, e.g. Bourdieu 1986: 193). The class structure is portrayed as determining practices of the body, with relatively little influence from gender, 'race'/ethnic, or other factors. Although Bourdieu acknowledges gender differences in body practices – particularly in relation to food preferences – this is a minor sub-theme in his work and tends to be submerged by the focus on class differences (see, e.g. 1986: 190–191, 382–383). He overlooks the *engendering of the norms* of body practices and the fact that women are more inclined than men to engage in practices of body modification, such as cosmetic surgery. Feminists have emphasised the gender biases at work in norms pertaining to body size, shape and appearance. Western ideals of feminine beauty may lead many women to practise radical forms of body management leading to eating disorders (e.g. bulimia, anorexia nervosa) that have been disproportionately experienced by women (e.g. Orbach 1989; Bordo 1993; Faludi 1992; MacSween 1993; Wolf 1990). Susie Orbach (1978, 1993), and others since, have drawn attention to how the constructions of femininity may lead women to adopt an 'unhealthy' relationship to their bodies. However, increasingly, it is recognised that men, too, are subject to the ideals of the thin, toned youthful body, leading in some cases to obsessive exercising, eating disorders and submission to surgery, though to a lesser extent than women (Grogan and Richards 2002; Monaghan 2005).

With the breakdown of old class categories and affiliations, and the growing view that with biomedical technologies the body can be modified and moulded according to one's desires and means, there are growing expectations that women and men from *all* classes and backgrounds will be able to recreate identity – to fashion a new *unique* self – via the modification of the body. Increasingly, modern societies are affected by the spread of neo-liberal philosophies and policies which involve a form of power contingent on regulated autonomy rather than coercion or domination (Rose 1999). Individuals are called upon to 'take charge of their lives', to live life 'like an enterprise' and exercise choice as a right, indeed an obligation of citizenship. A growing array of policies and practices and expertise is oriented to supporting the conditions for the exercise of choice and active citizenship, particularly through the generation of the growing marketplace of techniques of body modification and management. In healthcare, for example, there is a growing emphasis on health as a product and on providing 'consumers' with 'choice' (see Henderson and Petersen 2002). Government policies converge with corporate rhetoric in the stated concern with promoting individual 'freedom through choice'. The question of whether neo-liberal thinking has also affected critical, particularly feminist interpretations of the significance of body modification and management practices – through an over-emphasis on individual agency and choice – is discussed later in the chapter. First, to help cast light on the significance of choice and constraint in this area, I wish to turn attention to what has been identified by many commentators as a major force in the forging of views and identities in the contemporary period, namely what may be termed the body shape industry.

The body shape industry

I use the term 'the body shape industry' to designate what is, in effect, a highly diverse array of interests, including the business sector (e.g. food and beverage industry, private medical groups), self-help groups, departments of health/public health authorities, various expert groups (medical and other health professionals, psychologists, psychiatrists, psychotherapists), non-government organisations, and diverse media. Although having different objectives, these interests tend to share the view that bodies and lives can be improved through the use of the various body modification technologies and management techniques available in the market-place. It may seem odd to describe government departments and public authorities as part of an 'industry'. However, increasingly, the rationality and language of the market informs decisions about body management and healthcare, and the boundary between public and private provision is becoming blurred. Within health-care in a number of contemporary societies, including the UK, Canada and Australia, 'patient choice' and 'consumer rights' have been increasingly emphasised, and individuals are called upon to play their part in reducing healthcare costs by taking a 'proactive' approach to health, and participating in practices of self-care and risk management. The competent, responsible citizen should pay attention to their weight, eat 'healthily' including avoiding eating certain (e.g. 'high cholesterol') foods and make efforts to get fit (through regular exercise). 'Excessive' weight and failure to achieve a healthy body have become signifiers of a lack of self control, poor decision-making and social failure (Crawford 1994: 1354) – though solvable through hard work, deployment of the advice of various experts, and judicious purchases from the now vast and rapidly growing range of body products and services available in the market-place. Individuals are rewarded for their efforts to adopt healthy lifestyles through exercising and giving up smoking, for example, by being offered discounted insurance premiums and by other means. Achieving health and autonomy takes hard work and financial commitment – a point recognised by insurers, pension funds, self-help gurus, and diverse sectors of business, including fitness centres, health food shops and private medical groups offering cosmetic surgery and other body treat-ments. It is in this context of heightened concern about body size/weight and health, and growing expectations of 'care for the self', that the emergence of programmes of body modification and management promoted by the body shape industry need to be understood. As I will show later, if recent evidence of increasing practices of body modification and body maintenance (e.g. health and beauty treatments) is to be believed, the body shape industry has had considerable success thus far in winning new 'customers'.

Heightened concern about the 'obesity epidemic' and the obese individual

One area of considerable concern to the body shape industry in the final years of the twentieth century and opening years of the twenty-first century has been the over-sized/over-weight or 'obese' body. Increasingly, 'obesity' has been the subject of a growing number of policies and programmes, as well as the focus of considerable media coverage, in a number of countries.

In recent years, in the UK, the news media carried stories on the 'fight against fat' (Wintour 2006: 1), concerns about childhood obesity (e.g. Boseley 2005; BBC News 2005) and the health problems associated with what one article describes as 'the rising tide of obesity' (Meikle 2005). One news article, appearing in *The Guardian*, quoting a report from the Trust for American's Health, notes that 'Americans are getting fatter at a pace never seen before while government-led attempts to hold in bulging waistlines are doomed to failure'. It went on to say that 'More than 119 million people, 64.5% of the US population, are now considered overweight or obese' and that 'almost three-quarters of American adults could be overweight in less than three years' time' (Luscombe 2005: 13). Another article, in *The Independent on Sunday*, reports that 'The number of Britain's resorting to drastic weight-loss surgery will double in the next 12 months, say medical researchers, in a further sign of the growing obesity epidemic'. It notes that 'an estimated 1.2 million people in Britain are morbidly obese' and that 'a survey of British surgeons specialising in the field showed that at least 4,300 operations will be carried out this year, up from 2,287 in 2004' (Bloomfield 2005a: 12). Such articles reflect considerable anxieties about changes in body size and weight, in particular with what is seen to be a recent massive *spread* of 'obesity' within populations, particularly in the developed world, but also increasingly in some developing countries.

In her recent book, *Fat Wars: The Inside Story of the Obesity Industry*, Ellen Shell refers to the 'obesity pandemic' which she argues is 'by far the fastest growing public health crisis in the industrialized world' (2003: xiii). New forms of body weight expertise and a range of advice and new treatments for the 'obese' individual have emerged in the market-place, including a range of new weight loss drugs (Shell 2003). Various official reports have highlighted the nature of 'the problem' pointing to the health, social and economic implications of the 'epidemic of obesity' or the 'obesity problem' and the measures needed to tackle it (British Nutrition Foundation 1999; House of Commons Health Committee 2004; National Audit Office 2001). The growth of the internet and proliferation of diverse media have helped to fuel concerns about this 'epidemic' while at the same time providing a means of promoting a diverse array of treatments to consumers via direct-to-consumer advertising and other avenues. Concerns about 'the problem of obesity' have been articulated in a number of recent reports published by various authorities.

As these reports explain, obesity is a *growing global problem*, with considerable health, economic and social significance. The World Health Organization declares that 'Obesity has reached epidemic proportions globally, with more than 1 billion adults overweight – with at least 3 million of them clinically obese – and is a major contributor to the global burden of disease and disability'.[17] In its report, *Obesity*, the British Nutrition Foundation emphasises the failure to prevent and treat the global dimension of the problem:

The prevalence of obesity is rising steadily in many developed countries and also in eastern countries such as China and Japan. The global trend of increasing prevalence demonstrates that current measures to prevent and treat obesity are failing. Despite a vast research effort there are no practical population-based solutions on the immediate horizon.

(British Nutrition Foundation 1999: 1)

Although a number of reports claim that 'obesity' is a *global* problem with significant health and economic implications, rarely is there discussion about the actual distribution of 'obesity' in geographical and demographic terms and about what can be learnt from this about the sources and solutions to 'the problem'. Little data is offered to show whether the burden of 'the problem' falls disproportionately on peoples from particular parts of the globe or groups within the population and, if so, why this might be so and what might be done. If particular groups are vulnerable, what may this tell us about the economic, political, social and cultural contexts predisposing to being 'overweight' or 'obese'? Further, there is an absence of discussion about why 'obesity' has recently become a concern to public health and medical authorities. Reports fail to ask whether there have been changes in norms of body weight, which may result in a growing number of people being classified this way. The categories of 'obese' and 'overweight' are constructions and, as noted, norms around ideal body weight vary across cultures and through time, underlining their instability and potential to change. In the absence of such contextual information and analysis, it is difficult for readers of the reports to adequately assess the claims or to know what individual and collective responses should be made. Public discourse (particularly in news media reporting) about 'the problem of obesity' is strongly associated with images of over-abundance and over-consumption (poor diets), a problem which is often assumed to be, and sometimes explicitly stated to be, a problem associated with growing affluence. As also indicated above, in the West, body shape and size is formulated as a project of the self, with 'fatness' having a number of derogatory connotations, such as lack of self-control and laziness and it is seen as indicative of ill-health. Industrial development is seen as associated with particular patterns of illness – cardiovascular disease, cancer and 'obesity' – arising from the adoption of particular lifestyles; this is replicated in countries which follow the Western pattern of development.

Further, the above reports have nothing to say about the 'healthiness' and desirability of the Western model of development and associated lifestyles, and about how this may help create body size and weight problems of a different kind in large parts of the developing world; namely malnutrition and underweight bodies. In the news media, stories about 'the problem of obesity' in richer countries sometimes appear alongside reports about the problem of a lack of nutritious food or malnutrition in poorer countries, underlining the contrasts in people's experiences of problems with body sustenance and management at the global level. For example, in August 2005, a short news item ('Fat busting, New York style') appearing in the UK's *The Guardian* reported that 'New York City wants restaurants to cut their list of ingredients – and maybe some waistlines – by eliminating out trans fats'. The article noted that many restaurants were eliminating many kinds of margarine and frying oils in order to comply with the 'voluntary change', which was supported by the Department of Health and Mental Hygiene'.[18] The item appeared on the very same page as a news item ('Food crisis "threatens 20m people"') reporting that 'more than 20 million people in 12 African countries, from Niger in the West to Zimbabwe in the South, face serious food shortages and donor nations must do more to ease the crisis'.[19] The item cited the 'latest report' of 'the US government-funded Famine Early Warning Systems Network', which 'tracks "food insecurity" in 20 African countries'. It also noted that another organisation, the International Food Policy Research Institute 'projected that hunger could be a reality for nearly 42 million children by 2025'. Such issues tend not to achieve the same prominence in the news as 'the problem of obesity', however, unless linked to high-profile events such as G8 Summit and the Live 8 concerts, held in July 2005. When placed in a global, economic and political context, 'the problem of obesity' raises new questions for policy and social action, including whether 'the fight on fat' should be a priority of authorities in the absence of fundamental change in economic, political and social conditions predisposing to inequalities and illness.

The economic and health *burdens* posed by the rapidly growing dimensions of the 'obesity problem', however, has been a subject which has preoccupied many governments and health authorities in recent years. The UK's House of Commons Health Committee, in its Third Report, *Obesity*, published in 2004, for example, notes:

> Around two-thirds of the population of England are overweight or obese. Obesity has grown by almost 400% in the last 25 years and on present trends will soon surpass smoking as the greatest cause of premature loss of life. It will entail levels of sickness that will put enormous strains on the health service. On some predictions, today's generation of children will be the first for over a century for whom life expectancy falls.
>
> (House of Commons Health Committee 2004: 3)

Here, as in other reports, 'obesity' is defined in biomedical terms and measured via the 'body mass index' (BMI) which is 'calculated by dividing an individual's weight measured in kilograms by their height in metres squared' (House of Commons Health Committee 2004: 12). That is, an arbitrarily defined measure of body dimensions and weight has become the yardstick for evaluating health risk and classifying pathologies. A BMI of greater than 30 is widely accepted as the definition of 'obese', with figures higher and lower being classified variously, from 'morbid obesity' through to 'underweight'. Using this Index, entire populations have been categorised according to the percentage of people measured as 'healthy weight', 'over-weight', 'obese' and 'morbid obese'. Employed retrospectively over time, this measure has led many authorities to conclude that 'obesity' has become an 'epidemic' that poses a substantial risk to 'the public's' health. The National Audit Office defines obesity as 'a condition in which weight gain has reached the point of seriously endangering health' (2001: 7). Drawing on evidence provided by the UK Public Health Association and Faculty of Public Health Medicine, the House of Commons Health Committee defines obesity as 'an excess of body fat frequently resulting in a significant impairment of health and longevity'. Like these reports, the World Health Organisation defines obesity in terms of the BMI, noting that 'A BMI over 25 kg/m² is defined as overweight, and a BMI of over 30 kg/m² as obese'. Further, it notes, 'These markers provide common benchmarks for assessment, but the risks of disease in all populations can increase progressively from lower BMI levels.[20] On the basis of the BMI, the WHO observes:

Adult mean BMI levels of 22–23 kg/m² are found in Africa and Asia, while levels of 25–27 kg/m² are prevalent across North America, Europe, and in some Latin American, North African and Pacific Island countries. BMI increases amongst middle-aged elderly people, who are at the greatest risk of health complications. In countries undergoing nutrition transition, overnutrition often co-exists with undernutri-tion. People with a BMI below 18.5 kg/m² tend to be underweight. The distribution of BMI is shifting upwards in many populations. And recent studies have shown that people who were undernourished in early life and then become obese in adulthood, tend to develop conditions such as high blood pressure, heart disease and diabetes at an earlier age and in more severe form than those who were never undernourished.[21]

The question of whether 'obesity' as defined by the BMI is meaningful and valid given the large variety of body heights and differences in norms of body size across cultures and nations is not raised. Further, there is no discussion of whether certain sectors of the population are disproportion-ately affected and, if so, why this might be so. However, in these reports, the effect of obesity on health, particularly younger people's health has been the focus of particular concern. For example, the House of Commons Health Committee notes: 'A generation is growing up in a obesogenic environment in which the forces behind sedentary behaviour are growing, not declining'. And, 'Most overweight or obese children become overweight or obese adults; overweight and obese adults are more likely to bring up overweight or obese children' (2004: 7). The WHO also notes, 'Childhood obesity is already epidemic in some areas and on the rise in others', and cites some statistics from the USA and Thailand in support of the view that 'The problem is global and increasingly extends into the developing world'.[22]

Schools have been identified as a key site for identifying and tackling obesity, and new school-based programmes have been devised to address what is perceived to be a deficit in parents' abilities to control their children's weight. A recent recommendation of the House of Commons Health Committee suggests that parents are incapable of identifying that their children have a problem or of knowing how to deal with it:

> We recommend that throughout their time at school, children should have their Body Mass Index measured annually at school, perhaps by the school nurse, a health visitor, or other appropriate health professional. The results should be sent home in confidence to their parents, together with, where appropriate, advice on lifestyle, follow-up, and referral to more specialised services. . . . Care will need to be taken to avoid stigmatising children who are overweight or obese, but given that research indicates that many parents are no longer even able to identify whether their children are overweight or not, this seems to us a vital step in tackling obesity.
>
> (House of Commons Health Committee 2004: 95)

As some reports explain, a major 'cause' has been identified as a drop in 'energy expenditure', a change in 'energy balance' or an 'energy-dense diet' due to societal changes, particularly alterations in eating patterns, levels of physical activity, loss of skills to prepare healthy meals, and media, particularly advertising, influence. The above report of the House of Commons Health Committee, for example, notes that 'At its simplest level, obesity is caused when people overeat in relation to their energy needs' and that 'as *energy expenditure* has dropped considerably, environmental factors have combined to make it increasingly easy for people to consume more calories than they need' (2004: 3; emphasis added). It notes the increasing availability of '*energy-dense foods*' and that while people are generally aware of what constitutes a healthy diet, 'there are multiple barriers to their putting this into practice', such as loss of skills in preparing healthy meals and thus reliance on convenience foods, the prevalence of advertising of 'energy-dense foods', and 'confusing or absent' food labelling (House of Commons Health Committee 2004: 3; emphasis added). The WHO report notes that 'While genes are important in determining a person's susceptibility to weight gain, *energy balance* is determined by calorie intake and physical activity'.[23] The National Audit Office (NAO), which 'scrutinises public spending on behalf of Parliament', identified 'Changes in eating patterns and increasingly sedentary lifestyles' as 'the most likely explanation for the upward trend in obesity' (2001: 13). It notes that the increase in obesity has occurred in too short a time to be explained by 'significant genetic changes in the population' and that the most likely explanation is 'environmental and behavioural changes which have led to a more *energy-dense diet* and a rise in the level of sedentary behaviour' (NAO 2001: 13; emphasis added). Among the identified changes are shifts in eating patterns with more people eating outside the home, where people tend to eat more high-fat foods, and declining levels of exercise attributed to increased use of the motor car and other energy-saving devices in public places (escalators, lifts, automatic doors) and reduced levels of walking due to concerns about personal safety (NAO 2001: 13). Similarly, the World Health Organization identifies the problem as due to changes in diets, with 'a higher proportion of fats, saturated fats and sugars', combined with 'less physically demanding work' globally, as a result of 'economic growth, modernization, and globalization of food markets'.[24]

A number of comments can be made about the discourse of obesity as it pertains to practices of body modification. First, the concern about the problem of excessive body size and how to solve it is by no means historically recent. As Shell indicates, discussion about the nature, causes and cures of 'corpulency' was evident in Europe in the eighteenth century, if not earlier, and was the subject of some 30 doctoral theses. Anxiety about obesity, then called 'polysarcia', continued to rise in the nineteenth century as did belief that the problem could be controlled through concerted effort (2003: 28–30). The development of scientific medicine and the application of quantitative methods ('statistical medicine') eventually led to the Quetelet Index (after Adolphe Quetelet) which offered the first statistical measure of body weight. As Shell explains, this index, which was based on Quetelet's observation that 'the weight of normal adults was proportional to their height squared', 'a century or so later became the body mass index that is the gold standard today' (2003: 33). As Ian Hacking's and Georges Canguilhem's work makes clear, the BMI has its origins in efforts, beginning in the early nineteenth century, to quantify, measure and 'normalise' virtually all aspects of life (Hacking 1990) including the height, weight and lifespan of the 'average man' – a project to which Quetelet contributed significantly (Canguilhem 1989: 154–160). (See Chapter 4.) The idea that obesity was due to an imbalance in the energy value of foods consumed, and that individuals and groups 'burned energy' to different degrees (i.e. had different metabolisms) can also be traced back to an earlier period, namely the late nineteenth and early twentieth centuries. As Shell notes, the view that food intake could be calculated scientifically by counting calories began to gain favour as the twentieth century progressed and eventually 'calorie counting became a national – and international – obsession' (2003: 41). The relationship between amount of food intake and body size became established as did the notion that human metabolism was subject to a set of natural laws (2003: 37). In other words, ideas and practices that developed within the historical and culturally specific context of Western capitalist societies – and which contributed to 'making up people' (Hacking 1986) in particular ways – are now being imposed on populations of diverse average body heights, weights, and dimensions and with varying views on foods and sustenance.

Second, it is interesting to note the references to 'epidemic' in descriptions of 'the obesity problem' and to intergenerational transmission in recent reports on obesity. Those who use the term 'obesity epidemic' imply that there is consensus on the nature and extent of 'the problem' when in fact the scientific knowledge about overweight and obesity is 'confused and replete with flawed and misleading assumptions' (Gard and Wright 2005: 5). The use of 'epidemic' reveals the application of a contagion model used within public health in relation to a range of infectious conditions, including smallpox, HIV/AIDs and SARS. It suggests that problems can be isolated to particular 'infectious' sections of the population and solved through the same kind of rational administrative approach applied to other public health issues, such as quarantine or education. However, as noted above, specific details of the geographic and demographic distribution of 'the problem' are mostly absent in public discourse. The term 'epidemic' has strong rhetorical power, implying the need for urgent action, to bring the problem under control before others are infected. While it is acknowledged that factors such as food advertising and promotion may contribute to the 'epidemic', the emphasis remains resolutely on changing the lifestyles of individuals and on medical solutions. Thus, while the House of Commons Health Committee notes that 'it is critical that obesity is tackled first and foremost at a societal rather than an individual level' (2004: 47) and criticises NHS (National Health Service) decision-makers for treating obesity as 'a lifestyle problem for which treatment is an optional extra', at the outset it defines 'obesity as both a medical condition and a lifestyle disorder' (p. 12; see also p. 94) and it places a strong emphasis on biomedical (including surgical) and lifestyle measures along with voluntary agreements in the food industry in its proposed 'solutions' (2004: 46–107). In advancing this goal, education is seen as playing a key facilitative role in enabling individuals to choose a healthy diet. The Government is ascribed a role in 'addressing environmental factors in order to . . . make healthy choices easier to make' (2004: 54). This formulation of the problem as one of individual choice diverts attention from the question of why body size and weight has become a particular concern in the late twentieth and early twenty-first centuries and why the problem is constructed as it is (i.e. as a global epidemic).

Third, references to 'energy expenditure', 'energy balance' and 'energy-dense diet' in the above explanations of the cause of obesity reveal a conception of the body as a machine that is subject to control by its 'owner'. Learning how to properly 'service' the machine then becomes a priority: attention to a 'balanced' diet, developing skills in preparing food, adequate exercise, and so on. As one report notes, 'dietary factors and physical activity patterns strongly influence the energy balance equation and they are also the major modifiable factors' (Donnellan 2003: 7). Deirdre Davies (2003) has noted that the themes of energy balance and equilibrium are common in the discourse of weight control and suggest that the body-machine can be measured and calibrated in an accurate way, in terms of input and output and energy expenditure. The use of the body-machine model carries the assumption that the body 'owner' should take charge of monitoring and regulating the body so as to maintain or re-establish its balance. Attention to 'energy expenditure' and to maintaining or re-establishing 'energy balance' presupposes the need for constant intensive surveillance of the body by the self which has been associated with certain eating disorders (e.g. anorexia nervosa and bulimia) and with the use of often radical and dangerous biomedical procedures (e.g. bariatric surgery) (Davies 2003: Chapter 4).

Selling the ideal

It is against this background of widespread heightened concern about body size and weight that there has emerged a burgeoning market for 'obesity' and weight loss treatments and programmes, as well as services and products for those with eating disorders which have been linked to problems of 'body image'. 'Fat' like other 'conditions' such as short stature and large noses is denoted as 'ugly' which is viewed as a disease subject to medical treatment (Elliott 2003). Clearly, the body shape industry has become big business, with the development of new drugs, diets, exercise regimes, advice literature, and a range of surgical treatments. Pharmaceutical companies have invested heavily in new diet drugs and a range of surgical techniques are currently available to those who have been diagnosed as or judge themselves to be 'obese'. Increasingly, treatments and programmes for body modification and management are being advertised via news media and other media, particularly the Internet – often as part of a larger package of 'health and beauty' products and services – allowing individuals to 'shop around' for those deemed most appropriate to them. Internet forums dedicated to problems of 'obesity' and eating disorders (e.g. National Centre for Eating Disorders, National Obesity Forum, Weight Concern) serve to raise awareness of the problems associated with 'obesity' and act as a focal point for affected individuals and worried parents, allowing them to seek advice and counselling, training and support. Advertisements, sometimes cleverly disguised behind editorials ('advertorials'), imply that consumption of these products and services will allow those of non-normal body shape, size and appearance to gain control over their lives and that by creating a new body they will create a new self.

The commercial involvement in the promotion of a particular ideal of beauty, defined almost exclusively in terms of physical appearance – a certain body size (thin), height (tall), age (young) and colour (generally white) – can be seen in the vast array of glossy magazines and newspapers available through news agencies, supermarkets and other outlets, sometimes offered free of charge. Some are devoted specifically to health and beauty issues and are published or sponsored by parts of the health and beauty industry. An example is *Health and Beauty*, published by Boots, which presents itself as 'UK's leading health and beauty retailer'.[25] The brief editorial of the

May/June 2005 issue explains that the latest issue is 'designed to take the heat out of summer shopping. Our mission? To bring you an edited choice of the very best new buys at Boots. . . . ' The above ideal of beauty permeates the images on its pages, beginning with the cover image and encompassing the advertisements and stories, which portray predominantly young thin people, mostly women, with seemingly faultless complexions, smiling faces, sometimes posing in relaxed mode at home or in recreational settings (e.g. on the beach). Although including some advice columns on health issues (e.g. Diabetes, skin cancer, dieting), the magazine is basically a means for advertising the array of health and beauty products offered by Boots, including (in its May/June 2005 issue), apart from weight loss and diet products, creams 'to correct the appearance of expression wrinkles' (by L'Oréal) and to 'reduce signs of orange peel skin' (i.e. cellulite) (Nivea Sculpting and Smoothing Cream), fragrances for men and women, suncare products and tanning lotions, hair products, sexual aids, and dental care products.

In some newspapers, advertisements for body modification treatments appear in an 'advertorial' format, that is, they involve editorial comment which, advertisers have come to recognise, are more likely than straight advertisements to capture readers' attentions. One approach employs stories of 'experiments' involving people's (generally women's) use of different weight loss or other body modification treatments, often including a breakdown of costs of the treatments and contact details (phone numbers and website addresses) for those marketing the treatments, together with 'before and after' photographs showing supposed physical improvements and testimonials from those who have undertaken the treatments. A one and a half page article appearing in the UK's *Daily Mail*, reports six women's experiences with 'some of the latest treatments' for those with cellulite, including lipolysis injections ('made from an extract of soya beans and designed to break down fat so that it is expelled naturally from the body'), cellutites (which 'include a mocroweave that is designed to massage the skin, stimulating circulation and reducing water retention'), cream ('based on plant oils, marine extracts, vitamins and fruit acids'), chocolate therapy ('involves a chocolate mixture rich in minerals pasted on to troublesome areas'), cellulite doctor ('works with cycloid vibration, which is also used in hospitals to treat poor lymphatic drainage and poor circulation') and laser therapy ('emits laser energy that stimulates fat cells to release toxins and tightens skins'). The article includes women's assessments of the treatments (all positive) and photographs of the women before and after their cellulite treatments. In the 'after' photograph, the women appear in a confident, semi-clad pose, with cellulite-free legs exposed and with their eyes fixed on the viewer (Francis and Jackson 2005: 49). Another lengthy (one and a half page) article, in *The Daily Mirror* ('Boost your boobs . . . naturally') includes the 'before and after' photographs and testimonies of four women who used different non-surgical methods to achieve a bigger bust. The article includes details on the nature of the treatments ('eight sessions of Boob Aerobics at

Gymbox in Central London', 'listening to Inner Talk Breast Enlargement CD once a day for two months', 'BRAVA Breast Enlargement and Shaping System', and 'Erdic natural breast enhancement programme'), as well as their cost and the details of whom to contact for the treatments. Again, the subjects provide positive testimonials which are accompanied by 'before and after' photographs which supposedly show the improvement, with 'subjects' appearing in the latter in more confident pose – again gazing directly at the viewer. The use of before-and-after case studies and testimonials such as these, which speak directly to the reader and assist them to connect to the product or service by helping them imagine a new future self, is common in advertisements for beauty and health products and services.

The advertisements of the UK-based Hospital Group offer insight into not only the vast range of body modification services currently available in the market, but also the kinds of claims that are made and strategies adopted to sell products and services. One, which appears in the *Daily Mail*, is headed 'Obesity surgery, cosmetic surgery and more. . . . ' The advertisement includes the familiar 'before and after' photo of a middle-aged women showing evidence of the lost pounds, with the caption 'Francine Hodges, Gastric band and tummy tuck patient weightloss 11 stone'. It is accompanied by a quote, conveying the promises of obesity treatment: 'Since having my band I haven't felt that I'm missing out because I can still eat what I like – just smaller portions saving me money on food – it's the best investment I could have made for my health and well-being'. Underlying this are two lists of bullet points, under the headings of 'Obesity surgery' and 'Cosmetic surgery', respectively, which describe the nature of the services offered, as well as offering assurances about professionalism and the routine nature of the treatments, and help to allay any concerns potential consumers may have about the procedures. For example, the bulleted points under the 'Obesity surgery' are:

- Least invasive keyhole surgery
- 1000s of procedures carried out
- 24hr aftercare support available
- 6 & 12 month medical follow-up
- Fixed price band £6,950
- The UK's only dedicated Obesity Hospital Group.

Under 'Cosmetic surgery' is listed a range of services:

- Face Lift
- Breast Enlargement
- Breast Lift
- Breast Reduction
- Nose and Ear Reshaping
- Tummy Tuck

- Liposculpture
- Eyebag Removal and more . . .
- Free One-to-one Medical Consultation[26]

Except for the breast surgeries, most of these services are not overtly gender-biased, though descriptions and portrayals of models suggest that they are targeted particularly at older people who are assumed to be concerned about problems of ageing. That such surgery is generally expensive, as indicated by the 'fixed price band' of £6,950 would also restrict the treatments to particular socio-economic and older age groups who are most likely to be able to afford them. The advertisement does, however, include a note, 'Finance Available', which invites those who do not already have the ability to pay. Details are provided of the telephone number, a website address, and a list of outlets.[27]

When one visits the The Hospital Group's website one discovers a detailed list of services, providing a kind of 'one stop shop'. Services noted include cosmetic surgery, obesity surgery, hair loss surgery, non-surgical treatments ('Fat dissolving injection, frown line injections, cellulite treatments') and haemorrhoids/pile treatments ('A new and exciting 20 minute procedure for men and women which is relatively pain free and is now available'). Under 'Obesity surgery', it is explained that the Hospital Group is 'the leading obesity management group in the UK, our philosophy is to ensure that The Hospital Group remains at the forefront of where quality, patient care and value for money meet; working in partnership with patients, to meet their individual needs'. The website assures readers of the attention given to patient care and that 'Some of our specialist team have even undergone weight loss surgery themselves'. Further, it notes, 'Our Anaesthetists and Obesity Surgeons are fully qualified independent professionals practising within the NHS and private sector. They each hold their own relevant qualifications associated with their discipline, reassuring you of their abilities'. The website outlines the 'causes of obesity' ('energy balance', 'hereditary', 'metabolic disorders', 'eating and social habits', 'psychological disorders') and allows users to calculate their own BMI and provides a scale (from 'underweight' to 'superobesity'), to enable them to assess their own risk. It then directs the user through the available treatment options (the 'band system' and the 'balloon system') and their benefits, with accompanying patient testimonials, a 'weight loss diary' (with assurances from patients about the success of the operation and the improvements in their lives), and 'questions and answers', addressing the nature of the procedures, expected weight loss, and impacts on health and lifestyle. The website also provides information on the 'clinical team' who, it is stated 'will provide "bespoke" plans to enable success by helping you to change your lifestyle choices in the future'. It also provides a list of dietary and fitness 'tips for obesity patients'. Finally, it presents a map of UK-wide hospitals and clinics, with contact details, as well as 'click here' points to 'request a consultation' and a 'free brochure'.[28]

According to Khamsi (2005), who cites information from the American Society of Plastic Surgeons, in the USA alone, doctors perform 300,000 liposuction operations a year, with the number of such operations increasing fivefold between 1992 and 2003. As Khamsi explains, currently there are a vast variety of weight loss methods available on the market including, apart from those mentioned above, palm-held gadgets produced by Weight Watchers International that allow people access to a 25,000-item food database, obviating the need to carry a weekly logbook; a similar product for the low-carbohydrate Atkins diet which can be linked to mobile phones and personal digital assistants (PDAs); an oven (designed by Sharp Electronics) designed to heat food to a temperature high enough to 'melt away the grease'; and a light-weight stomach stimulator implanted just under the skin below the rib cage which 'sends electrical pulses to the stomach, creating a feeling of fullness'. There is also a host of 'easy-to-swallow pills or potions to suppress appetite' in development (Khamsi 2005: 103). Further, one should not forget the vast number of diets available and heavily promoted, including the Atkins Diet, which became fashionable among many celebrities and a large selection of the population in recent years. Datamonitor, a consumer-research firm, notes that in 2004 at least 44 per cent of American adults and 29 per cent of Europeans were on a diet. It predicts that the market for diet food will grow by $17 billion between 2004 and 2007, to over $100 billion, partly due to the availability of a range of 'tastier, low-calorie foods using artificial sweeteners like Slenda' (Khamsi 2005: 104). Clearly, the 'obesity'-focused sector of the body shape industry is huge and growing and creating many opportunities for 'spin-off' industries, like the market research companies that track trends in this sector and sell their reports at high prices – some in the order of tens of thousands of dollars.

The growth of 'body image problems'

Broadly corresponding with the period of growing concern about the 'obesity epidemic' and a burgeoning market of beauty and body modification products such as those described above, body shape experts, psychiatrists, mental health professionals, primary care physicians, and cosmetic specialists have documented increasing problems related to 'body image' or 'low body satisfaction'. From the 1990s onwards, more and more literature addressed the nature, management and treatment of 'body image' and related 'eating disorders' and 'compulsive exercising' (see, e.g. Abraham and Llewellyn-Jones 2001: 117–118). In their book, *Body Image: A Handbook of Theory, Research and Clinical Practice*, Cash and Pruzinsky described the 1990s as 'a pivotal era in the evolution of body image scholarship and as a 'productive period of conceptual, psychometric, and psychotherapeutic developments' (2002: 5–6). More recently, Sylvia Blood has commented that, in experimental psychology, the discourse of 'body image problems' 'has become an increasingly dominant explanation for women's distressing experience of their bodies' (Blood 2005: 1). A professional and self-help literature oriented to the treatment of 'obesity' and 'eating disorders' and drawing substantially on psychological and psychotherapeutic approaches claims to offer an 'inside view' of physical appearance and how this may affect psychological functioning (Sarwer and Didie 2002: 41). Books published between 2002 and 2005 include titles such as: *Eating Disorders: A Parent's Guide* (Bryant-Waugh and Lask 2004); *'I'm, Like, SO fat!': Helping your Teen Make Healthy Choices about Eating and Exercise in a Weight-Obsessed World* (Neumark-Sztainer 2005); *Assessment of Eating Disorders* (Mitchell and Peterson 2005); *Beyond a Shadow of a Diet: the Therapist's Guide to Treating Compulsive Eating* (Matz and Frankel 2004); *Weight Wisdom: Affirmations to Free you from Food and Body Concerns* (Kingsbury and Williams 2003); *Self-harm Behaviour and Eating Disorders: Dynamics, Assessment and Treatment* (Levitt *et al.* 2004); *Eating Disorders and Cultures in Transition* (Nasser *et al.* 2002). These books include advice to professionals on how to diagnose, classify, assess and treat people with eating disorders and to 'consumers' on how to cope with problems. As the blurb for one of the above books (*Weight Wisdom*) explains: 'Pity and positive statements replace compulsive, perfectionist rules with new strategies to cope with blame, guilt, vulnerability, and self-criticism. Concrete activities help people with eating problems get off the scale, get in touch with their feelings, and make friends with their bodies'.

The pursuit of slimness has itself become a psychopathology in need of treatment, via counselling, cognitive behaviour therapy, psychoeducation, and pharmacotherapy. Thus, the pursuit of cosmetic surgery and dermatological treatments has been described as 'an adaptive coping strategy' or diagnosed as indicative of a 'body dysmorphic disorder', 'obsessive-compulsive disorder' or one of a number of 'eating disorders' such as anorexia and bulimia (e.g. Sarwer and Didie 2002; Castle and Phillips 2002; Phillips and Castle 2002). Dieting, widely promoted in the past as a panacea for 'obesity', is also beginning to be recognised as a potential health problem. One recent headline in *The Guardian*, for example, announced 'Overweight who diet risk dying earlier, says study' (Sample 2005: 1). The study, which was reported to be carried out in Finland, and involving '2,957 overweight or obese people who had been screened to ensure they had no underlying illnesses', was claimed to show that 'those who wanted to lose weight and succeeded were significantly more likely to die young than those who stayed fat'. The article goes on to say that although it is not clear why the dieters were at greater risk of dying younger, they believe that it may be due to 'fat being lost from lean organs as well as other body tissues' (Sample 2005:1).

In the body image and the feminist literatures it is acknowledged that girls and women are particularly dissatisfied with their bodies and that ideals of female beauty may lead them to develop a poor self conception, compulsive dieting, eating disorders, and to pursue radical surgery. Gender norms prescribe different body ideals for women and men that have different implications for each gender. Views differ, however, in relation to the question of how much agency women have in their negotiations with cultural norms. Striegel-Moore and Franko (2002) express a commonly held view that body dissatisfaction stems from the fact that women's identity is seen as inextricably linked with 'looking beautiful' and with complying with social expectations regarding femininity.

> Females' bodies are more likely than males' bodies to be regarded in a way that is evaluative – and therefore objectifying. When males' bodies are evaluated, it is in terms of functionality more than aesthetics. Early on, girls are exposed to the societal expectations to pursue physical attractiveness. They gradually internalize the objectifying gaze, thereafter engaging in self-monitoring and self-improvement behaviours aimed at meeting the cultural beauty standard.
>
> (Striegel-Moore and Franko 2002: 187)

From this perspective, young girl's internalisation of dominant cultural ideals of feminine beauty combined with mass media influence, participation in gender-typical activities, parents' attitudes and behaviours in regard to their own body image, and peer pressure affect their body image development in adolescence (Levine and Smolak 2002). According to Susie Orbach, writing in the mid-1980s, women's obsession with regulating body size, which may result in anorexia is depicted as a 'metaphor for our age'. In her view, anorexia symbolises 'the battle for autonomy in which every woman is engaged': it is 'a dramatic expression of the internal compromise wrought by Western women in the 1980s in their attempt to negotiate their passions and desires in a time of extraordinary confusion' (Orbach 1993: 4). As Orbach argues, the body has become a commodity in the market-place and is so viewed by women themselves. Women have become receptive to the message that the body-commodity is 'deficient and in need of attention' (1993: 16). More recently, Pitts has pointed to the ways in which women may attempt to *reclaim* the body through such modification practices within the limits imposed by the fact that the body is always *already* inscribed by culture (e.g. Pitts 2003: 72–86). Cosmetic surgery and other forms of body modification can therefore be examined as a site for both the technological reproduction of the gendered body and a means by which women use their bodies as 'a vehicle for staging cultural identities' (Balsamo 1996: 78). In MacSween's (1993) view, anorexia and bulimia can be explained as a 'strategy of resistance' – an attempt to control the feminine body – albeit one which is ultimately doomed to failure because of the individualization of these problems within the patriarchal order.

Feminists have drawn attention to the female gender bias of the discourses and practices of body modification and management and the imperatives and pressures that pertain disproportionately to women. However, although insightful and interesting, feminist work to date has paid less attention to the connections between, on the one hand, constructions of gender or gender difference and, on the other hand, the global political economy of the body shape industry. This includes the workings of the transnational biomedical and the pharmaceutical industries, which fabricate categories of disease, some gender-specific, which are then promoted to prescribers and consumers, through the media and other forums, often with the assistance of public relations practitioners (see Moynihan *et al.* 2002; Moynihan and Cassels 2005; Zuckerman 2003). Increasingly, the body shape industry is oriented to a highly segmented market, with products, services and strategies oriented and promoted to different 'niches', according to different combinations of gender, sexuality, age, socio-economic status, 'race' or ethnicity, lifestyle, place of residence, and a host of other factors. Men and specifically gay men, for example, increasingly have been recognised as also suffering 'body dissatisfaction', 'appearance obsession' and eating disorders as a result of pressures to have the 'body beautiful' (particularly muscularity) and to be sexually attractive (see, e.g. Donnellan 2003; Corson and Andersen 2002). Reporting on a review of specialist healthcare provision across the UK for men with eating disorders, published in 2000 on behalf of the Eating Disorders Association, Donnellan notes that 'approximately 10% of people with eating disorders are men and approximately 20% of men with eating disorders identify as gay, which is double the proportion of gay men in the population' (2003: 21). However, although a growing proportion of men suffer such disorders and undertake cosmetic surgery and other treatments, one can question the extent to which this reflects growing parity between men and women in relation to physical appearance or other spheres (Davis 2002). The evidence suggests that women are most at risk of problems of 'body image' and 'eating disorders', and are seen as in need of surgical and other enhancement techniques, and are subject to more body modification procedures and management practices. Having said that, the subject of new body modification and management techniques is multifarious and shifting as the body shape industry constantly expands to encompass a diverse range of lifestyles, worldviews and cultural and sexual practices. Thus, at the global level, one can see a proliferation of body modification and management practices, but with particular ideals – especially the thin, white European, heterosexual and physically abled body dominating – reflecting the outward spread of discourses and practices from the rich urban centres of the dominant Western world to other economically poorer parts of the globe. In short, although the technologies of body modification and management have developed and proliferated considerably since the nineteenth century, the drive to establish a normative standard of beauty and health, against which deviations are then measured, assessed and controlled has a long history in the West. A major development in recent years, however, has been the burgeoning of the so-called beauty industry, which offers the promise of transforming lives through a vast array of cosmetics, skin treatments, and potions and lotions of various kinds to enhance one's appearance.

Buying beauty

The modern shopper cannot help but notice the considerable number of beauty products available on the High Street and through magazines, newspapers and other media. Most large department stores have a perfume counter, including, apart from perfumes, a range of beauty products, such as skins creams, moisturisers, bath and shower products, toners, eye-care products and lipsticks, and associated paraphernalia (e.g. hair brushes, make-up tools, skin accessories, bags and cases), generally on the ground floor near the entrance to entice female customers in particular. The Body Shop, acquired by the French cosmetics company L'Oréal in 2006, has an especially strong presence in many town centres in Europe, and has expanded to become a major global concern, with shops located in shopping centres throughout the world. Increasingly, beauty has been presented as a consumer product, which can be bought and whose price and quality is differentiated according to market 'niches'. Those who have the financial wherewithal and who are seen to have most at stake in maintaining the beautiful body, such as celebrities, often spend considerable sums on the purchase of beauty products and services. The link between celebrity status or fame and beauty is constantly reinforced through media, in advertisements and promotional packages which are used to promote beauty and body care products, and in numerous stories about the supposedly glamorous lives of celebrities, for which 'consumers' seem to have an insatiable appetite (Rojek 2001). The UK football star, David Beckham is a classic example of the use of a celebrity to sell beauty products. In the early 2000s, he has promoted a range of beauty and fashion products, in the UK (e.g. for Marks and Spencers) and other countries (Japan) and has developed a lucrative advertising career in this field. According to a survey by *France Football* magazine published in 2005, the 'star has annual earnings of £17 million, including £12.5 million from advertising contracts' (Culf 2005: 12), making him the highest paid football player in the world.[29] As advertisers and those working in the media know, celebrity status, like sex, sells. Many feminists, on the other hand, see the beauty industry as exploiting people's, particularly women's, insecurity by peddling an illusory 'beauty myth' (e.g. Wolf 1990). However, although some writers have strong views about the nature of the beauty industry and its effects, its nature and operations have been relatively unexplored, reflecting a general neglect in the social study of what are viewed as feminised spheres (Black 2004: 8–10). Further, until recently, there has been little empirical research on the 'consumers' themselves; on how they view and engage with beauty products and services.

If data provided by the beauty industry's market surveys can be taken as a guide, beauty products and services constitute a huge and apparently growing sector, comprising diverse aspects and operations. In 2004, the European and US personal care market alone was worth $US86 billion and was predicted to grow to $US102 billion in 2009 (Datamonitor 2005). Companies like Beiersdorf AG, Clarins, Yves Rocher Group, L'Oréal Groupe, Colgate-Palmolive, Avon Products Inc., The Gillette Company, Revlon Inc., Unilever Group, and GlaxoSmithKline Plc are among the better known larger companies involved in cosmetics and toiletries. Many of these are expanding outside the rich countries of the north into the Asia Pacific, Eastern Europe, Latin America, Africa and the Middle East. Beiersdorf AG which has 100 affiliates worldwide and produces Nivea among a host of other cosmetic, toiletry and medicinal products, like many other companies has undergone massive restructuring and repositioning in the market as a result of a global downturn or levelling of sales in the USA and some Western European countries, increasing competition, and currency fluctuations and has looked to expanding into other markets and products (e.g. extension of men's toiletries) and employing new technologies and marketing techniques. Between 1999 and 2003, it saw its greatest growth (58 per cent) in its Africa, Australia and Asian operations (Euromonitor 2004: 3). As with other multi-national companies, it is looking to expand into Eastern Europe and Asia to position itself in these rapidly developing regions and to benefit from the cheap production costs and highly skilled but low paid labour force. A Euromonitor report, which produces profiles for different companies in cosmetics and toiletries, and other industries, acknowledges the benefits of using local staff who identify with the company and the strategy of focusing on a small number of internationally recognised brands (e.g. Nivea) which assists with entry to new markets and new product areas (2004: 9). This increasing entry of major global companies involved in cosmetics and toiletries into Eastern Europe, the Asia-Pacific, Latin America, Middle East and Africa parallels observations of growing body dissatisfaction among at least some minority ethic groups from these regions (see, e.g. Gimlin 2002: 79, 99–100; Grogan 1999: 136–137).

Despite substantial, long-standing feminist criticism of the promulgation of ideals of beauty, the beauty industry would seem to be expanding. In the UK, the 2004 annual Survey of the Beauty Industry, comprising salon owners, salon managers, beauty therapists, nail technicians, and others, showed an increase in every category of business over the previous year, with a growth of 17.54 per cent rise overall. In the introduction to the report of the survey findings (a summary of which is provided on a website) it is stated that 'The information is extremely useful for beauty professionals, enabling them to judge who their customers are, what treatments and products they like, and how much the salon should charge for treatments; in other words, vital information for anyone wanting to run a successful beauty business'.[30] The report showed that the industry is a large employer, encompassing 14,440 salon businesses, with 31,288 therapists working full- and part-time. This services a huge client population, with 7,150,814 people visiting a salon over the previous 12 months, up from 6,925,922 in 2003. The survey reveals that manicures, pedicures and basic facial treatments are the top three most popular salon treatments. Interestingly, it also notes the number of salons accepting male clients had increased 'slightly by 1% from 78% to 79%', and that for salons accepting male clients there was an increase of those visiting every month, from 7.5 to 10.2.[31]

Market analysts such as Datamonitor have noted the growing segmentation of the cosmetic and toiletry industry, and drawn attention to recent trends, offering profiles for different countries. This company offers some 'highlights' for Europe and the USA:

> Seniors represent the fastest growing demographic group in terms of [personal care] occasions, representing not only socio-demographic changes, but also a growing desire among these consumers to 'look good for their age'. The growth in male grooming is not solely attributable to fashion; across Europe and the US 89% of men consider that good grooming and presentation is essential to their success in the workplace.
>
> (Datamonitor 2005)

Armed with detailed data derived from market surveys, such information has become a valuable commodity in its own right (some reports sell for hundreds and even thousands of pounds), with companies that seek to gain a market lead needing to know exactly what their customers want and desire. But exactly what is being promised through glossy advertising and what conceptions of the body and self do they convey? What assumptions about human subjects and subjectivity or 'sense of self' underlie promotional efforts and what techniques are used to sell the ever growing array of products and services available in the market-place? Is it reasonable to argue that the beauty industry is promoting a 'beauty myth'? To what extent are 'consumers' exercising 'freedom of choice' and making an 'informed' decision when buying beauty products and services?

Feminist debates

The questions of whether the beauty industry is promulgating false promises or a 'myth' about beauty and whether the women who mostly participate in beauty treatments are 'dupes' of an exploitative system has been the subject of considerable ongoing debate among feminist scholars over many decades. They continue to provoke debate for a number of reasons, not least of which is that writers on either side of the debate tend to have deeply held views about the nature of society and human agency and in particular about the question of the extent to which women are able to exercise 'freedom of choice' within a sexist society. Feminism is a diverse field and not easy to categorise, but encompasses radical, socialist, liberal and postmodern/ poststructural positions. Early feminist writers of the 1970s and early 1980s

such as Andrea Dworkin, Katherine MacKinnon and Sandra Bartky tended
to adopt a radical stance in that they viewed the beauty industry as exploitative of women and a manifestation of 'patriarchy', and the pursuit of beauty
as a damaging cultural practice (see Jeffreys 2005: 6–8). Debate was reignited
in 1990 with the publication of Naomi Wolf's *The Beauty Myth*, which
argued that women were compelled to engage in beauty practices and that
this imperative became more intense as a consequence of the 1980s backlash
against the threat of women's liberation and greater access to opportunities,
particularly through the labour market. Although writers on this subject have
emphasised different themes, the beauty industry tends to be seen as reflecting
a sexist culture and beauty practices as having harmful effects on women's
bodies and lives. The industry and the practices are viewed as indicative
of the cultural domination of women, which involves the treatment of
women as sex objects. Women who participate in beauty practices are seen
as implicated in the objectification of their own bodies and thus the perpet-
uation of sexist culture (Jeffreys 2005: 8). Given this view, it is not surprising
that beauty pageants (e.g. Miss World) and media portrayals, particularly
advertising, of 'beautiful' women and of beauty products has been the target
of much feminist criticism. In some versions of this argument, women appear
as 'victims' of an all-dominating 'patriarchy' who, like workers in Karl
Marx's depiction of capitalist social relations, suffer 'false consciousness'
in failing to recognise how they have been duped by an exploitative all-
dominating system.

Recently, a new 'wave' of feminist writing on beauty and the beauty
industry, sometimes drawing on postmodern/poststructural theory, and some
based on fieldwork in settings where women engage in different forms of
body modification or management, has presented a more complex picture of
the beauty industry and of women's engagement with beauty practices (e.g.
Davis 1995; Gimlin 2002; Black 2004). In these writings, the beauty industry
is seen as multi-faceted rather than homogenous (as tended to be depicted
by earlier writers) and as being more or less exploitative and dangerous, and
women are seen to express their agency through variable and active engagements with beauty practices. Women buy beauty products and services for
a range of reasons and engage with beauty service providers (e.g. beauty
salons) for various purposes on different occasions or at different times in
their lives, including for sociability and a break with daily routines. Cosmetic
surgery may be a strategy adopted by women for reclaiming control over
their lives in a context offering restricted opportunities for self-fulfilment (e.g.
Davis 1995). Indeed, it may have subversive potential, in undermining the
dominant ideals of feminine beauty and for undermining notions of the fixed
human subject (e.g. Balsamo 1996; Morgan 1991, citing Negrin 2002: 22).
A number of these themes are evident in the work of Gimlin (2002) and Black
(2004), writing in the contexts of the USA and UK, respectively.

In researching her book, *Body Work: Beauty and Self-Image in American
Culture*, Debra Gimlin (2002) examined a range of different 'sites' for beauty

treatments and different beauty practices: the hair salon, aerobics and cosmetic surgery. She also explored the views of people within a civil rights organisation (the National Association to Advance Fat Acceptance (NAAFA)) devoted to advancing the well-being of people with non-'normal' bodies; for example, through pursuing anti-size-discrimination legislation. Grimlin challenges the notion that women 'blindly submit to [body work] or choose to make their bodies physical manifestations of their own subordination' (Gimlin 2002: 2). While she accepts that women face particular and more intense pressure than men to conform to certain ideals of beauty and that for women the link between body and identity is more explicit, the women whom she encountered were found to be 'savvy cultural negotiators, attempting to make out as best they can within a culture that limits their options' (Gimlin 2002: 4, 106). They were reflective and critical consumers of the treatments and, for those undergoing plastic surgery, tended to see this as a 'final option for correcting a tormenting problem' rather than as a means of meeting an enforced standard of beauty imposed by others (Gimlin 2002: 73–109). Gimlin's work with NAAFA, however, underlined the limits of women's capacity to negotiate the non-normal identities which their large bodies represented. For example, women in the group refused to date fat men, rejected approaches from men who have a sexual preference for a fat partner, and continued to try to lose weight. In stigmatising members of their own group, they reinforced rather than challenged 'the cultural fear and repudiation of fat' (Gimlin 2002: 140).

In her UK-based study, *The Beauty Industry*: *Gender, Culture, Pleasure*, Paula Black (2004) also portrays a complex view of the beauty industry – or at least a segment of this industry – and of beauty practices in her examination of women's interactions with beauty salons. According to the testimonials of clients, treatments offered by beauty salons fall into a number of categories; namely, pampering, routine grooming, health treatments, corrective procedures, and counselling (Black 2004: 15–19). In Black's view, the women whom she encountered 'were in no sense unambiguously oppressed in their use of the salon' and 'None of the women were in the salon for reasons of beauty' (2004: 40, 51). Indeed, all were 'highly sceptical of the operations of the beauty industry' (2004: 99) with many expressing ambivalence about their own engagement with beauty practices and showing an awareness of feminist arguments. The women had diverse rationales for their use of the salon, including 'time for themselves' away from the demands of home life and sociability with other women, and were reflective in their use of different treatments. Women's narratives reflected the influence of class, gender, age, income, ethnicity and other factors on their preferences and priorities. The discourse of choice was found to permeate both the arguments of the 'consumers' and also those within the beauty industry itself, with the idea of the body as a project and using the salon to fabricate a particular self-view being evident in the accounts of respondents. Decisions to use salons were found to vary according to the women's age and their point in the life-course. Important life events, such as weddings, holidays and pregnancy may be marked by attention to the body and its display, and act as triggers for an initial visit. Rather than striving for an idealised version of beauty, the women who attend beauty salons sought treatments that were 'suitable' or 'appropriate' for them as women, given the time, occasion, and their age – decisions that were assisted through the purchasing of the skills possessed by others, namely, the beauty therapist (Black 2004: 43–99).

Such work underlines the need to differentiate between sectors of the beauty industry and types of beauty practice. Further, it emphasises the need to recognise women's agency, which was often denied in earlier feminist accounts, where women tend to appear as 'dupes' or uncritical consumers of practices and services. Women are recognised as having diverse experiences, which are strongly shaped by various factors including age, ethnicity, socio-economic status, family role, and so on. However, recent feminist contributions of this kind have themselves been criticised for over-emphasising 'agency', 'choice', 'empowerment' and 'liberation' and underplaying constraint (Jeffreys 2005: 13). Negrin (2002) argues that the surgical restyling of the body, promoted by writers such as Balsamo and Morgan and the French performance artist, Orlan, overlook the complicity of such body modification efforts with commodification processes within consumer culture and deny the inequitable contexts within which such body transformations occur. Jeffreys, writing from a radical feminist position, criticises what she labels 'liberal feminists' for their failure to acknowledge 'the forces that restrict and can even eliminate women's ability to choose' (2005: 13).She sees the move towards emphasising women's capacity to choose and to express agency and downplaying coercion as indicative of 'the postmodern takeover of leftwing thinking' and of 'the cultural turn' in social theory. In her view, this represents a denial of the key significance of beauty practices for the creation and maintenance of difference between the sexes (Jeffreys 2005: 13–14, 29–30). She views beauty practices in Western culture as harmful cultural practices, which 'in recent decades' have become 'more and more invasive of the body' (2005: 28ff, 149ff).

Recent developments, new questions

Debates such as those above will no doubt continue as feminism itself evolves and the beauty industry develops new products, services and strategies. 'Beauty' and its representations, production and promotion has long been a subject of popular interest and academic analysis and criticism and is likely to continue to be so in the future. However, I would argue that fresh questions and new avenues of investigation are needed to make sense of these and other developments in technologies of body modification and management, particularly in light of recent shifts in power and politics, described earlier. While one should not lose sight of how these technologies of the body may reinforce stereotypes of gender and create 'difference', there needs to be greater acknowledgement of the ever-changing norms and practices of body modification and management, pertaining as they do to both women and men of different ethnicities, sexualities, ages, socio-economic statuses, and so on, and what this reveals about the contemporary workings of power. The beauty industry is shifting its attention to newer populations, including younger people (who are increasingly targeted by advertisers; e.g. Nivea), with recent claims that cosmetic manufacturers are 'making profits from teenagers who . . . may damage their young complexions by using unsuitable products' (Bloomfield 2005b: 4) and that beauty treatments are being offered to young girls who are 'treated like "Barbie Dolls"' (Hill 2005: 9). The questions that need asking include: What forces are underpinning this trend and what are the broader social, economic and political implications? How is the increasing availability of body modification and maintenance treatments changing conceptions of the body, age and ageing, health and illness, and the self? What are the implications of these treatments for the 'consumers' themselves, in terms of their physical and mental health and self-identities?

Cosmetic surgery, it would appear, is becoming 'normalised' within medical practice, which is no doubt assisted by television programmes such as *Extreme Makeover* and *Ten Years Younger*, which show the 'wonders' of surgical and other body modification techniques. The Internet and other advertising media promise potential 'consumers' considerable 'choice' and expectations of success in treatments and easy access to products and services. For example, the Harley Medical Group, which advertises its services on the Internet indicates that it has 11 cosmetic surgery clinics throughout the UK, and provides a range of 'reshaping, reducing or enlarging' procedures for both men and women. The Group offers 'free consultations at convenient locations around the country, so you will not have to travel far to discuss how we can make a real difference to your life'.[32] According to a news report published in 2005, the Harley Medical Group 'had seen surgery among those in their 50s and 60s quadruple in the past five years' and that 'Apart from wanting to look younger, the main reasons for surgery were "job prospects" and "second marriages"'.[33] Another article reports that 'Record numbers of Britons are travelling abroad for plastic surgery amid growing complaints about soaring prices for straightforward procedures in the UK' (Bloomfield 2005c: 3). The article goes on to note that 'the surge in demand' for cosmetic surgery, combined with the prospect of an overseas holiday, 'is persuading 10,000 Britons a year to travel as far afield as Brazil, South Africa and Malaysia for cheap plastic surgery' (Bloomfield 2005c: 3). Such reports suggest that the boundary between surgery for reasons of health or restoration and surgery for enhancement for 'social' reasons is becoming blurred. It may be that some body modification treatments which are currently used or being developed for body restoration after injury or disease – for example, face transplants for patients who are seriously disfigured (see Revill 2002: 1) – may in the future become routine for those wanting to 'restore' youth or create a new identity. Concerns about the blurring of the distinction between treatment and enhancement have been voiced in relation to genetic technologies which, proponents claim, will change the nature of healthcare practice in the years ahead. (See Chapter 6.) The implications of the routine use and 'normalisation' of cosmetic surgery and other body modification or maintenance treatments needs fuller analysis and debate, especially in regards to the significance for concepts of health, illness and normality, people's expectations about the healthcare, and the future allocation of healthcare resources.

Such analysis and debate needs to encompass global as well as local contexts, given evidence, noted earlier, showing growing concerns about weight and appearance in some societies which apparently did not previously exhibit anxieties about these issues (Grogan 1999: 136–137; Nasser 1997: 46; Seed *et al.* undated). The dispersion of Western ideals of perfection or 'beauty', it has been suggested, may account for these concerns. Reviewing the literature pertaining to women from Asian and Hispanic ethnic groups and body dissatisfaction in the late 1990s, Grogan argues that there may be a 'cultural shift' in attitudes to thinness. Although in her assessment more white women are 'at more risk of "feeling fat", and are more likely to diet, than British Afro-Caribbean and Asian women, or Afro-American, Asian-American or Hispanic groups', there is some evidence indicating that this disparity is disappearing leading to more body dissatisfaction among the latter groups and that this may be 'a result of adoption of dominant white socio-cultural values in relation to body image' (Grogan 1999: 137). Seed *et al.* (undated) in their UK study of the socio-cultural factors and perceptions of attractiveness in Black South African (Zulu) female university students found that 'the pursuit of thinness among black females was strongly linked to the desire to attract men' who, it was perceived, 'now preferred thinner women, leaving the women with "little choice" but to respond'. Other reasons given included: 'lack of modern clothes in bigger body sizes; teasing from friends; media portrayals of thin black ideals; [and] perceived empowerment – because they now have a "right" to choose for themselves'. The authors conclude that the pursuit of thinness among black South African female university students 'appears to constitute just one aspect of a broader cultural *emphasis upon thinness* and *disparagement of overweight* previously not observed among the black community' (Seed *et al.* undated; emphases in original). Such findings indicate that the impacts of the diffusion of Western body ideals on groups of different cultures and ethnicities may be profound and reinforced through various means.

The emergence of powerful transnational business interests in beauty and body modification/maintenance products and treatments (e.g. Beiersdorf AG, Clarins, Yves Rocher Group and L'Oréal) calls for study of the national and international economic, political and socio-cultural implications of the production, marketing, distribution and consumption of products and services. Some beauty products have become everyday 'essentials', finding their place in bathroom cabinets alongside the toothpaste, soap, and toilet paper. The 'hand and body care' sector of the beauty industry, which includes lotions, creams, sprays and moisturisers, alone is a sizeable and rapidly growing market. According to a Datamonitor report: 'In 2004 the overall European and US personal care market was worth US$86bn growing to US$102bn in 2009'. Further, '86.9% of all personal care usage occurred on everyday occasions such as daily personal hygiene routines or beauty regimes, making everyday use by far the most valuable type of personal care occasion'.[34] How do medicines, potions, tissues and treatments circulate within global and local economies and how does this impact on people's everyday lives and 'sense of self'. Who are the producers and who are the consumers of these products and services and who stands to profit and lose from their exchange? What are the attendant dangers, unrecognised or unacknowledged, associated with this exchange? And how adequate is legislation governing the marketing of beauty products and body modification treatments?

Recent news reports highlight some pertinent specific issues in need of analysis. One relates to the reinforcement of social inequalities and the health dangers arising from the economic exchanges associated with beauty and other body modification/maintenance treatments. One recent news report notes that 'Aborted foetuses from girls and young women are being exported from the Ukraine for use in illegal beauty treatment costing thousands of pounds' (Parfitt 2005: 17). The article goes on to say:

> The foetuses are cryogenically frozen and sold to clinics offering 'youth injections', claiming to rejuvenate skin and cure a raft of diseases. It is thought that women in the former Soviet republic are being paid £100 a time to persuade them to have abortions and allow their foetuses to be used in treatments. Most of the foetuses are sold in Russia for up to £5,000 each. Some are paid extra to have abortions late in their pregnancy.
>
> (Parfitt 2005: 17)

The article notes that although 'Ukraine law allows an aborted human foetus to be passed to research institutes if the woman involved consents and her anonymity is protected', 'staff at state health institutions are selling them to private clinics offering illegal therapy' – a practice which is difficult to detect due to corrupt agreements between doctors and academics. Beauty salons in Moscow that purchase the aborted material to provide the 'foetal therapy' are flourishing, with salons charging up to £10,000 to wealthy clients 'who are told the treatment can stop the ageing process, or eliminate such debilitating conditions as Parkinson's disease or Alzheimer's' (Parfitt 2005: 17). If this report is true, then it would seem that the pursuit of 'beauty' by some rich female 'consumers' – who themselves are at risk of being duped by those promoting these treatments – may be at the expense of the health and well-being of other, poorer women. As the article indicates, there may be health dangers associated with these illegal treatments that 'us[e] stem cells which are often untested for viruses such as Aids' (Parfiff 2005: 17).

Another issue relates to the particular use of science in advertising to lend credibility to claims, to entice 'consumers' to purchase products or services. Scientific claims have long been used in advertising to sell products. However, the validity of such claims is often questionable, especially when studies involve a small sample size, and studies are not subject to the process of peer review and publication in science journals where work is available for public scrutiny. Some months after the above report, one company, L'Oréal, was ordered to withdraw and amend some television advertisements starring the model Claudia Schiffer, after the Advertising Standards Authority (ASA) 'found it could not back up the claims made for creams to combat cellulite and wrinkles' (Gibson 2005: 9). The two products in question were Anti-Wrinkle De-Crease cream and Perfect Slim anti-cellulite cream. For the former, it was claimed that 76 per cent of women had 'visibly reduced expression lines', while for the latter, 71 per cent of women found that the product 'visibly reduced the appearance of cellulite' (McCartney 2005: 2). The ruling was described as 'one of the most damning to date' of the 'highly competitive' (£15 billion) cosmetic market (Gibson 2005: 9). As the original article notes, the ruling was the latest in a series of criticisms of 'misleading' advertising by multinational companies involved in the marketing of cosmetic and shampoo products, including Estée Lauder, Chanel, Max Huber and Procter & Gamble. In a detailed piece on the scientific claims in advertising, including skin-care products, published in *The Guardian's* G2 the following day, and evidently prepared in response to this news, it was pointed out that such claims are often based on studies with small samples. For example, the studies for L'Oréal's Perfect Slim anti-cellulite cream, which was the subject of the ASA ruling, 'was tested on just 48 women, meaning that the number of women who noticed a difference was in fact only 34' (McCartney 2005: 2). The article also noted that since staff at the ASA are unable to scrutinise 'an estimated 30m adverts printed every year in the UK', they rely heavily on public complaints, 14,000 of which are made annually. It questioned the scientific rigour of many of the studies and the validity of some scientific claims cited in advertisements for other beauty products, as well as for 'several medicines that have come "off prescription" and are now available for over-the-counter purchase' (McCartney 2005: 9). As this case indicates, there is a need for analysis of the way in which science is deployed in the advertising of beauty products and other body modification/maintenance products and services and to reveal how this may shape publics' responses.

Finally, it needs to be asked how adequate are current ways of conceiving 'consumers' and their engagements with the body shape and appearance industries. In particular, the question of 'free will' or 'social determinism', which prefigures and serves to polarise feminist and other debates about the beauty industry and body modification practices, needs rethinking. It is possible to acknowledge both agency and structural constraint at the same time and avoid the voluntarism or social determinism that is evident in many accounts; i.e. the view that individuals are *either* unconstrained decision-makers or 'dupes' *or* victims of an all-dominating, oppressive system. As noted, increasingly, agency or 'choice' (active citizenship) has become central to the workings of power. One can acknowledge that individuals may express agency through participation in practices of body modification and management and thereby constitute themselves as particular kinds of selves, while at the same time recognising that the options for thinking and acting are prescribed or suggested by the social context. Practices may be more or less pleasurable, 'oppressive' and dangerous, according to time, the situation, and participants' interactions. Different times and contexts present different degrees of constraint and different opportunities for contesting, negotiating or changing norms. The concept of beauty itself is contested, if a recent Dove report is any guide. This showed that many women in the USA at least do not equate 'beauty' with physical appearance and that (contrary to the expectations of the research team) women were found to have a 'high level of satisfaction with their looks'.[35] While the increasing commodification of culture does present a constraint and physical and other dangers – for example, in the use or over-use of certain hazardous products and services and the reinforcement of inequalities, as noted above – there needs to be greater acknowledgement of the pleasures and emotional appeal of using particular products and treatments. Women's pleasurable engagements with beauty salons were apparent in the accounts of Black's (2004) respondents, for example. Some of the growing numbers of men using beauty products and body modification treatments no doubt derive similar pleasure from their 'consumption' of these products and treatments. Rather than offering generalised assessments of the significance of body modification and maintenance practices, there is a need for close scrutiny of body norms and how they are (re-)constructed and maintained, and of the claims of those who suggest or promote forms of body modification and management. I would contend that the same argument pertains to biomedical treatments for illnesses and disabilities, which has been the focus of considerable debate and a topic to which I turn in the next chapter.

4   The classification and regulation of bodies

What do bodies reveal about their 'owners'? Is it possible to accurately assess a person's character or well-being, for example, from an initial meeting with them? The belief that one can classify and judge the trustworthiness, personality, outlook, health or mental disposition of another person or a group of people from their face or body shape, size, age or appearance is deeply rooted in Western culture. This suggests that there is a close relationship between the external, physical body, and the inner self. The long-held idea that appearance reveals an essential nature has been mirrored and extended in studies of human types (Porter 2003: 247). Regardless of whether or not it is valid for one to classify and evaluate others on the basis of appearance or public presentation alone, people do routinely make such judgements which affect whether or not and how they interact with others. In contemporary societies, classificatory schemes affect how we view and conduct ourselves; that is, our self identity. But is classification and judgement a universal and inevitable human trait? And, what are the broader social implications of our particular ways of classifying bodies? This chapter examines the mechanisms and socio-political dimensions of body classification in the contemporary West, particularly in the context of growing consumerism in healthcare and more generally, and explores some of the concerns and opposition to classification that have arisen in response. Making reference to examples drawn from a number of different spheres of everyday life, it is shown how processes of body classification are inextricably connected to broader workings of power and political economy.

Classification in context

As Bowker and Star (2000) argue, to classify – that is, to sort things into categories or classes of categories – would seem to be an inherent part of being human. Whether animals classify in a similar way is difficult to determine. However, within much of the animal world, there exist hierarchies and patterns of animal-to-animal and animal-to-human interaction which suggest that some kind of classificatory process is at work. The question of whether this is comparable to what happens among humans, however, is debatable.

As far as is known, all human societies classify objects to some degree; however, the nature, degree and visibility of classification, and the means of classifying, vary considerably through time and across cultures. In many traditional or pre-modern societies there seems to have been no need to classify and order with the kind of statistical precision that is common in many societies today. Space, time and quantity were measured according to criteria relevant to the pertaining conditions of existence. For example, in Australian indigenous communities, which traditionally were based on a hunter-and-gatherer mode of production, there is an apparent lack of precision about the measurement of age in terms of time, despite recognition of broad age differences and their significance for social standing. The notion of a working age and a retirement age, which are significant concepts and categories in contemporary industrial societies, were of little relevance in traditional societies. Similarly, insofar as is known, among Australian indigenous peoples, aggregates of phenomena were not measured by the kinds of quantitative criteria used by European-Australians. For example, broad categories like 'mob' were used, and among more traditional groups continue to be used, rather than a precise population figure (e.g. 50 people) (Tonkinson 1974). With the rise of industrial capitalism and a growing emphasis on the scientific understanding and rational organisation of economic and social life, however, there was a growing interest in the use of statistics to quantify, classify and predict. As Ian Hacking (1990) notes, in Europe from around 1820, there was what he describes as an 'avalanche of printed numbers', with enumeration of all kinds of phenomena, such as births, suicides, deaths and diseases. More and more, information was needed about the population, including details of city planning, housing and transport systems, as well as the problems associated with large urban conglomerations, such as sewerage disposal, pollution, and disease. Writing at the end of the nineteenth century, Max Weber, one of the acknowledged founders of sociology, noted the increasing rationalisation of modern society, as manifest in a particular bureaucratic organisation and organisation of social life. In Weber's view, the rationalisation, classification and enumeration of life threatened to become an 'iron cage' which imprisoned the human soul. While many take a dim view of rationalisation and classification, many of the purported successes of the modern period have been linked to processes of rationalisation and categorisation. The nineteenth century saw the rise of the public health movement, which is noted for its extensive use of statistical categories used to establish links between poor housing, sanitation, education, and so on, and the incidence of diseases in particular areas or among certain populations (Petersen and Lupton 1996). Epidemiology, the science of statistical correlation and a central tool of public health, has its origins in efforts to map the spread of epidemics among urban populations during this period.

The normal and the pathological

At the same time, the emergence of scientific medicine relied heavily on the classification of diseases and diseased bodies, assisted by new techniques of measurement, which allowed the calibration of difference and the establishment of the normal and the pathological (Canguillhem 1989). As Hacking indicates, although the word 'normal' has a long history, 'it acquired its present most common meaning [i.e. usual or typical] only in the 1820s'. It was defined in opposition to the pathological which was for a time confined mainly to the medical domain. However, increasingly, it came to encompass almost all spheres, including 'people, behaviour, states of affairs, diplomatic relations, [and] molecules' (Hacking 1990: 160). In medicine, 'normal' health became defined objectively in terms of a diagnosis showing freedom from disease and adherence to ideals of body weight and size. For example, the measurement of abnormal or high blood pressure (hypertension), which is considered to be dangerous because it makes the heart work harder to pump blood to the body and contributes to hardening of the arteries or atherosclerosis, has become standard in medical assessments, as has the calculation of BMI (Body Mass Index) to assess 'normal, healthy' body weight (see Chapter 3).

Although in medicine, normality may be classified on the basis of statistical criteria, as Armstrong notes, statistics are unable to provide a definitive boundary between normal and abnormal since the exact cut-off point where normal variation becomes pathological is often difficult to determine (1989: 119). Further, as he explains, 'there are so-called pathological phenomena or processes which are statistically normal in some populations' and 'many "abnormal" or "unsual" biological states and processes' (e.g. height, eye colour, hair length) which cannot sensibly be described as diseases (1989: 119). As Armstrong notes, normality may also be defined in terms of acceptable or desirable social values. This meaning of normality often informs medical judgements, including the designation of certain classes of phenomena or behaviours as 'pathological', and thus in need of 'treatment'. Thus, social ideals, such as a preference for people of a certain height, weight, skin or eye colour, physical form, or sex or sexual orientation may lead to certain characteristics being classified as 'pathological'. It might be argued that social definitions of a normal human being, a normal life and when life begins routinely inform medical judgements in relation to prenatal tests and in decisions on whether or not and when to terminate a pregnancy. The influence on medical decisions of social assumptions about normality can be seen in many areas of biomedical practice.

The belief that disability is a 'burden' for parents of the disabled, for disabled people themselves, and for society may lead many doctors to suggest termination in cases where a genetic mutation is detected through prenatal testing. In modern Western society, female bodies have been viewed as 'non-normal' or 'unruly' and as a kind of pathology in need of particular forms of biomedical treatment. They are viewed as soft, fleshy and undisciplined, in contrast to the male body which is hard, muscular and disciplined (Petersen 1998a: 42–43). In multiple edition anatomy texts, such as Gray's *Anatomy*, the male body has been consistently posited as the norm and given greater prominence than the female, which is presented as an 'imperfect' version and hence worthy of less discussion (Petersen 1998b). As Ehrenreich and English (1979) noted many years ago, women's bodies have been the subject of biomedical and other expert control throughout the nineteenth and twentieth centuries. Since modern societies have little tolerance for ambiguity of physical sex and gender, children who are born of 'ambiguous' sex (i.e. where genitalia are not clearly female or male; e.g. a micro-penis) are often subjected to genital reconstruction and then 're-socialisation' in order to align their assumed 'true' identity with their new physical body (Colapinto 2000; Fausto-Stirling 1992). Further, given the absence of openness to unusual anatomies, conjoined twins are viewed as a 'deformed' anatomy which needs to be 'normalised' through surgery (Dreger 2004). Intolerance of same-sex attraction has meant that in the recent past people who have been attracted to people of the same sex ('homosexuals') were often treated through chemical and other means to 'correct' their supposed 'pathological' urges. These are but some examples of how a social definition of 'normal' may inform clinical decision-making and the classification of phenomena as 'pathological', with profound implications for those individuals so classed as well as entire groups.

Although classification is inescapable and arguably an essential aspect of what makes us human, as noted, the nature, degree and visibility of classification, and the means of classifying may vary considerably through time and across societies. Phenomena which are classified as deviance may in time become classified as indicative of pathology and in need of medical intervention. In their influential book, *Deviance and Medicalization: From Badness to Sickness* (1992), Peter Conrad and Joseph Schneider document a gradual redefinition of deviance designations in American society from 'badness' to 'sickness' over approximately the last 200 years. These include mental illness, inebriation, opiate addiction, hyperactivity in children, same-sex sexuality, and criminal behaviour. These changing definitions involve changing attributions of responsibility and blame, and new policy responses and regulatory institutions. The trends these authors identify for the USA would seem to find parallels in many other contemporary societies. When a phenomenon is defined as 'badness' or 'evil' it will tend to attract physical punishment or imprisonment, but when it is defined as a 'sickness', it will be 'treated' or 'cured' through biomedical means, including the use of surgery and drugs. This process of 'medicalisation' of social phenonemona has been noted for other societies, too, but often those with a different set of questions and political agenda. The question of whether it is better to be punished or 'treated' is open to debate and is likely to depend on the particular phenomenon, the context, and the nature and severity of the punishment or treatment. While, in some instances, control through punishment may be considered harmful, substituting this with control via 'treatment' may prove equally (and perhaps more) pernicious. Being locked up for conduct considered to be deviant may be preferable for those involved in some instances to being subject to, for example, electroconvulsive therapy or powerful drugs, which may lead to mental trauma or physical harm. The perceived implications and harmfulness of a system of classification for individuals and groups often varies considerably through time and in different places. Ongoing debate at the international level about what constitutes 'torture' and its legality illustrates the variability in definitions of harm and acceptability.

One interpretation of medicalisation is offered by Michel Foucault, referred to in Chapter 1. His main contribution in this area is *The Birth of the Clinic: An Archaeology of Medical Perception* (1975). As noted, Foucault was interested in the emergence of discursive formations, such as medicine, sexuality and regimes of discipline and punishment, and the reconfiguring of the relationship between knowledge and power that these entailed. The emergence of what Foucault calls the 'medical gaze' involved a re-orientation between the visible and the invisible, bringing into view classes of phenomena previously imperceptible and hence indescribable. In the introduction to the above book he writes:

> At the beginning of the nineteenth century, doctors described what for centuries had remained below the threshold of the visible and the expressible, but this did not mean that, after over-indulging in speculation, they had begun to perceive once again, or that they listened to reason rather than to imagination; it meant that the relation between the visible and the invisible – which is necessary to all concrete knowledge – changed its structure, revealing through gaze and language what had previously been below and beyond their domain.
>
> (Foucault 1975: xii)

The 'medical gaze' involved a reorganisation of space, in particular the hospital, a new definition of the status of the patient in society, a new conception of 'the body', and new classifications of 'diseases' and their signs and symptoms. Clinicians come to see and know the body in ways previously unimagined and techniques such as dissection become crucial to understanding how the body 'works' and the basis for 'pathology' (Foucault 1975: Chapter 8). Although, in modern Western culture, 'biology' is generally depicted as separate and separable from 'society', Foucault's concept of biopower draws attention to the inherently political nature of the biological categories and classifications that have become increasingly pervasive. However, as Agamben (1998) argues, political rule has long involved some element of effort to control life processes. Historical and cross-cultural work has highlighted the fact that modes of classification change through time and across contexts, and are thus inherently unstable. How individuals and groups classify themselves and others – as 'normal' or 'abnormal', 'strong' or 'weak', 'healthy' or 'ill', and so on – therefore are also subject to change through time. Ian Hacking has noted the close correspondence between self identity and ways of being and the classificatory systems or societal ways of 'making up people' (Hacking 1986).

The International Classification of Diseases (ICD) and the Diagnostic and Statistical Manual of Mental Disorders (DSM) which are formal classifications for morbidity and mortality, and mental disorders, respectively, are powerful technologies of the medical gaze, bringing into visibility discrete classes of disease and the diseased through the use of precise, supposedly objective criteria. These classifications, which provide the basis for medical judgements and public health strategies at the international level, include a description of every disease or group of related diseases along with their diagnoses and a unique code. The history of the ICD can be traced back to the 1850s and efforts to develop a uniform international classification of causes of death, which was extended later to diseases which affect health but which do not necessary lead to death. The classification has since undergone a series of revisions, culminating in the Tenth Revision (ICD-10), which came into use by the World Health Organization (WHO) member states in 1994.[36] The DSM, published by the American Psychiatric Association, was published in 1952 and has also undergone various revisions, with the most recent edition (DSM–IV) published in 1994.[37] Both systems of classification provide a key resource for healthcare workers and inform the development of health policy at national and international levels. The World Health Organization, which is the United Nations specialized agency for health, has used the ICD as the basis for monitoring population health and for healthcare planning since 1948 when the WHO was created. The WHO took over responsibility for the ICD, when its Sixth Revision, which included causes of morbidity for the first time, was published.[38]

As the WHO's website explains,

> [The ICD] is used to classify diseases and other health problems recorded on many types of health and vital records including death certificates and hospital records. In addition to enabling the storage and retrieval of diagnostic information for clinical and epidemiological purposes, these records also provide the basis for the compilation of national mortality and morbidity statistics by WHO member states.[39]

These classifications aim to provide a concise and universal means of identifying conditions which, in essence, are often subject to considerable debate about their causes, symptoms and precise delineation. The question of how best to classify mental conditions such as depression and schizophrenia, for example, has been extensively discussed over a very long period of time. Some writers have even questioned the applicability of the disease or illness model to what is in effect a complex psycho-social phenomenon (Szaz 1974). Clinicians, however, tend to work on the basis that mental illnesses can be objectively diagnosed according to clearly defined symptoms. In relation to depression, for example, they are advised to gather a range of data before deciding whether a patient is suffering from clinical depression and to evaluate whether a person has symptoms of conditions such as 'major depression', 'dysthymia', or 'bipolar disorder' – all of which are subject to a precise diagnostic criteria within the DSM1V.[40] For instance, the entry for 'Major depressive disorder, single episode' within DSM1V includes the following among its diagnostic criteria:

> A For a major depressive episode a person must have experienced at least five of the nine symptoms below for the same two weeks or more, for most of the time almost every day, and this is a change from his/her prior level of functioning. One of the symptoms must be either (a) depressed mood, or (b) loss of interest.
> a Depressed mood. For children and adolescents, this may be irritable mood.
> b A significantly reduced level of interest or pleasure in most or all activities.
> c A considerable loss or gain of weight (e.g., 5% or more change of weight in a month when not dieting). This may also be an increase or decrease in appetite. For children, they may not gain an expected amount of weight.
> d Difficulty falling or staying asleep (insomnia), or sleeping more than usual (hypersomnia).
> e Behavior that is agitated or slowed down. Others should be able to observe this.
> f Feeling fatigued, or diminished energy.
> g Thoughts of worthlessness or extreme guilt (not about being ill).
> h Ability to think, concentrate, or make decisions is reduced.
> i Frequent thoughts of death or suicide (with or without a specific plan), or attempt of suicide.

As can be seen, this classification entails a combination of subjective assessments of internal mental state (e.g. 'thoughts of worthlessness or extreme guilt') and supposedly objective evaluations of external bodily state (e.g. 'A considerable loss or gain of weight'). Both, however, rely on the subjective evaluations of the clinician as to what constitutes 'normal' or 'abnormal' in the case of all the symptoms. While the criteria may appear to be objective and thus beyond dispute, evaluations about how conditions are to be classified are likely to vary considerably between clinicians, across different cultural contexts and through time.

The development of the ICD and DSM which allow diseases to be classified according to precise biophysical criteria is indicative of the growing 'politicization of life' in the modern age (Agamben 1998). Questions about the origins of life, the value of life, and the end of life have become central to how contemporary societies are governed. Economic considerations are obviously significant in debates about prolonging life or continuing life which is deemed to be unproductive, for example the profoundly disabled. Especially in a 'post-welfare' context, with an emphasis on efficiency, value-for-money, and so on, increasingly cost–benefit factors influence judgements about whether life should be preserved and when it should end. Recent developments in biomedical classifications, as determined, for instance, through tests for genetic 'markers' for disease can be seen as means of extending power over newer populations and potentially discriminating between lives that are valued and those that are not. As explained in Chapter 1, one of the promises of the new genetics is to provide the basis for a new predictive, personalised medicine. Knowing that the individual has a 'faulty' gene, it is argued, allows health professionals to predict the onset of disease and identify the 'pre-symptomatic' ill who need treatment through drugs or changes in lifestyle or who may need to terminate their pregnancy if found to be a carrier of a genetic condition. Some writers predict that a growing emphasis on individual responsibility in healthcare and more generally will mean that, in the future, individuals who do not 'do the right thing', that is undergo a gene test where these are available and terminate a pregnancy when found to carry a faulty gene will be judged to be 'irresponsible' (Crossley 1996; King 1995).

Numerous criteria and means have been deployed for categorising and differentiating between bodies. At different times to varying degrees, bodies have been classified according to criteria of class background, skin colour, shape or dimension (including head shape and cranial capacity), facial features, age, sexuality, and height. The idea that appearance, for example facial features (the chin, brow, smile, lips, eyes), could provide insight into the inner state of mind or soul can be traced back to the ancient Greeks (Porter 2003: 245). Physiognomy which was concerned with the interpretation of outer appearance, especially faces, as an indicator of the character or temper of the person became popular towards the end of the eighteenth century and for the entirety of the nineteenth century (Twine 2002). For example, the Italian criminologist Cesare Lombroso produced a detailed classification of bodies into criminal types. Darwin, in his *The Expression of Emotions in Man and Animals* explored the physiognomy of insanity and the classification of emotional states and saw a continuum in the modes of expression throughout the animal kingdom (Gilman 1988: 129–139). During the nineteenth century, anthropology, psychology, sociology, criminology, and other scholarly disciplines began to delineate the physical diversity of human types and experiences as part of an evolving 'master' classificatory scheme based upon particular assumptions about the ideal body and rationality; viz. that pertaining to the white European male. Differentiations began to be made on the basis of all kinds of biophysical criteria, particularly skin colour, sex, and sexual preference. Since the eighteenth century, 'race' has been a key marker of difference and since the late nineteenth century differences of sex (i.e. male versus female) and sexuality (e.g. 'homosexual' versus 'heterosexual') have achieved increasing significance (see Chapter 2). Although 'race' has been a contentious concept, because of the practical difficulty and the recognised political implications of classifying people according to biophysical differences, recently there has been a resurgence of scientific interest in 'race', with debates about the utility of the category in understanding inequalities in health and mental abilities. A major theme in recent social science work and a focus for activist groups has been the regulatory implications of efforts to classify, intervene into and regulate bodies. The exercise of power through classification has almost invariably given rise to resistance. Gay rights emerged out of resistance to viewing same-sex sexual attraction as a medical problem or pathology, while feminism emerged out of resistance to the biomedical classification and regulation of women's bodies. Similarly, minority ethnic rights movements emerged out of resistance to the social discriminations arising from the imposition of biologically defined, 'racial' classifications. In some cases, resistance has taken the form of utilising the descriptive categories in a subversive way, such as the use of 'queer' as an identity label by those of non-normatives sexualities, to emphasise difference and legitimacy outside the dominant heterosexuality (Petersen 1998a). I will turn to the question of resistance to classification later in the discussion. First, it is worth examining in more detail some contemporary forms and mechanisms of classification and pointing to some of their often unrecognised implications. As I argue, in the contemporary period, a number of converging processes are at work in the classification of bodies. Changes in modes of governance, with a greater emphasis on individualism combined with commodification and medicalisation have altered the character and processes of classification. More and more, the rationality of the market has affected definitions of the normal and the natural, and criteria of inclusion and exclusion, and consequently the basis upon which physical and social distinctions are made. New biomedical and other technologies increasingly available in the medical market-place enable and facilitate mechanisms for classifying and regulating bodies and minds. The character and implications of these developments will become clear, hopefully, by reference to recent examples drawn from a number of domains.

The changing classifications of health and illness

The influence of the rationality of the market on the formation of classificatory categories is perhaps most evident in the field of healthcare, particularly in the re-conceptualisation of 'health'. The rapid development and increasing availability of new medical technologies, combined with commodification and consumerism in healthcare, has occurred hand-in-hand with the rise of new categories of 'condition' or 'disorder' or 'dysfunction' in need of 'treatment'. More and more, people are classified as ill or potentially ('pre-symptomatic') ill on the basis of such categories. Some of these 'conditions' or 'disorders' are arguably mostly problems of personal relationships or related to physical environments or economic, political and social conditions rather than manifestations of biophysical disturbances within the individual. These include 'social anxiety disorder', 'pre-menstrual dysphoric disorder' and 'female sexual dysfunction' (Moynihan and Cassels 2005). Sometimes conditions appear to have some biophysical basis, but have been defined as being more extensive than is justified by the available evidence; for example, 'irritable bowel syndrome' and 'osteoporosis' (Moynihan and Cassels 2005). Further, they may be better 'treated' by changes to the physical or social environment, or to diet or lifestyle. For example, osteoporosis measures may include making physical environments safer for vulnerable (generally older age) groups to minimise the possibility of falls. Labelling people as having osteoporosis and treating them with drugs may discourage them from taking measures to reduce the risk of fractures. For instance they might reduce exercise which actually helps muscle development and balance and helps prevent falls and hip fractures (Moynihan and Cassels 2005: 152–153). As some writers have recently argued, many conditions such as the above have been 'constructed' or 'manufactured' by big pharmaceutical companies who are keen to expand the market for their drugs in the relentless pursuit of profit (Law 2005; Moynihan and Cassels 2005). Advertisers may work closely with drug companies to help create new diseases. One individual who works on marketing campaigns for drug companies revealed that little-known conditions may be given renewed attention, existing diseases may be redefined, or new conditions may be created (Moynihan and Cassels 2005: xi). Drugs are then developed and marketed on the basis of satisfying an 'unmet need' of consumers.

Evidence from the above and other studies indicates that pharmaceutical companies do exert considerable influence over definitions of health and illness via extensive advertising, the employment of public relations and other experts, and, to varying degrees in different countries, control over medicine and regulatory authorities. There is nothing especially new in many of these claims: such practices and links were noted over twenty years ago (Braithwaite 1984). However, since then, 'health' has become increasingly commodified and the pharmaceutical and other health industries have become even more powerful and less subject to effective regulation. There are growing doubts about the ability of regulatory authorities, such as the US Federal Drug Administration (FDA) and the UK's Department of Health to adequately regulate the pharmaceutical industry because of their close relationship with industry (e.g. Law 2005: 15–16, 97, 102, 174). In an increasingly de-regulated global market dominated by powerful companies, nation states are less able than in the past to control companies' activities. Pharmaceutical, biotech and diagnostic companies have sought newer markets within the developed Western world and increasingly the developing world through targeting previously unidentified populations of the diseased and ill. In recent years, medical technologies, including MRI, ultrasound and amniocentesis, as well as newer diagnostic technologies, such as gene tests and neuro-imaging (see Chapter 2) have also increasingly become available in the global market-place, allowing the detection of new conditions, or potential conditions, in a growing proportion of the population. There are predictions that, in the future, nanotechnologies may complement or replace these technologies, allowing for new means of disease diagnosis and molecular imaging, as well as novel techniques of drug delivery for treating cancers and other conditions.[41] Big pharmaceutical companies like Pfizer see huge business opportunities for nanotechnologies in the future. According to the Senior Director of Pfizer's Global Research and Development, in an article published in early 2006,

> Nano-formulation could be critical to helping us achieve specific therapeutic characteristics for some compounds, for lowering toxicity and adverse effects of some drugs, and even improving their efficacy. Another benefit could be to help us create novel and innovative drug delivery [approaches] that would also help patients.[42]

Considerable expectations are associated with genetics, the neurosciences and, increasingly, nanotechnologies, especially as a result of the anticipated merging of these technologies in the future (RS/RAE 2004). Whether these technologies will develop in expected ways and deliver what is promised remains to be seen (see Chapter 6). It seems that with genetics at least, it seems highly unlikely that many of the promised developments will eventuate (Holtzman and Marteau 2000). However, the visions held by pharmaceutical companies and other biomedical concerns strongly shape research agenda and policies which affect how health and illness are defined and who is classified as 'healthy' and 'ill'.

Genetic testing

The increasingly widespread use of genetic tests has served to create ever growing new categories of the diseased and 'at risk'. As findings on the genetic bases of disease accumulate, a burgeoning number of people will be classified as having or being 'at risk' of developing a genetic-related condition. The use of prenatal genetic tests allows the identification of those at risk of giving birth to disabled children, for example those with Down's Syndrome or spina bifida. The question of whether such testing is 'beneficial' is debatable. From the perspective of many healthcare workers and health policy makers, genetic testing has the potential to offer parents 'choice' in health decision-making and savings in healthcare provision through allowing termination of a pregnancy in cases where there is the prospect of a disabled child requiring expensive ongoing treatment and care. Some people in the disability rights movement, however, believe that routine testing presents the danger of eugenics entering by the 'back door' (Duster 1990). Individual decisions 'freely' exercised will have an unintended eugenic outcome and will reinforce discrimination against disabled people by implicitly devaluing their lives (Bailey 1996; Shakespeare 1998). There is some evidence to suggest that these concerns are justified. A 36 nation study on patients' and professionals' views on autonomy, disability and discrimination, conducted between 1993 and 1995, revealed that patients, geneticists and primary care physicians share a similar pessimistic view on disability and few believed that people with disabilities added to society (Wertz 1999: 174). In an increasingly deregulated healthcare system, characterised by growing competition and financial pressures and the imperative to demonstrate cost–benefit efficiencies, physicians and patients are likely to feel compelled to terminate a pregnancy in cases where a genetic mutation is found, to avoid ongoing costs of treatment and care in the future. Patients who know they are 'at risk' of carrying an affected foetus will feel obliged to 'do the right thing' and terminate the pregnancy rather than 'leave things to chance'. In such instances, 'freedom of choice' is an illusion: there is a compulsion to make a choice and the options on offer are limited. Some writers argue that, in the future, genetic selection is likely to reach a new level. Rather than selecting out foetuses 'at risk' of being diseased and disabled, parents may seek to enhance their embryos with genes that have characteristics which they themselves do not have; for example, by ensuring that they have certain 'desirable' characteristics – tallness, intelligence, fair complexion, and so on. This so-called 'germline genetic engineering' is supported by some scientists, who argue that it has the potential to eliminate all 'faulty' genes from the gene pool thus avoiding suffering and reducing healthcare costs in the future (see, e.g. Stock and Campbell 2000).

Pharmacogenetics

The field of pharmacogenetics, on the face of it, seems less contentious than prenatal genetic testing, since its focus is not on the bodies and lives of future generations but rather on the health and well-being of current generations. Pharmacogenetics promises the development of new drugs 'tailored' to the individual rather than a population suffering a common health condition. Medicine, it is claimed, will be 'personalised' in that it will be 'targeted' to the individual's genetic profile and 'predictive' in that it will allow determination of who will become ill (Hedgecoe 2004). As Hedgecoe points out, in Britain, pharmaceutical companies have made great efforts to change the testing culture within the healthcare system (2004: 106–121). Testing for genetic-related conditions (evident after birth and 'late onset') is expected to become standard in healthcare in Britain and many other countries in the future, as suggested by the UK's Genetics White Paper, *Our Inheritance,*

Our Future: Realising the Potential of Genetics in the NHS (Department of Health 2003). This outlines a vision of genetics in the NHS in the future, including testing for single gene disorders, improving preventive and monitoring services for those at risk of developing disease, and developing new drugs and novel therapies. In 2005, an article published in the journal *Nature* reported that Japanese companies had developed a machine that would allow doctors to check patients' DNA from a single drop of blood before writing a prescription (Cyranoski 2005). Such reports suggest that personalised medicine is imminent. At about the same time of the publication of this article, the UK's Royal Society released a report which argued that pharmacogenetics had been 'overhyped' and that its implementation will be a 'gradual rather than revolutionary process' and that it will take 15–20 years to live up to its promise in clinical practice (Royal Society 2005). Regardless of which of these claims can be believed, it is clear that policy is being developed in many contemporary societies on the premise that genetics *will* deliver what is promised and that people's lives will be healthier and happier as a consequence. References to 'health' and to 'public benefit' have strong rhetorical power and are seen as sufficient justification for adopted policies. Critical voices are often muted by the mostly positive media coverage of new genetic discoveries and imminent new treatments, with little attention paid to the considerable complexities of interpretation, uncertainties in the field, and to environmental and ethical issues (Petersen 2001, 2002). (See Chapter 2.)

The growing availability of new medical diagnostic tests and procedures raises the question of whether medical treatments should be restricted to conditions which affect one's 'normal' state of health and well-being (generally defined as being free of obvious disease or disability) or be allowed to be used to improve or enhance one's appearance, performance or pleasure. Sometimes 'treatments' are undertaken or technologies used for reasons of lifestyle or leisure, rather than for 'health'. Cosmetic surgery, which was referred to extensively in the last chapter, is often undertaken to improve appearance rather than to correct deformities resulting from disease (e.g. cancer), burns or injury. The dramatic rise in cosmetic surgery in recent years cannot be attributed to its increased use in medical treatment alone. (See Chapter 3.) Do people have a right to have access to what are often expensive treatments to improve appearance when resources might better be used for helping those who are 'genuinely' sick? How may one legitimately draw the line between 'health' and 'enhancement'? How does a shift in this boundary affect people's conceptions of their bodies and selves? To help cast light on these questions, valuable insights can be drawn from the example of the rise of Viagra. The growing popularity and availability of Viagra – the pill for 'erectile dysfunction' – illustrates clearly the difficulty of drawing the line between 'health' and 'enhancement' and the implications of shifting definitions of health and responsibility for the provision of healthcare and notions of normality and identity.

Viagra

Like all technologies, Viagra embodies assumptions about the categories of users, their needs, and social relationships (Mamo and Fishman 2001), which are worth examining in some detail. The drug's designers had envisaged an 'ideal' user in mind which, in turn has affected users interactions with the drug, although the intended meaning or ideal use may be modified or subverted by users (Mamo and Fishman 2001: 19). Following the approval of Viagra in the USA in 1998, millions of men (primarily white, middle- and upper-class heterosexual men) began to seek medical assistance for problems of erection (Loe 2004). This group may have previously had difficulties with erections (although it is hard to tell how widespread or chronic) due to any number of reasons. In the past, difficulties with erection were likely to have been classified as 'impotence' and defined as a psychological and relational 'problem' in need of psychotherapeutic interventions; however, with the biomedical diagnosis of 'erectile dysfunction' it was seen as a physiological 'disorder' treatable through pharmacological intervention (Mamo and Fishman 2001: 20). The 'little blue pill' became seen as the 'quick fix'. The demographic target group comprising white middle- and upper-class heterosexual men also happened to be those with the best health cover and who were willing to spend ten dollars on a pill (Loe 2004: 23). Loe's analysis of news articles and conversations with doctors, pharmacists, consumers and marketers confirmed that this narrow demographic group was indeed the target and that other groups, such as racial minority groups, gay men, working-class men, and disabled men were 'not accounted for by Pfizer' (2004: 24). As Loe argues, Viagra has contributed to a redefinition of 'normal' sex. However, as she found in her study, definitions went beyond erections to affect definitions of 'normal masculinity, normal femininity, normal sexuality, normal aging, normal bodies, and normal medicine' (Loe 2004: 19). Implicit within the technology are assumptions about what some groups will judge to be intolerable in life, about the ability of medicine to fix the 'broken male machine' and conquer supposed 'declines of aging', and about what constitutes 'normal, healthy' sexual relations (that is, heterosexual penetrative sex). Normal male sexual desire is presumed to be 'readily available and unproblematic', which is opposed to female sexual desire which is seen as lacking and problematic (Mamo and Fishman 2001: 20).

More and more, technologies of the body, such as Viagra, are routinely used and find application for problems and populations for which they were not originally envisaged. Once discoveries are made and new technologies become established there is pressure to find new applications. This pressure arises, first of all, from companies that have expended considerable amounts of money on drug trials and approval processes and, second, from 'consumers' who have been informed and have come to expect that they should have access to these technologies. Viagra itself was originally developed by Pfizer to treat high blood pressure, although with the failure to achieve this in clinical trials researchers sought to capitalise on their 'unintended consequences' (Leland *et al.* 1997). Viagra has recently been identified as having potential for treating Crohn's disease, a condition which affects the bowel (Marks *et al.* 2006). In February 2006, it was reported in *The Lancet* that a research team had discovered that the condition was due not to an auto-immune disease, where a person's immune system attacks the tissues of the body, but rather due to 'defective innate immunity' due to a poor flow of blood. The researchers found that the administration of Viagra to five healthy individuals and ten patients with Crohn's disease 'resulted in marked increases in bloodflow . . . in most participants' (Marks *et al.* 2006: 668). In this instance, the research was not financially supported by Pfizer. However, the case illustrates how, once a new drug becomes available, it may soon be seen to have potential applications in treating other conditions of similar aetiology – regardless of the associated dangers. Viagra, for example, has been known to cause blindness by inducing an optic stroke and a number of deaths have been linked to the use of the drug, especially when combined with recreational drugs such as Ecstacy and crystal meth. (Law 2005: 12; Loe 2004: 176–177). As Loe notes, the dangers associated with Viagra are exacerbated in the largely unregulated context of 'virtual' pharmacies and the black market. (Viagra was one of the first drugs to be made available on the internet, a development which, as Loe notes, was undoubtedly helped by the stigma attached to using and asking for the drug (2004: 177).)

Pharmaceutical companies have worked hard to market drugs to a large segment of the population so that their use becomes an ordinary part of living and means for coping. Since the release of Viagra, pharmaceutical companies have sought to expand the market for this drug, and have targeted women in particular who are defined as suffering 'sexual dysfunction' (see Loe 2004: 171–172; Moynihan 2003). Soon after the launch of Viagra, pharmaceutical companies, including Pfizer began to establish new research and clinical trials for a 'female Viagra' for treating 'the "other half" of the sexually dysfunctional' (Loe 2004: 126). In an article, 'Sexual dysfunction in the United States: prevalence and predictors', published in February 1999 in *Journal of American Medical Association (JAMA)*, it was noted that 43 per cent of women aged 18–59 suffer 'sexual dysfunction' – a figure which is widely cited in scientific and lay media (Moynihan 2003: 46). Two of the authors disclosed close links to Pfizer (Moynihan 2003: 46). Despite efforts to medicalise women's sexual experience, however, it has proved difficult to easily 'diagnose' the 'problem'. As Loe notes, considerable effort has gone into developing a new classificatory system for 'female sexual dysfunction', through for example changes to the aforementioned ICD-10 and a series of (unsuccessful) drug trials (2004: 138–143). Given the reduction of sexuality to a biophysical response, and the view that sexual difficulties arise from body 'malfunctioning' (a problem of blood flow or hormones), it is hardly surprising that research efforts have proved fruitless. Research failure has been attributed to women's 'complicated' physiology, rather than to flawed assumptions underpinning the research. The effort to apply a biomedical classification to female sexual experience and to treat diagnosed 'dysfunction' with drugs has parallels with earlier efforts to treat female 'frigidity' through therapeutic intervention (Ehrenreich and English 1979).

As with other drugs that have proved popular, efforts have also been made to expand the market for Viagra at the global level. With the rapid development of the internet and global media, Viagra is readily available, legally or illegally, and sought after worldwide (Loe 2004: 171). In December 2005, it was reported in the press that Pfizer was introducing Viagra to the Indian market 'after holding it back for seven years until the country passed firmer patent laws'. The article noted that 'as many as 40 local versions' had entered the Indian market, and that Viagra 'will cost about 20 times the price of its imitators when it goes on sale'.[43] It also reported that doctors had noted a growing demand for treatment for 'impotence complaints' and that more people would demand the product 'once they were educated about its benefits'. This is in a country with considerable economic and social inequalities and where a large proportion of the population still does not have basic amenities such as sewerage and clean water. Drug companies such as Pfizer are keen to expand their markets for established products within less developed or developing countries such as India as competition among companies marketing generic brands within more developed countries becomes more intense and the total number of approvals for pharmaceutical products with significant new therapeutic benefits declines (Law 2005: 10). The Viagra phenomenon exemplifies the increasing privatisation of medicine and the interdependence between experts and marketers (Loe 2004: 172).

Age and ageing

The market pressures and rationalities that are shaping the classifications of health and illness are also shaping the classifications of age and ageing. As a number of social theorists have recently noted, definitions of age and 'the aged' are undergoing rapid change (e.g. Faircloth 2003; Gilleard and Higgs 2005; Vincent 2003). A number of factors are seen to have contributed to this, including alterations in work patterns with less stability in the labour market and patterns of employment, and shifts in the pattern of family life including increasing divorce rates, solo living, and co-habitation (Vincent 2003: 115). In the event, there seems little doubt that concepts of 'retirement', 'pensioner' and 'old person' and of what it means to be a person of a certain age category have become less clear than in the past. For example, laws pertaining to mandatory (i.e. legally prescribed) retirement ages (e.g. 65 in the UK) have been altered in a number of countries. Increasingly, it is recognised that chronological age may not closely correspond with age identity, or 'conception of self', and health and lifestyle. The 'first wave' of the English Longitudinal Study of Ageing (conducted 2001–2003), which tracked a group of 12,100 individuals over 50 to explore patterns of health and lifestyle found that the majority rated their health as 'excellent', 'very good' or 'good' and the vast majority of men (84 per cent) indicated that that they had no mobility problems. (The self-rating did vary however among groups, with those with the lowest incomes, poorest jobs, and with the least education having the worst health.) The study also found that half 'go to the cinema, opera or museums at least once a month' and that 'more and more people are leaving work before state retirement age'. Further, 'Only 3 in 10 men who are working in their fifties are 100 per cent certain that they will still be working after the age of 60'.[44] A Swedish study that aimed to measure people's subjective ages (how old they felt and how they think other people see them) found that although men and women of all ages 'internalized' 'images of youthfulness', people's subjective or experienced age is somewhat less than their chronological age. Approximately half of those over 65 still consider themselves to be 'youthful persons', however, there was found to be a gender difference with women reporting more negative experiences than men, which increases with successive age groups (Öberg 2003: 127–128). Such work challenges the perception that ageing is necessarily a negative experience, marked by physical and mental decline, passivity, and widespread experience of illness and disability. There is a growing belief that medical scientific advances combined with the active participation of older people in matters of health and other spheres can help people surpass some of the previously assumed 'natural' constraints of age and facilitate 'positive' or 'successful' ageing experiences.

As with other fields of biomedicine, gerontology increasingly embraces the belief that 'nature' has the potential to be substantially controlled through the pursuit of rational science. In recent years, policy makers and scientists have become increasingly interested in the biological mechanisms of ageing (see, e.g. House of Lords Science and Technology Committee 2005), the assumption being that the resulting enhanced understanding will eventually enable improved healthcare, particularly via the use of more effective drugs, for example, for the control of Alzheimer's disease. An ageing population, it is assumed will bring new pressures on healthcare related to deterioration of minds and bodies. For the biotechnology and biomedical sectors of industry the ageing of the population increasingly is seen to offer significant opportunities for developing and marketing new drugs (e.g. for osteoporosis and Alzheimer's disease) and other technologies, including replacement body parts, including knee joints, hips, and so on. The marketing opportunities presented by an ageing population were noted by the UK's House of Lords Select Committee on Science and Technology, in its report, *Ageing: Scientific Aspects*, published in July 2005.[45]

Older people are often regarded as being the generation with the assets, and the leisure to spend those assets. This is an over-simplification,

Mr Mervyn Kohler, the Head of Public Affairs at Help the Aged, made it plain that half of pensioners do not have a large enough income to pay tax, and that many are eligible for means-tested benefits. Despite this, it is true that the UK's wealth, savings and spending power are now heavily concentrated within the over-50s. They hold 80% of all assets and 60% of savings, while over 75% of UK residents with assets of £50,000 or more are over 50. Some of the savings are tied up in the equities of their homes. Nevertheless, this group controls 40% of UK disposable income, making them a key group for buying in high-profile sectors such as cars, holidays and IT. They purchase 25% of all children's toys, and are the single biggest buyers of gifts at Christmas.[46]

At the level of the individual, the links between chronological age and expected conduct is undergoing rapid transformation. There is less pressure than in the past to 'act one's age' and to dress in particular ways, or engage in certain presumed age-specific activities. In public policy and wider discourse, 'retirement' has tended to be associated with 'pensioner', as seen in the term 'pensionable age'. Caricatures of 'the aged' as infirm, child-like, needy, and so on, although still evident, have become less acceptable in public discourse and, in some countries, are seen as evidence of 'ageism'. In advertising and more generally, although stereotypes of age and age discrimination persist, these are gradually being eroded by new models and popular cultural depictions of ageing, and by evidence of how individuals actually experience and live their lives and conduct their relationships. These changes are reflected in fashions in clothing, in advertisements for holidays and other leisure activities, and in discussions about financial planning for the potentially long period of 'later life'.

In the West, the dominant construction of ageing for much of the last one hundred years or more has been one of linear progression through life with growing decline, incapacity and dependence in the years preceding death. The life course is structured by a series of normative expectations, among which is that ageing should comprise an 'appropriate' sequence of stages, the duration of each stage is less important than that they follow sequentially (Vincent 2003: 115). That is, the expectation is that one will complete school before moving to University and then to work, and that people of certain ages will undertake certain kinds of work and leisure activities appropriate to those ages. This concept of ageing is reinforced through diverse policies and practices, including registries of births, age-based school grades, laws regulating driving, passport and alcohol consumption, and access to cheap fares, for example bus passes. It emerged and became dominant during a period in which industrial manufacturing comprised a large sector of the economy, of which productive activity and output was the key defining feature. The concept of the working body within the manufacturing economy was based on an assumed gendered division of labour, in that men's bodies occupied the sphere of paid work, while women's bodies occupied the sphere of unpaid domestic labours (Petersen 1998a: 49). Masculine identity was demonstrated through being *at work* (i.e. visible in the public domain), being seen to be physically active and occupying the 'breadwinner' or 'provider' role. As people's bodies aged they were seen as less productive and hence less valuable to the economy. 'Retirement' was seen as marking a sharp break between the productive and unproductive life, a 'reward' for one's past contributions to the economy, and a prelude to death, which was assumed to generally follow within 10–15 years.

The above model of ageing has never been an accurate reflection of many people's experiences of ageing and has become even less so in recent years. For a start, the model does not reflect the reality of most women's lives, which is more often than for men marked by discontinuous employment in full-time paid work and a major role in unpaid home and child care, especially when relationships have broken down. The so-called gender wage gap is still large, and many women will never accumulate enough pension or superannuation benefits to live comfortably in old age (Curtis and Branigan 2006: 4). Prevailing cultural conceptions of femininity closely link the female body to unpaid reproductive and caring labour undertaken largely in the private sphere. The dominant model of ageing on the other hand reflects the experience of a particular stratum of society which is in full-time relatively well-paid employment and is able to save for 'retirement' through pension or superannuation contributions. For casual workers and those from low-paid groups, such as many disabled and minority ethnic groups, the relationship between age-based identity and work has always been weaker than this model suggests. In any event, it has long been acknowledged that there is a mismatch between classifications of physical age and people's experience as reflected in the notion of 'mask of ageing', which draws attention to the distance between one's interior age (conception of self) and one's external appearance (the physical body) to which others respond (Vincent 2003: 7). People may 'look old' but 'feel young inside' in that they still experience good health and are active and are excited by the things which excited them as young people.

From the perspective of governments, the ageing of the population is generally viewed as a problem for policy, reflected in references to the 'time bomb'. In the future, it is argued, societies will have difficulty caring for older people 'in retirement' who are assumed to be increasingly dependent on the diminishing working population and hence a 'burden'. Responding to this perceived challenge, in recent years, governments and funders of research (e.g. national research councils, such as the UK's Economic and Social Research Council and the Biotechnology and Biological Sciences Research Council) have initiated a number of programmes on ageing. Recent news and science reports on age and ageing provide insight into the perceived nature of 'the problem'.

A recent news article, on 'The future of old age' commenced:

Every minute that you spend reading this article, the average life expectancy in Britain will rise by 12 seconds. By the time you finish reading G2 [the source of the item], your life expectancy will have gone up six minutes. This time tomorrow, it will have increased by almost five hours. The reason is clear: rapid advances in medicine and biology have been one of the biggest achievements of the past century and we are all living longer. Where anyone reaching the age of 60 was considered to be near death's door at the turn of the 20th century, it is barely old enough for retirement at the turn of the 21st century. And scientists are still not holding back. Shripad Tuljapurkare, a population studies expert at Stanford University, told a recent meeting of the American Association for the Advancement of Science that, as new anti-ageing treatments become available, our species will get even older. Soon, the average age will jump by a year every year – five times the current rate. While few would argue that living longer is an attractive idea, the rapid increase in the number of years begs the question: what will life be like for our increasingly elderly population? Is it such a good idea to live for an extra decade if it just involves 10 more years of illness or frailty?

(Jha 2006: 6)

The questions being raised here are those typically found in recent publications of ageing and reveal concerns encapsulated by the term 'time bomb', which suggests a looming healthcare and socio-economic catastrophe. In this and many other articles, 'the problem' is attributed to the successes of medicine. The article goes on to describe growing scientific interest in 'the mechanisms behind ageing' and cites studies on genetics which have cast light on ageing processes, and the potential for stem cell technologies, drugs and other treatments for 'dealing with the problems of age' (Jha 2006: 8). Underlying this discourse is the continuing view that ageing equates with increasing disease and disability and, hence, presents a potential societal burden, the corollary being that 'the problem' must be 'fixed' through biomedical solutions.

Belief in the power of biomedical solutions to the 'problem' of ageing is seen in an article published in *The Scientist* in early 2006. It is interesting to note the negative portrayal of ageing in the article: ageing is presented as a series of risks and 'undesirable' side effects, begging for remedy, with no acknowledgement made of its positive aspects. The article opens with:

Imagine an intervention, such as a pill, that could significantly reduce your risk of cancer. Imagine an intervention that could reduce your risk of stroke, or dementia, or arthritis. Now, imagine an intervention that does all these things, and at the same time reduces your risk of everything else undesirable about growing older: including heart disease, diabetes, Alzheimer and Parkinson disease, hip fractures, osteoporosis, sensory impairments, and sexual dysfunction. Such a pill may sound like fantasy, but ageing interventions already do this in animal models. And many scientists believe that such an intervention is a realistically achievable goal for people. People already place a high value on both quality and length of life, which is why children are immunized against infectious diseases. In the same spirit, we suggest that a concerted effort to slow ageing begin immediately – because it will save and extend lives, improve health, and create wealth.

(Olshansky *et al.* 2006: 28)

The article goes on to argue for urgent research into the 'causes of ageing' and points to the health and economic benefits that are likely to accrue from resulting improvements. For example, 'Healthy older individuals accumulate more savings and investments than those beset by illness. They tend to remain productively engaged in society. They spark economic booms in so-called mature markets, including financial services, travel, hospitality, and intergenerational transfers to younger generations'. Further, 'This compression of mortality and morbidity would create financial gains not only because aging populations will have more years to contribute, but also because there will be more years during which age-entitlement and healthcare programs are not used'. And so on. Such comments reflect growing recognition that 'the aged' are a potential major economic resource and, if not 'healthy', present a likely 'burden' and that, therefore, an 'investment' in their needs is likely to pay 'dividends' in the future.

The focus on ageing as a process of physiological decline and a potential economic problem obscures the politics of the classification of age and historically and culturally diverse evaluations of ageing; the fact that what is seen to constitute 'old age', 'working age', 'retirement age' and how these are viewed varies through time and across societies and is shaped by economic contexts and political priorities. As with classifications of many other contemporary phenomena, the classification of age and age identities (e.g. 'youth', 'the aged') in contemporary societies reflects processes of individualisation and commodification. It is recognised by gerontologists, policy makers, and producers of various goods and services targeted to the growing 'grey market', that individuals should seek to 'halt the ravages of time' and take active steps to keep their bodies and minds active, so as to avoid disease and disability, including mental decline, or at least limit the period for which they are likely to be ill. That is, individuals are expected to play an active role in ageing so that, as policy makers increasingly express it, they may age 'successfully' and experience ageing as a 'positive' experience. 'Success' can be demonstrated through active involvement in the market as active consumers of goods, services and experiences. Researchers and businesses have 'discovered' that there is a rapidly growing cohort of older, relatively affluent 'consumers' who are healthy, active and have considerable potential purchasing power (e.g. Hill and McKie 2006). The leisure industry has identified a massive market for 'packaged' holidays and adventure pursuits, while pharmaceutical companies see a large and rapidly expanding market for 'anti-ageing' or 'rejuvenating' products and services for 'body-conscious' older people. The development of a Alzheimer's drug, to 'help people think sharper and remember things better', it was announced in a recent news item, 'could be available in chemists within a decade' (Curtis 2006: 5).

Another news article, 'Video games for the elderly: an answer to dementia or a marketing tool?', announces the development of a new computer game, Brain Training for Adults, which is 'a package of cerebral workouts aimed at the over-45s by the Japanese game console and software maker Nintendo' (McCurry 2006: 23). The game is said to 'improve mental agility and even slow the onset of dementia and Alzheimer's disease'. The article notes that 'Targeting grey gamers is a smart move by Nintendo as software makers try to wean themselves off the shrinking teen market'.

> About 20% of Japan's 127 million people are 65 and older, and the number is expected to rise to almost 30% by 2025. More than 3.3 million of the games have been sold in Japan since they went on sale in May, with the second package in the series selling 500,000 units in the first week.
>
> (McCurry 2006)

If such figures are to be believed, it would seem that many older people are endeavouring to keep themselves 'healthy' and 'engaged' members of society through consumption of goods and services oriented to keeping both body and mind active. There would seem to be little doubt that among the non-working older age groups there has been a rise in *overall* levels of consumption in recent decades. For the USA, Gilleard and Higgs (2005) have noted an increase in expenditure among these groups between 1984 and 1999 to a pattern increasingly in line with that of all adults, with expenditure on entertainment rising even more dramatically, from 56 per cent to 83 per cent of average adult expenditure during this period. They observe a similar increase in Europe (2005: 9). However, it is difficult to ascertain the extent to which particular patterns of consumption can be taken as an indication of wider perceptions of ageing and health. It could be that many sections of the population ignore or resist such marketing pressures. Further, it needs to be recognised that many groups are marginalised from consumer society because of their economic circumstances and are less likely to be the targets of the potentially persuasive techniques of mass marketing. It is much more difficult to gain insight into the views of those who resist or are marginalised from consumption than those who actually consume. In any event, it would appear that the imperatives confronting 'the aged' today in relation to responsibility for health and active participation in society are different from those confronting earlier generations. With predictions that people will live to an increasingly older age, it is expected that the 'responsible' citizen will make concerted efforts to ward off illness and to extend their productivity and participate in society beyond the prescribed 'working age'. Indeed, as with those who do not take active steps to prevent illness, increasingly, those who do not endeavour to age 'successfully' are liable to be judged 'irresponsible', failed citizens.

The future of classification

While classification would seem to be universal and inevitable, as noted, the nature, degree and visibility of classification, and the means of classifying may vary considerably through time and across societies. In the modern period, the classification of bodies would seem to be central to the workings of power and specifically 'bio-politics'. This chapter identified a number of factors that are shaping body classification in contemporary societies, in particular processes of individualisation, commodification and medicalisation. In the chapter, some examples of changes in classification in the fields of health and illness and ageing were presented. While it is difficult to predict the character and implications of classificatory systems in the future, recent developments suggest the potential for the development of increasingly detailed means of classifying and regulating bodies and lives. An anticipated convergence of new biomedical and other technologies may allow new, more efficient means of surveillance (e.g. Bogard 1996). In early 2006, the UK Government announced its intention to introduce 'biometric' passports and identity cards. (Whether this will be 'voluntary', at least initially, or compulsory was still being debated.) The idea for such passports and cards, though discussed for some time, gained momentum in the wake of 9/11 and the so-called 'war on terrorism' as well as concerns about 'identity fraud' (see, e.g. Ford and Charter 2006). A new politics of fear surrounding personal and national security has helped lend legitimacy to new forms of risk assessment and security in the UK, USA, Australia, and many other countries, leading to the erosion of individual and group rights once deemed to be defining features of a liberal democratic society. The use of unique biological information for means of identification and demonstration of citizenship status may seem relatively innocuous to some and perhaps the 'price to be paid' for tighter security. However, it would seem to represent one step closer to the surveillance society feared by some people, and foreseen by some science fiction writers like George Orwell (*1984*). Concerns are heightened when, at the very same time, new genetic databases, for criminal investigation and medical research (UK Biobank) are being developed, which, according to some commentators, may allow the linking of personal information in novel ways. The combination of such developments may mean that, in the future, every person will be precisely located in space and time and subject to ongoing control of the body and mind. As Foucault (1977) indicated, with reference to the panopticon, the ultimate aim of surveillance technologies is to elicit self-regulation, the monitoring of one's own thoughts and behaviour (see Chapter 1). Foucault recognised that power works most effectively when there is a close connection between the control of the body and the control of the mind. The next chapter examines the changing connections between 'the mind' and 'the body' and identifies some unacknowledged regulatory implications of efforts to 'integrate' body and mind.

5   Powers of mind over body

The significance of 'the power of the mind', to concentrate one's energies, to heal the body, and to endure pain, are well recognised in both science and the wider culture. Examples of heroic feats, including instances where individuals have been able to overcome extensive physical isolation, trauma, and hunger permeate news media, fictional writings and cinema portrayals. The political activist, Nelson Mandela endured many years of imprisonment, sometimes involving solitary confinement, for his beliefs and actions and emerged as a political leader and significant international figure in the human rights movement well into his later years. Similarly the artist Frida Kahlo, despite childhood polio and a bus accident that broke her spine and created other injuries resulting in years of suffering, became widely known and respected as a painter and loved by people throughout the world. Indeed, much of what makes these people well known and respected is their demonstration of being able to overcome adversity and show courage and commitment to ideals and values despite great personal physical and emotional trauma. However, many much less celebrated examples of the 'power of the mind' can be cited. Some of these may seem mundane, but have profound significance for those directly involved. These include people who undergo rigorous training to perform particular specialist body feats, including mountain climbing, military manoeuvres, body building and competition in sports, or who undergo highly disciplined regimes of self-treatment or illness prevention, or who practice many hours each day to learn a musical instrument, to dance, or to undertake some other creative activity, or who starve themselves for a political cause or other reasons. Sometimes this 'mind control' may appear to be extreme, indeed pathological, as in the case of the anorexic or the obsessive exerciser who may cease to see beyond the detail of their obsession. However, in many cases, a 'highly focused mind' is what is required of those in particular occupations or undertaking certain activities. The kinds of emotional display called upon by those in the growing service sector, involving for example the happy smile, the deferential demeanour and/or the demonstration of concern for the other, are part of the job and, if not performed well, may constitute grounds for one's dismissal.

This chapter examines some aspects and implications of the contemporary focus on 'power of the mind', with specific reference to the arenas of health and healing and self-care. Continuing the themes of the earlier chapters, it draws attention to how the changing contexts of contemporary Western society, and particularly the values and expectations of individualism, medicalisation, and consumerism, shape thinking and action in this domain. In many societies there is growing dissatisfaction with the tendency within medicine and more generally to view the mind as separate from the body, and consequently many people have turned to 'holistic' approaches with the hope of 'integrating' or 're-aligning' mind and body (and sometimes spirit). The chapter describes the nature of this development and critically examines some of the associated practices and claims. Philosophies and practices oriented to the 'whole person' have considerable appeal in contemporary society and help sustain an ever growing array of products and services. A host of mind–body therapies are promoted on the basis that they will 'empower' individuals and create 'healthier', more 'balanced' lives. The chapter asks: What kinds of assumptions underlie this contemporary emphasis on 'holism' and 'the power of the mind'? Who is seen as best able to facilitate and who is called upon to undertake this mind–body work, and what technologies and techniques are being developed and utilised to this end? To what extent and how is the recent emphasis on 'the power of the mind' changing practices in medicine and self-care? And, what are the broader socio-political implications of these trends? To speak of 'the mind' as an entity separate from 'the body' at all is based on a series of assumptions that need to be examined. It is a distinction which is strongly associated with the philosopher René Descartes whose work is widely cited as a source in debates on the so-called 'mind–body problem'. Because his work has had such enduring influence, it is useful to begin by offering some brief assessment of the significance of his contribution and legacy.

The mind–body dualism

Much has been written about so-called Cartesian dualism, and Descartes' writings continue to provoke discussion. It is not the place here to revisit the details of these arguments which can be found elsewhere (e.g. Rozemond 1998; Leder 1990). An important point to note about 'Cartesian dualism', however, is its reference to a particular way of thinking about 'the mind' and 'the body' and their relationship, rather than to an agreed and fixed set of principles or propositions. It is also important to place Descartes' views into broader historical perspective, and to see his reflections as part of a long history of philosophical thinking in the West about the relationship between the senses and reason that can be traced back to the ancient Greeks (Synnott 1991). A key influential text is Descartes' *Meditations on First Philosophy*, published in 1641. For a contemporary reader, it is difficult to discern the subtleties of a piece written 350 years ago within a radically different context and worldview. All texts are subject to multiple interpretations and, as with the Bible and Marx's *Communist Manifesto*, Descartes' text is infused with allegory and allusion, making interpretation difficult for later readers who bring a different set of concerns and questions. However, many scholars agree that Descartes' contribution in *Meditations* was the clear distinction he drew between the mind (or soul) and the body, and the recognition that the former 'can exist without' the latter (Descartes 1993: 91). This separateness of the mind and the body does not mean that he saw an actual separation but that there was a *conceptual possibility* of separation (Malcolm 1972: 6). Rozemond suggests that his interest in the idea that the mind can exist independently of the body, or that thinking can be split from sensing, stemmed from the fact that this provided hope for an after-life, as revealed in his synopsis to the *Meditations* (1998: 3). It has been suggested that Descartes' early experiences of sickness shaped his philosophy on the mind–body relationship in that they created a sense of alienation from and a desire to 'escape' his body (Leder 1990). His philosophy, like most philosophies, was undoubtedly influenced by a combination of personal experience and the social context which gave rise to a particular set of questions.

Descartes is widely credited with the phrase, 'I think therefore I am', which is often taken to characterise the ascendance of the disembodied rationalist worldview associated with the modern age. In his *Meditations*, he notes that the human mind 'is more easily known than the body' and that 'I am not much more than a thing which thinks, that is to say a mind or a soul, or an understanding, or a reason'. In his *Meditations* he sought to demonstrate that 'the mind or soul of man is entirely different from the body' noting, as an example, that the 'body is by nature always divisible, and the mind is entirely indivisible' (Descartes 1993: 97). That is, since one is a 'thinking thing' one perceives oneself as a unitary being. The faculties of thinking, feeling, conceiving, etc. cannot be said to be in parts since they are all 'one and the same mind'. If one loses a part of one's body nothing is taken away from the mind. However, in his view, this does not apply to 'corporeal or extended objects' which can all be imagined as divided into parts (1993: 97). Descartes' reasoning has been questioned (see, e.g. Malcolm 1972); however, this does not disprove the dualism. As Malcolm notes,

> Familiar facts would seem to support [the dualism]. People have thoughts, make decisions and experience feelings, without there being any physical occurrences corresponding to these mental occurrences. This would seem to present a case for the independence of mind and body.
>
> (Malcolm 1972: 5)

Many examples can be found to support this conceptual separation, including the well-known placebo effect in medicine, whereby belief in the curative powers of a medicine may make one 'feel better' (Morris 1998: 67, 125).

As Rozemond observes, despite his attention to the 'mind–body problem', Descartes 'had more to say about the physical world than about the mind' (1998: xiv). She attributes this to Descartes' commitment to mechanistic science; that is, the idea that the body like other aspects of the physical world operated like a machine and could be understood through universal laws. In *Meditations* Descartes devotes some discussion to the structure and physical workings of the body, as evident in his account of various sensual experiences, such as hunger, thirst, and pain (see, e.g. Descartes 1993: 95–100). In reading his views on 'sensations', one cannot help but see parallels with much later writers from evolutionary biology (e.g. Darwin) and psychology, who postulated a physiological basis of emotional expression. (See Chapter 2.) His ideas also seem to have antecedence with the ancient Greeks, who drew a clear distinction between the senses and the mind and attributed epistemological and metaphysical superiority to the latter. That is, although the senses were seen to have a place, it was low and associated with the animal part of humanity (Synnott 1991: 62).

There has been much debate about how Descartes envisaged the *relationship* between the body and the mind. Some of Descartes' reflections suggest that he saw a close interaction between the body and the mind. At one point in *Meditations* he notes that 'there is nothing which this nature teaches me more expressly [or sensibly] than that I have a body which is adversely affected when I feel pain, which has need for food or drink when I experience the feelings of hunger and thirst, and so on'. He goes on to say:

> Nature also teaches me by these sensations of pain, hunger, thirst, etc., that I am not only lodged in my body as a pilot in a vessel, but that I am very closely united to it, and so to speak so intermingled with it that I seem to compose with it one whole. For if that were not the case, when my body is hurt, I, who am merely a thinking thing, should not feel pain, for I should perceive this wound by the understanding only, just as the sailor perceives by sight when something is damaged in his vessel; and when my body has need of drink or food, I should clearly understand the fact without being warned of it by confused feelings of hunger and thirst. For all these sensations of hunger, thirst, pain, etc are in truth none other than certain confused modes of thought which are produced by the union and apparent intermingling of mind and body.
>
> (Descartes 1993: 93)

In this excerpt, Descartes seems to be suggesting the primacy of the body in one's perception of self as a sensorial being and the close connection between body and mind. However, as Rozemond comments, Descartes does not really provide detail about how mind and body are united, or how this union gives rise to sensations (1998: 212). Rehearsing long-standing arguments about the fallibility of the senses or sense deception, he concluded that 'it is easier not to trust entirely to anything by which we have once been deceived'. Consequently, 'I shall consider myself as having no hands, no eyes, no flesh, no blood, nor any senses'. (1973: 145, 148, citing Synnott 1991: 71). Descartes has hardly had the last word on 'the mind–body problem', which has been a recurring theme over the centuries and continues to dominate discussion in many fields, both inside and outside academe.

Enduring influence and implications of Cartesian dualism

The continuing salience of Descartes' ideas in the modern period may be explained by their congruence with a broader view on the separation of mind and body within modern, capitalist society, characterised by class and gender exploitation and a sharp division between mental and physical labour. Writing in the nineteenth century, Marx observed the psychic and social alienation of workers in the developing capitalist society who had only their labour power to sell. In Marx's view, the capitalist mode of production was responsible for the sensory deprivation of the proletariat and the 'animalization' of humanity: 'man (the worker) only feels himself freely active in his animal functions – eating, drinking, procreating, or at most in his dwelling and in dressing-up, etc.; and in his human functions he no longer feels himself to be anything but an animal. What is animal becomes human and what is human becomes animal' (Marx 1972: 111, citing Synnott 1991: 74). As Synnott explains, Marx 'situated his discourse on the senses squarely within the arena of real material life – the arena of "eating, drinking, procreating"' (1991: 74). Marx was writing during a period in which the mode of production was dominated by manufacturing processes and the majority of workers only had their labour power to sell. However, increasingly, during the twentieth century, the division of labour was based on the distinction between mental and physical work, paralleling the growth of the state bureaucracy and the rise of the middle-class 'white collar' workers. This was followed by the emergence, in the late twentieth century and early twenty-first centuries of a new class of service workers, who were valued for their emotional labour. In Marx's writings, the body of the worker is a male body and he gave little attention to the role of women within the spheres of production and reproduction. Marx could not have anticipated the significance of service work and emotional labour within advanced capitalism. Like other male thinkers of the period and since, whose writings have dominated public discourse, issues of difference along lines of 'sex' or 'gender' have been largely absent in his theories. In contemporary rich Western economies, the growing service sector is comprised largely of women, many of whom are from lower socio-economic groups and, increasingly, from poor countries of the developing world who serve as nannies, maids and sex workers for the wealthy (Ehrenreich and Hoschild 2002)

One of the important contributions of feminist scholarship especially since the late 1960s has been to draw attention to the significance of gender dualism within Western thought: the fact that women's bodies and minds are seen as different and differently related and as inferior to men's bodies and minds. As Lloyd (1984) writes, male rationality has been seen as the paradigm of reason, while the male body has long been viewed as the ideal, according to which the female body has been viewed variously as an aberration, inversion or under-developed version. For women, the mind and body are seen as more closely related than for men; that is, they are 'more in touch' with their bodies and prone to its 'unruliness'; for example, menstruation, childbirth. They are also seen as being more 'in touch' with their feelings than men – the 'more rational sex' – and therefore better suited to perform certain roles, such as caring. According to Laqueur (1990), since the Enlightenment period of the eighteenth century, the 'two sex model' has predominated: the female body has been seen as different though complementary to the male rather than, as previously, an inverted male (the 'one-sex model'). The focus on complementary opposites was seen as part of an array of efforts to define essential differences between men and women in anatomies and in mental abilities as a consequence of the threat posed by the increasing demands of women to the dominant relations of gender following the rise of liberal democracy (Laqueur 1990: 194–207; Schiebinger 1989: 216–227). The implications of gendered constructions of the mind–body relationship will be spelt out in greater detail later in the chapter. However, the important point to note here is that such work has served to unsettle the apparent 'naturalness' of the relationship between mind and body by showing that this is posited differently for men and women and has shifted and may shift in line with changing economic, political and social contexts.

What has also become increasingly evident is that the so-called mind–body dualism is an abstraction based upon a particular idealised conception of the 'normal, healthy' mind and body; namely that of the white European middle-class male who self-identifies as heterosexual. The bodies and minds of women, black and coloured people, working-class people, and people who do not self-identify as heterosexual have been viewed implicitly as physically and/or mentally inferior, and in some instances pathological. People with 'black' and 'coloured' bodies have often been viewed as a different species from and 'closer to nature' than people with white bodies. Concerns about racial hybridity or the mixing of 'races' was strongly evident in many societies in the nineteenth and twentieth centuries, and arguably still is to some extent (see, e.g. Young 1995). People of same-sex sexuality have been persecuted because of their perceived threat to normative heterosexuality and since the late nineteenth century male 'homosexuality' has been constructed as a sexual deviance and a kind of pathology that stands in opposition to the 'healthy' 'manly man' (Cohen 1993: 17–18). During the twentieth century, many efforts were made to intervene into the minds, bodies and lives of 'homosexuals' in order to better understand and 'treat' their 'pathology'. For example, the so-called Sex Variants study, which was conducted between 1935 and 1941 and involved the physical examination and interviews with individuals from New York's homosexual community, sought to learn as much as possible about homosexuality so as to assist physicians in identifying and treating 'sexually maladjusted' individuals (Minton 1996: 452; Terry 1995: 138). Such studies were often undertaken with the consent of the homosexual communities who believed that the resulting information would advance the rights of homosexual people (Minton 1996: 437). (See Petersen 1998a: 60–64 and Petersen 2000 for a discussion of the pathologisation of homosexuality.) Further, the bodies of peoples of the working class have been viewed differently from and inferior to those of the middle and upper classes. Different physical indicators have been taken to differentiate classes, including body shape, size, colour, bearing, and dress. As was noted in Chapter 3, in Bourdieu's view, in contemporary societies aesthetic judgements in relation to bodies involve class distinctions. Thus, tastes in food, clothing, and body adornment and modification can all be 'read' as indicators of one's class position and serve as means to distinguish classes. A common distinction in the context of work has been between 'blue-collar' and 'white collar' occupations, associated with the office and factory or outdoors, respectively. Sometimes the term 'pink collar' is used to identify workers in traditionally female occupations, such as cleaning or nursing. It is interesting to note the significance of clothing type in these distinctions, which are often taken as a surrogate for class in official statistics and academic studies. In the past, skin colour and degree of musculature also served as surrogates for class, with 'lower class' peoples being distinguished by their tanned skins and muscular development and 'upper classes' by their pale skins and lean bodies, with the latter being implicitly valued above the former; however, in late modern, consumer societies this distinction has eroded.

Health, healing and the body-machine

One of the legacies of this mind–body dualism, many critics contend, has been the tendency to view the body and its health and development in isolation of the mind. The philosopher, Drew Leder (1990), for example, argues that one legacy of Cartesian dualism is the experience of 'bodily absence' or a tendency of the self to disregard the body in everyday life, unless it becomes diseased. That is, the mind-dualism, it is argued, has led to a conception of self that is 'disembodied' often leading to the neglect or objectification of our bodies which involves personal and social costs. We are often not as *caring of* or *careful with* our bodies as we should be and therefore do not undertake requisite kinds of body maintenance and preventive healthcare. Compulsive over-eating, extreme physical risk-taking, drug-taking (including the over-use of medications) and the failure to exercise are often cited by health promoters and other body specialists as examples of body neglect. Caring for the body, however, presupposes a certain kind of self-discipline or mind–body relation, the nature and degree of which varies through time, across contexts, and among groups. As Marcel Mauss (1973) pointed out many years ago, 'techniques of the body' – the way we hold, train and conduct our bodies (e.g. to walk, run, eat, sleep, reproduce, defecate, bath) are highly diverse reflecting the expectations (or 'habitus') of the social milieu. Different contexts present different opportunities and imperatives in relation to the conduct of the body. In the contemporary West, such differences are perhaps most evident between genders, for which there are specific norms pertaining to body bearing and personal conduct.

The literature on men and masculinities and on men's health indicates that the particular techniques pertaining to the male body can make men more vulnerable to physical disability and premature death and to inflicting violence on others and themselves (Connell 1995; Lois 2005; Sabo and Gordon 1995). The 'ideal' male body in the contemporary West is hard, muscular, controlled and impenetrable. Involvement in 'risky' leisure and competitive or combative activities provides an occasion for demonstrating one's 'manliness'. Sport and warfare are key sites for the disciplining of male bodies, the regulation of the mind, and the undertaking of risk. The soldier is trained to view their body as part of the machinery of war, to maintain it in a state of preparedness for fighting, and to keep the emotions under tight control. The male sportsman exercises a similar level of mind–body discipline. Pushing one's body to the limits in competitive sports and in other contexts of risk-taking, and displaying emotional and physical control, are means of enacting masculinity (Lois 2005: 121–122). In her *Dismembering the Male: Men's Bodies, Britain and the Great War* (1996), Joanna Bourke describes how male bodies were trained during the First World War, to make them more compliant and useful while confirming particular masculine norms. A comprehensive regulatory apparatus developed around the disciplining of male bodies, including the grading of recruits according to their levels of fitness. These definitions of fitness were adopted within the civilian population. Military drill was also applied to the civilian population, along with organised games which were promoted as a means of moulding bodies (Bourke 1996: 172–175). The body of the soldier has to be disciplined to kill with 'emotional detachment'. Although portrayed in psychology and popular discourse as innate, aggression needs to be learnt and controlled and instilled in recruits through psychological conditioning and rituals, such as drill involving the use of the bayonette. Both in competitive sports and warfare, training the mind is integral to the disciplining of the body. As Bourke points out in her *An Intimate History of Killing: Face-to-Face Killing in Twentieth Century Warfare*, killing does not come 'naturally' (Bourke 1999: 72–75). Officers in the front line of combat have repeatedly reported concerns about the success of training in terms of motivating recruits to kill. Further, studies have shown that soldiers are disinclined to shoot the enemy and that of those who fire their weapons generally only a small proportion hit their targets (Bourke 1999: 74–75). Women who are in combat roles face similar difficulties to men and, notwithstanding the argument about women's lesser 'capacity for aggression' which is used to exclude women from combat roles, they, like men, can be trained and can train themselves to kill when necessary (Petersen 2004: 69–79).

Western medicine is built upon the notion of the body-as-machine which can be broken down and understood in terms of its component parts and without relation to the feelings and experiences of its 'owner'. The 'emotional detachment' that is part of the traditional training of doctors, requires the practitioner to treat patients 'dispassionately' or without empathy. The use of cadavers in medical education is arguably part of this training in mind–body separation. Dissection, like sports and warfare, serves as a root metaphor of male culture which expresses 'a competitive, Social Darwinist moral order' (Larsen and Pleck 1998: 51). Through undertaking dissection, the medical student acquires and demonstrates a mastery over both the subject and himself (Sappol 2002: 80). This notion of the body emerged during the ascendance of the modern scientific age which inaugurated a mechanistic conception of the universe (Capra 1983). The resulting so-called biological reductionism, many writers point out, has contributed to viewing the body like an object and commodity which is subject to the 'quick fix' cure through the use of technologies and treatments available for purchase in the medical market-place. Like machines, bodies are seen to 'wear out' and 'malfunction' and are seen as subject to 'repair'. The body shape industry, increasingly oriented to the older population operates with an implicit conception of the body-as-machine (see Chapters 3 and 4). Even where the mind does figure in biomedical practice, such as in psychiatry, illnesses tend to be defined in biophysical terms (e.g. an imbalance in body chemistry) and seen as needing 'treatment', via the use of drugs, probes, or other bodily interventions. As Brian Broom, a consultant physician and psychotherapist who promotes the use of a mind–body approach in clinical practice, observes: 'Most psychiatrists do not try to act as mind/body integrationists. They sit comfortably on one side of the dualistic split' (1997: 43).

'Reconnecting' mind and body

In the view of critics of biomedicine, healing practices need to 'reconnect' or 'integrate' body and mind through the adoption of a more 'humanistic', 'holistic' healthcare that is seen to have existed in the pre-modern world. Modern medicine, it is claimed, has led people to experience illness as disruption and fragmentation and to feel alienated from their bodies. Pain is narrowly and inadequately conceptualised as *sensation*, the implication being that it can be rationally and objectively understood (Bendelow and Williams

1995: 84). As Bendelow and Williams note, the medico-psychological conception of pain devalues subjectivity and emotional experience (1995: 89–91). Recognising the limits and implications of biomedicine, a number of writers have proposed new metaphors and descriptions of illness, consistent with the changed and changing contexts of healthcare. David Morris (1998), for example, argues for new metaphors to reflect a shift from the modern experience of illness to the postmodern experience of illness. The latter he notes is 'biocultural', in that illness depends not on biological mechanisms (as has been the case with modern beliefs about illness), but rather on 'convergences between biology and culture' (Morris 1998: 6, 71). In Morris' view, 'Illness in the postmodern age is understood as fragmentation' and thus 'what we seek from the process of healing is to be made whole'. (1998: 67, 71) As Morris explains, systems theory has become the dominant metaphor for illness, replacing the outdated machine metaphor, which was dominant in the modern age. Some two decades earlier, George Engel suggested a similar, 'biopsychosocial' approach, which combined various element of the classical biomedical model with the newer insights of the social sciences (Armstrong 2003: 29). This has been influential within nursing which has sought to develop an identity and theory of practice distinct from that of medicine (see Petersen and Winkler 1992), and to some extent within medicine itself. However, this model has not given equal priority to the different dimensions and in practice biomedicine continues to occupy prime place (Armstrong 2003: 29). As Morris observes, the reality of clinical practice allows little time for psychosocial therapies, and financial pressures discourage a focus on the complex, non-biological dimensions of illness (1998: 73). Nevertheless, within medicine and other health professions, as well as within public health, there is growing recognition of the need to 'reconnect', 'integrate' or 'bridge' mind and body; to develop a 'whole person' approach.

The concern to 'reconnect' body and mind is manifest in various spheres, in medicine and other healthcare professions and sociology and other social sciences. The following paragraphs examine some of these diverse theoretical and practical efforts and draw attention to a number of their unacknowledged implications.

The patient's experience

Within healthcare and the sociology and anthropology of health and illness, one response to the reductionism of biomedicine has been to emphasise the importance of the patient's views and experiences. Positioning themselves in opposition to Cartesian dualism, Hahn and Kleinman, for example, propose that we conceive 'the body as mindful and the mind as embodied' (1981, citing Daniel 1991: 109). Rather than simply document the clinical manifestations of disease in the body, it is argued, clinicians should 'listen to' the patient's 'illness narratives'. Arthur Kleinman (1988), who works at the interface between anthropology and psychiatry, is a key exponent of the illness narrative approach. Many illnesses that are seen within medicine as strictly biophysical conditions in need of specialist technologies or treatment, such as depression and mental illnesses, Kleinman argues, are often more adequately understood as manifestations of psycho-social trauma that find expression in culturally specific metaphors. Patients who consult doctors not only bring their physical symptoms of disease, but also their biographies and experiences that are shaped throughout their lives and in interactions with their families and communities. The clinical interview itself, then, aims not to derive objective information about the patient's 'symptoms' which are 'diagnosed' with reference to universal classificatory systems (e.g. DSM1V and ICD) (see Chapter 4) and then 'treated', but rather to provide the means for patients to *re*-present their 'stories' in their own terms. The clinician is seen to undertake a facilitative rather than a directive role, as tends to occur in medical practice. Since patients' stories pertain to particular experiences and are told to specific audiences, they can be closely examined by the clinician with reference to their context and metaphorical content. Stories about physical and mental disorders, for example, may provide a 'window' for examining more general psycho-social and relational difficulties in the life of the individual. Cross-cultural work on health and illness in non-Western societies, such as that undertaken by Kleinman (1980, 1986) (e.g. in China) and others (e.g. Daniel 1991) (in India) disturb the taken-for-granted biomedical notion that illness is simply a matter of biology. For example, within Siddha, the traditional medical system of India, 'small pox is no more "real" than a "depressed heart", even though one may well be a more serious condition than the other' (Daniel 1991: 109).

Considerable success has been claimed for the use of narrative approaches in clinical practice, for overcoming problems of the 'body-only' approaches of biomedicine. Narrative analysis is claimed to offer insight into the 'lived experience' of patients, to 'empower' the individual and to contribute to a more humane and effective healthcare practice. Accounts of clinical success are common, though few reveal details about failures, the typicality of clinical groups, and the dangers associated with the practices of the confession. There has been little reflection upon how the power relations of the medical encounter may shape patients' responses and the nature and amount of information that they reveal. In his account of the use of the narrative approach, a clinician, Brian Broom, describes himself as being in a 'collaborative relationship' with the patient and on a 'collaborative journey of discovery and healing', which denies the inequalities of power and knowledge existing between clinician and patient (see Broom 1997: 4). The clinician, who proposes a 'mind/body approach' 'to assist the doctor and psychotherapist to work well with patients and clients' describes how they seek to establish 'connections between the presenting physical symptoms and the patient's story' (Broom 1997: 3–4).

The particular clinical group of concern here is comprised of people who, in the first place, come to the clinician (usually the medical doctor) with physical symptoms. The clinician is willing to listen for the 'story', and this story is taken as very important and relevant, in some way, to the physical illness presentation. The clinician encourages the patient to undergo an exploration of the connections between symptoms and story and, in many cases, the result is restoration to health, or at least a loss of the physical symptoms. . . . The focus is on the person as a whole. This person presents to the clinician with symptoms in the body. The bodily symptoms are considered carefully, along with the 'story' of the whole person, and a working hypothesis is developed as to the meaning of the symptoms. The clinician and patient then join in a collaborative journey of discovery and healing.

(Broom 1997: 4)

Broom goes on to describe the limitations of diagnostic categories and his own experiences of trying to 'fit' patients into some 'known' category. He writes: 'Medicine is much less tidy than our taxonomic systems might suggest', and that 'Over the years I have learned that these patients with untidy syndromes have much to teach us' (Broom 1997: 40). As he explains, he became increasingly dissatisfied with the 'restrictive biological model' and the tendency to ignore 'crucial data relating to the cause' of illness (1997: 29). Consequently, in developing his 'mind/body integrative approach' he has sought to overcome the 'dualistic suppositions' which lead to 'fiddling with the machine' and develop alternative metaphors for clinical work. It is interesting that he proposes the metaphor of the prism, 'which not only permits a conceptualisation of the person as a whole (as also does the machine metaphor) but also encourages the observer to see the person from very different vantage points (the machine metaphor does not do this), and from there to respond to the person as a whole' (Broom 1997: 50). This visual metaphor positions the expert-observer in a kind of panoptic relation to the patient and suggests that the data collected via the 'collaborative journey' will produce a 'fuller', and thus 'truer' picture of the nature of the patient's illness. By 'listening' to the patient, rather than just 'reading' the patient's physical symptoms, as generally happens in the clinic, it is assumed, the clinician comes to understand the patient in the context of their everyday life and relationships rather than solely in terms of the illness category.

Arthur Frank (1990), an influential sociologist in the illness narrative field, adopts a somewhat different approach, in that patients' illness narratives are presented as struggles against medical colonisation. In *The Wounded Storyteller*, he argues that the illness experience has been 'colonised' by modernist medicine and 'overtaken by technical expertise' and that the aim of the 'post-colonial ill person' is to have their 'own suffering recognized in its individual particularity' (Frank 1995: 10–11). Telling one's story is an attempt to 'give a voice to an experience that medicine cannot describe'.

This voice is embodied in a specific person, but it is equally social, taking its speech from the postmodern times we live in. The voice of the ill person is made possible by modernist medicine, but it cannot be contained with modernist assumptions, particularly those about medical professional dominance and the narrative surrender this dominance requires. . . . As a post-colonial voice, the storyteller seeks to reclaim her own experience of suffering.

(Frank 1995: 18)

Frank's approach is confessional in style. He talks of the individual needing to bear responsibility for their narrative self and asks whether it is possible to be 'successfully ill' (1995: 63). In *The Wounded Storyteller*, he emphasises the importance of 'becoming a witness' or 'offering testimony' to one's illness (1995: 137–167; see also pp. 62, 140–141), at one point citing the authority of St Paul (in the Corinthians) who 'expressed the embodiment of witness passionately' (1995: 165). As Frank argues, while modern medicine demands 'narrative surrender' – that is, experiencing and expressing one's illness in biomedical terms – the postmodern experience of illness demands that '*the capacity for telling one's own story is reclaimed*' (Frank 1995: 6–7; emphasis in original). In a later article, Frank (2001: 353) acknowledges the challenges of adequately representing suffering and notes how social science may actually increase suffering through its 'attempts to organize local experience within extralocal categories'. Drawing on the work of the feminist scholar Dorothy Smith (1987, 1999), Frank argues that research which starts from the 'discourse of ruling relations' is unable to adequately conceptualise the experience of suffering. The dilemma for the ill person is recognising and writing about those things which are most salient to them 'without making them fit some explanatory scheme'. Reflecting on his own illness experiences, he notes, for example, that 'I suffered at having to submit my suffering to medical workers for whom I was another instance of a category requiring that this and that be done' (Frank 2001: 361).

It may come as something of a shock to healthcare workers to be told that they are implicated in their patient's suffering. However, the work of Frank and others highlights how medical classifications and processes may lead to such an experience and should lead to reflection upon how healthcare practices may be transformed without them becoming part of the technology of governance. While the benefits that may derive from narrative approaches should not be denied, it needs to be recognised how the use of the language of empowerment may obscure the power relations within the clinic and the surveillance associated with 'getting to know' the patient (May 1992). The imperative to relate one's illness narrative bears close resemblance to the religious confession which, as Foucault noted, has achieved a central role in the 'production of truth' in Western culture. As Foucault observed, 'Western man has become a confessing animal' evidence of which can be found in the practices of a diverse array of institutions, including the judicial system, medicine, pedagogy, family relations, and in intimate relations (Foucault 1980: 59).

Sociology's 'discovery' of emotions

Within sociology and the other social sciences, increasingly it is recognised that the mind–body dualism has led to the failure to recognise the *social* significance of the emotions. The experiences of pain and suffering, for example, have not been *explicitly* addressed in social theory thus far (see, e.g. Wilkinson 2005). In sociology, the focus has been on the disembodied rational actor and on social action, to the neglect of a consideration of how feelings shape subjectivity and conduct. The suffering associated with class exploitation or gender discrimination, for example, not only affects people's 'sense of self' but also serves as a motivator to action and a catalyst for change. Social movements, for example, are usually motivated by outrage at some injustice and a shared vision of some ideal alternative social order. Although a nascent sociology of emotions can be found in the work of Emile Durkheim (Fisher and Chon 1989) and of the later scholar Norbert Elias (1978), Arlie Hochschild (1983) has been a seminal influence in the recent development of this field. Hochschild is credited with the concept of 'emotional labour', which emphasises the unacknowledged hard work and commercialisation of feeling involved in service occupations, caring, and intimate relations (see, e.g. Duncombe and Marsden 1993, 1996, 1998, 2002; Freund 1998; James 1989; Wouters 1991, 1998). Significantly, Hochschild's work has focused on the emotional labours of the new class of service workers which, as noted above, emerged in the late twentieth century. The changing context of capitalist social relations has served to make visible the significance of this form of labour for the generation of surplus value; i.e. profit.

Thinking of the emotions as involving 'work' implies an active self, and the necessity for presenting one's body in particular prescribed ways – maintaining a smiling face, a cheerful disposition, and a deferential demeanour, showing a concern for the other, and so on. Such techniques of the body are learnt in context and imply certain dispositions, commitments and abilities. As the sociologist Erving Goffman (1959) noted, 'impression management', or the enactment of a positive conception of self, is integral to smooth interactions in everyday life. Emotional management, however, can exact considerable costs for the individual and their relations, when this is insincere or when one's performance is disrupted in some way. With the growing service sector of advanced consumer capitalism, increasingly people are required to 'act a part', either through changing their outward appearance through body language, that is 'surface acting', or by 'deep acting', which involves altering one's feelings so that one expresses feeling spontaneously. The latter may be especially harmful for the individual and interpersonal relations (Hochschild 1983: 35–39). Those who 'over-identify' with particular jobs, however, may suffer 'burnout' and become remote from those they serve (1983: 186–189).

While the sociology of emotions has been insightful and served to make visible an aspect of social relations that has been largely invisible within social theory and everyday life, the wider social and political significance of emotional experience and expression remains largely unacknowledged and unexplored by sociologists and other social scientists. As Reddy (2001) argues, the emotions are subject to profound social influence and thus are of 'the highest political significance' (2001: 124). In Reddy's view, in order that political regimes can endure they must establish a normative order for the expression of emotions – what he terms an 'emotional regime'. These include prescriptions about how to express oneself, the degree of required emotional constraint, the forms of self-control, and so on. Although Reddy's ideas are insightful, he has little to say about the interplay between social norms and individual conduct or about the gendered dimension of emotions, including beliefs about enduring emotional differences between men and women (Petersen 2004: 8). Further, he and other sociologists have not extensively explored how emotional pain may accumulate in the body and shape the self and social interactions. A study of emotional pain and responses to it may deepen understanding of a range of sociological topics, such as consumption, media, civil and international conflict, marriage and divorce, juvenile and adult crime, economic trends and political movements, and face-to-face interaction rituals (Davetian 2005: 5.3, 5.4). Sociology's 'discovery' of emotions parallels official concern with emotional management, and is therefore not devoid of political implications. Increasingly, the emotions have become central to political rule in contemporary societies, with diverse authorities increasingly interested in levels of 'emotional literacy' and emotional health. The questions of how people feel and how they relate to others in their personal and work lives have become public issues, with programmes addressing the 'deficits' in people's (particularly men's and boy's) emotional responses, through training in emotional skills and access to appropriate support. Individuals are called upon to 'get in touch' with their emotions and become 'emotionally literate' as a duty of citizenship, for the sake of their own health and well-being and for the advancement of economic prosperity and social cohesion (Petersen 2004: Chapter 5).

In recent decades, there has been a burgeoning interest and a growing body of expertise oriented to bringing body and mind in closer unity (i.e. 'psychosomatic unity'), through various forms of 'mind training' and specialised mind/body practice. The emotions have become a key site for the work of 'integrating' mind and body, and 'getting in touch' with one's emotions has become essential for those seeking to optimise 'health' and 'well-being'. The philosophy of holism has provided the basis for a thriving complementary and alternative medical industry, the socio-political implications of which have barely begun to be explored. Here I examine some recent trends, highlighting the significance of individualism and consumerism.

Treating the 'whole person'

> In reality, every cell in your body is both structurally and functionally
> related to every other cell in your body. Similarly, all your thoughts,
> beliefs, fears, and dreams are dynamically connected within the structure
> and function of your psyche. I would also like to suggest that your cells
> and your thoughts are more directly interconnected than you probably
> believe at present. As you experience and study the various bodymind
> parts and processes that I will be isolating and discussing, please be
> continually aware that each and every aspect of you is attached and
> related in some remarkable way to every other aspect of you. By dis-
> covering and integrating these relationships, you allow yourself to bring
> greater harmony into your bodymind, thereby diminishing the conflicts
> that live within you and increasing your overall health and psychological
> well-being.
>
> (Dychtwald 1986: 23)

This quote from Ken Dychtwald, an influential proponent of the 'whole
body' approach, reflects widespread concerns about the 'imbalances'
resulting from the separation of mind and body and belief in the benefits to
be had from mind–body therapies. Even a cursory view of pertinent websites
in this field reveals a bewildering array of holistic practices and expertise
on offer, and discussions about the benefits of particular therapies. A diverse
array of expert groups, including medical practitioners, nurses and other
allied healthcare workers, alternative healers, and patient groups, has
promoted the 'holistic approach' for 'health and well-being'. CAM (complementary and alternative medicine) therapies are numerous, but common
ones include acupuncture, aromatherapy, chiropractic, homeopathy, hyp-
notherapy, herbal medicine, osteopathy and reflexology.[47] In one report,
it is estimated that between 6.6 per cent and 20 per cent of the British
population use CAMs ('using the stringent assumption that non-respondents
are non-users') and that the average number of visits per patient range from
2.8 to 5.3 per year (Ong and Banks 2003: 23). Studies also reveal gender
differences in usage: a number have found that women are significantly
higher users of CAMs than men (2003: 20). In recent years, there has
emerged a massive and rapidly expanding industry of 'complementary and
alternative medicines', much of which (though by no means all) claims to
be 'holistic'.

The definition of the field of CAM is contentious and there is ongoing
debate among healthcare professionals and scholars about the compatibility
of 'unconventional' approaches with biomedical treatments.[48] The terms
'complementary' and 'alternative' are often used to distinguish approaches
which are seen as either complementary to and compatible with orthodox
treatments from those which are in some sense fundamentally different or
oppositional. However, the distinction is not as clear and as stable as this

suggests since CAM itself designates a highly diverse field of philosophies and practices. Consequently the use of the term 'CAM' may conceal as much as it reveals (Willis and White 2004: 51–52). To further confuse matters, sometimes the term 'holistic' (or 'wholistic') or 'integrative' medicine or healthcare is used to distinguish approaches which offer a 'true' alternative to orthodox medicine, in that it is seen as the only field which can lay claim to treating the 'whole person' and not fragmented parts of the body 'which orthodox medicine does and alternative medicine can' (see, e.g. Bradshaw 1996; Donnellan 2004). As Saks argues, the knowledge base itself is not the critical decisive factor in determining whether a particular therapy is defined as part of 'orthodox' or 'non-orthodox' medicine, but rather the extent to which it receives recognition by the state with appropriate support from the medical profession (1996: 28). What is worthy of sociological note here is the increasing acknowledgement within medicine and healthcare of holistic approaches, and the question this raises for the conceptualisation of the mind–body relation.

The reference to the 'whole person', 'wholeness', or 'holistic care' in the literature signals that which is seen to be problematic in biomedicine; namely, the tendency to view and treat the individual, and more specifically their body in isolation of the mind, emotion, and spirituality. As David Morris observes,

> An interest in the spiritual dimensions of healing represents an important trend within postmodern culture. Healing, in this case, is a process distinct from cure, in the sense that people can gain a sense of peace and wholeness even in the grip of incurable disease. Wholeness is a key concept. . . . Health, healing, wholeness, and wellness thus are knit together in an ancient unity that holds great appeal for postmodern proponents of alternative or complementary medicine. Individuals and even corporations now promote the pursuit of this new goal called wellness – not just good health, which may be a stroke of luck, but a lifestyle attentive to diet and exercise, and spiritual satisfaction.
>
> (Morris 1998: 66)

Some approaches to CAM/holistic medicine include reference to 'environment' and 'societal' influences on health and well-being in addition to 'emotional' and 'spiritual' dimensions; however, many, if not the majority, are limited to seeking a 'realignment' of body and mind in order to enhance health and well-being; to create a 'well-balanced' person. It is recognised that 'stresses' and 'imbalances' in one's life may lead to one becoming ill. As one book, *The Handbook of Alternative and Complementary Medicine* explains, 'medicine has more or less ignored the mind as a cause of sickness ever since therapeutics ousted magic' (Fulder 1996: 232). As the book goes on to say, increasingly, research has revealed that 'the stress hormones of people who do not "switch off" properly get used to a round-the-clock mobilization, leading to tiredness, "burnout", irritability, insomnia, and then on to psychosomatic disease'.

> Most complementary practitioners, and anyone who holds a more subtle expansive view of man, can only state that all disease has a psychological as well as physical, environmental, social and sometimes even spiritual dimension. This is the assumption underlying all traditional medical systems.
>
> (Fulder 1996: 233)

As Fulder notes, a large number of psychotherapeutic or psychosomatic methods are now available within complementary medicine for preventing and treating disease, including 'meditation (especially visualization), relaxation, bioenergetics, prayer and faith, stress management, yoga, concentrated breathing exercises, counselling, autogenic therapy, and biofeedback' (Fulder 1996: 233).

Some evidence suggests that the increasing use of CAMs is in part due to dissatisfaction with biomedical knowledge and practice and individuals' preparedness to 'shop around' for alternatives. A study undertaken by Ong and Banks (2003) points to the influence of a consumerist approach in healthcare: people have higher expectations of their practitioner or therapist than in the past and want to feel more in control of their healthcare. As Ong and Banks report: 'They expect to be listened to, be given a personal approach and receive priority for their needs'. Further, 'Patients want to feel that they have had quality time with their practitioner, and a full and comprehensive examination resulting in a satisfactory diagnosis and effective intervention, without unwanted side effects' (Ong and Banks 2003: 29). Other studies also reveal dissatisfaction with conventional treatment, including poor doctor–patient relations and lack of attention by conventional medicine to the causes of problems (2003: 30).

The field of holistic medicine/CAMs is strongly individualistic with proponents often claiming that therapies are oriented to the 'empowerment' of the 'consumer'. As in other domains, such as public health and health promotion, 'empowerment' often equates with self-responsibility or care of the self (e.g. Petersen and Lupton 1996). As Fulder explains, mind–body therapies 'may begin with therapy but they all move on to growth, self-awareness, and personal development' (1996: 233–234). Further, 'they all attempt to elicit self-healing capacities' by giving individuals 'room to work, usually by removing, dissipating, or neutralizing attachments, negative emotions, anxieties, and destructive thought processes that lead to negative physiological reactions and negative behaviour patterns such as compulsions'. And, this assumes a certain kind of relation between the expert therapist and novice patient: 'the therapist is normally an instructor or even priest, and the patient a trainee'. As Fulder notes, 'the trainee must work on himself, largely by himself', with the implication being that, 'The prognosis or outcome is as much his responsibility as anyone else's' (Fulder 1996: 234). Individual responsibility can mean simply that one is responsible for finding solutions for one's health problems. However, in the extreme it can mean that individuals are also held responsible for having created the problem in the first place (Goldner 2004: 15) by, for example, 'not taking appropriate care of themselves', by 'internalising' anger or depression, or responding inappropriately to stresses of everyday life. The focus on individual responsibility in CAM/holistic medicine was emphasised in a study undertaken by Hughes (2004), involving in-depth interviews and focus groups with patients and practitioners in the UK's NHS and in private practice based in a Local Health Authority in West Yorkshire. Patients were understood and understood themselves to be centrally implicated in their own health maintenance and their illnesses. The patient was considered to require 're-education' and it was expected that this would occur through their active involvement in the therapy. As Hughes found in the case of osteotherapy, the body and the mind were 'considered to be re-educated both in understanding and communicating with each other, as part of the individual's education in practical techniques of self-care' (Hughes 2004: 35). However, CAM practitioners and patients struggled to avoid *responsibility* becoming *blame*.

Hughes' (2004) study also revealed that 'health' is not viewed as an endpoint of treatment but rather as 'work in progress' and as a matter for negotiation. The patient was seen to be in need of 'empowerment' through knowledge, training and participation in their own healthcare – initiating treatment, engaging in practices of health improvement, negotiating definitions of success and ending the therapeutic process with the CAM practitioner. This concept of responsibility, Hughes (2004) observes, is not dissimilar to contemporary biomedical discourses; for example, the focus on the 'expert patient' and patient participation in treatment within the NHS. In this respect, her analysis argues against a simplistic distinction between conventional medicine and CAM/holistic medicine in terms of assumptions about individual responsibility for care. Indeed, the forms of activism surrounding CAMs, involving individuals taking the initiative in seeking out and using therapies, asking their practitioners, informing their friends to use CAM, and demanding insurance reimbursement, can be viewed as expressions of growing consumerism and active citizenship in healthcare (Goldner 2004). The commodification of CAMs and their development from a 'cottage industry' into a mature market sector has created growing opportunities for providers of CAM goods and services, including orthodox medical practitioners (Collyer 2004). As Collyer notes, CAMs constitute a big industry and have the potential to generate considerable profits for producers and providers of services during a period of declining budgets and increasing pro-market policies in healthcare (2004: 94–96). In the UK, one recent estimate is that one in five people use CAMs and that the CAM industry is worth £1.6 billion (Kennedy 2004: 28). The philosophy of individualism and 'self-responsibility', the view of 'health' as 'work in progress', and consumerism in healthcare and more generally, converge to support a thriving market in CAM/holistic healthcare goods and services.

In recent years, there has been a proliferating number of CAM and holistic events (e.g. exhibitions, meetings, workshops, conferences, self-help courses) and publications (books, magazines, and other media), some of the self-help variety targeted at those who seek therapies, and others oriented to the medical or allied health practitioner or members of the 'interested public' who may wish to simply learn more about developments in the field. Some authors of books and other publications on CAM and holistic healthcare have become guru-like figures and would appear to have developed lucrative careers from developing tapes, CDs and DVDs, books, and giving lectures. The aforementioned Ken Dychtwald, author of *BodyMind* and numerous books on ageing, is described on the 'Leading Authorities' website as 'the nation's foremost visionary regarding the lifestyle, marketing and workforce implications of the "age wave"'.[49] He is described as having 'addressed nearly two million people worldwide in his speeches to corporate, association and government groups', and it is noted that he 'appears frequently on national television and radio programs'. He is promoted as, 'A highly sought-after public speaker and consultant, [who] is consistently praised for his unique ability to blend cutting edge social science and marketing wizardry with world-class presentation showmanship'. Accompanying videos show him in presentation pose and explain his skills and ability to tailor his presentations to the needs of particular audiences. The website also includes links to amazon.com, where readers may purchase his books. The website also notes Dychtwald's extensive corporate interests. For example, in 1986, in partnership with his wife he became 'the founding President and CEO of Age Wave, a firm created to guide Fortune 500 companies and government groups in product/service development for boomers and mature adults'. Further, 'In 2001, Ken Dychtwald became a Senior Advisor to North Castle Partners, a private equity firm focused on investment opportunities in the "healthy living and aging" sectors'. At the end of the entry, the reader is informed that his 'local fee range' is $30,001 to $50,000, with an accompanying note, 'Traveling from: California'.

Like some literature on illness narratives, some writings on CAM/holistic health is confessional in style, recounting the author's experiences of 'awakening' to their previously 'forgotten' or 'disregarded' body and bearing witness to one's 'discovery' of their 'embodiment'. The quasi-religious tone of a number of writings is striking. In his influential book, *BodyMind* (1986; orig. 1977), Dychtwald relates his early experiences of mind–body separation and of 'a long series of experiences and realizations that served to reshape totally the relationship I was having with my body' (Dychwald 1986: 8). According to Dychtwald his awakening began in 1970 at a workshop run by John Pierrakos on 'bioenergetics' (Reichian psychotherapy), which he describes as 'a form of psychotherapy that deals with emotional health and sickness from the perspective of psychosomatic unity'. He describes how, up until the point of his 'body awareness', he had 'ignored' his body or viewed it instrumentally. However, gradually he came to recognise the integration of his body and mind: 'The experience with John Pierrakos proved to be the first of a long series of experiences and realizations that served to reshape totally the relationship I was having with my body . . . with my self'. He adds, 'It was at this time that I stopped "having" a body and first began to realize that I "am" a body and that my body "is" *me*' (Dychtwald 1986: 5, 7–8; emphasis in original). Dychtwald goes on to explain the relevance of these insights for understanding 'the human bodymind', offering examples of what can be learnt from closely examining body anatomies and postures about body–mind relationships and 'how we create ourselves in our own image' (1986: 25). Acquisition of such knowledge is seen as having thera-peutic value. That is, 'By discovering and integrating these relationships, you allow yourself to bring greater harmony into your bodymind, thereby diminishing the conflicts that live within you and increasing your overall health and psychological well-being' (Dychtwald 1986: 25).

Dychtward's reference to the examination of the face for signs of tension or imbalance, in particular, has early antecedents with the diagnostic science, physiognomy, which, as noted in Chapter 4, has a long history as a classificatory tool in the West. As Dychtwald notes, the ears, eyes and forehead all tell stories about one's unique life and personal history and can be 'read' diagnostically. In his discussion of 'The forehead', for example, he writes:

> The muscles of the brow and forehead region are exercised in con-junction with almost every motion of the face, and, as a result, they tend to exhibit any chronic feelings and movements that we express with our faces. These muscles can become easily overstressed. I have found the single greatest contributor to tension in this bodymind region is thinking, and for this reason I have come to call the brow and forehead muscles the 'rationality' muscles. When people overuse their thinking capacities or superimpose their rationality upon their spontaneous feelings and excitations, these muscles can become armoured and tense.
>
> (Dychtwald 1986: 236)

Dychward goes on to describe the therapeutic value of being able to 'read faces' in the way he proposes, using a vivid hydraulic metaphor to convey the detrimental effects of identified suppressed emotions:

> Tension and tension headaches in the region of the forehead may indicate that the person has been suppressing feelings with thought and exaggerated rationality. When this happens, the pressure of the unreleased emotions can build up in the top of the head, in very much the same way as carbonation becomes congested at the top of a soda

bottle. When emotions are thus held down, they also can become distorted and wind up transforming themselves into feelings of anger, regardless of what they were to begin with. When people complain to me of headaches in this bodymind region, I often ask them who or what they are angry with. As soon as I say this, they usually smile and ask me, 'How did you know?' If the emotions have been held down long enough to be transformed into anger and rage, I try to provide a therapeutic opportunity for the person to vent the rage and 'blow his top' through appropriate psychoemotional exercises that might encourage yelling, complaining, biting, or crying. When the bottled up emotions are freed in this fashion, tension in the forehead is usually lessened and many headaches immediately disappear.

(Dychtwald 1986: 237)

The idea that the emotions, particularly the emotions of pain and anger, are pent up forces that are the source of illness and need release has been a recurring theme in the history of the psychology of emotion and psycho-analysis. Thus, various therapies, including 'talking cures', 'primal therapy', and encounter groups, have sought to allow contexts for the 'safe' release of repressed emotions. With the increasing emphasis on 'emotional literacy' and concerns about the destructive effects and psychological, social, and economic costs of violent outbursts of emotion particularly among men and boys (see Petersen 2004: 134–137), there has been increasing receptiveness among medical and other healthcare workers and policy makers to 'emo-tional training' and exploring means of addressing the emotions within healthcare.

The 'mainstreaming' of CAMs/holistic approaches

The recent 'mainstreaming' of CAMs and holistic approaches in medicine and healthcare, after a long period of medical opposition and hostility to non-orthodox healing practices (see, e.g. Saks 1995; Willis 1989), would seem to reflect growing recognition among members of the medical pro-fession that they need to respond to the challenge posed by holistic medicine/ CAMs to the authority of orthodox medicine. The effort to integrate different paradigms with sometimes fundamentally contradictory metaphysical beliefs and philosophies, however, has not been without difficulty (Coulter 2004). Complex debates about the compatibility of practices and ongoing political contestations over 'ownership' and boundaries of knowledge have been obscured by debates about how to 'integrate' CAM/holistic medicine within healthcare. Consideration of contextual issues, particularly political impli-cations of CAM/holistic medical knowledge and practice tend to be sidelined by narrow, policy-oriented questions and practical biomedical concerns such as 'does it work?', 'Is it safe?' 'How can it be integrated?' (Tovey *et al.* 2004: 6).

The available evidence suggests that patients will use CAMs in addition to orthodox medicine and frequently 'exercise choice' and 'shop around' for the 'best' treatments and that this cannot be ignored in practice (Ong and Banks 2003: 13; Sharma 1995: 53–56). The majority of CAM referrals are initiated by the patient rather than the doctor (Ong and Banks 2003: 40). According to one UK study, between 1995 and 2001 the proportion of CAM services supported by full or partial payments by patients increased from 26 per cent to 42 per cent in general practices in England (Dobson 2004: 21). Acupuncture and homeopathy were the therapies most frequently provided (Dobson 2004: 21). Studies in the history of medicine reveal that publics' use of non-orthodox medicine and medicine's efforts to accommodate and integrate alternative practices in response are not new. In the early nineteenth century, as today, criticisms were made of medicine's concern with 'treating symptoms and applying "heroic" drugs and technologies rather than meeting the emotional needs of patients' (Cooter 1988: xi). As Cooter explains, it should not be assumed that non-orthodox medical practices and self-help necessarily challenge the knowledge and practices of Western scientific medicine. Much of the interest in non-orthodox practices, as in the nineteenth century, has been initiated and promoted by persons *within* orthodox medicine (or on its margins) who have sought to bolster the prestige and power of the profession, as well as establishing their own reputations (Cooter 1988: xi). Medical and other healthcare professions have seized the opportunities provided by the 'freer' medical market and the exercise of individual choice in medical consumerism (Cooter 1988: xv).

In arguing the case for the integration of CAM/holistic approaches in medicine, medical writers and medically oriented CAM organisations often cite evidence supporting publics' growing use of complementary and alternative healers. In 2004, the Australasian Integrative Medical Association (AIMA) and Royal Australian College of General Practitioners (RACGP) released a Joint Position Statement on complementary medicine which opened by noting the increasing use of complementary medicines. It cited a survey undertaken in South Australia in 2000 (published in an article in *Preventive Medicine* (MacLennan *et al.* 2002: 166)) which revealed that 'approximately 52 per cent of the Australian population used complementary medicines'. And, further this represented 'an estimated out of pocket spending of $2.3 billion which is a 62% increase since 1993 and four times the out of pocket spending on pharmaceutical drugs'.[50] It was also noted that 'Some people use complementary medicine in situations where they perceive that conventional treatments do not offer successful intervention' and that 'People who use complementary medicine are generally not rejecting orthodox medicine' but 'Rather they are seeking effective care for their health needs'. The Statement went on to note the different varieties of CAMs, the need for consumers' and practitioners' 'access to quality information' ('so that they are empowered to make well-informed decisions'), and the necessity for CAMs to be 'assessed on an evidence basis'. Here, as elsewhere, CAMs are portrayed as not essentially different from orthodox medicine, but rather part of a range of medical therapeutic choices available to 'consumers' in the medical market-place. Further, 'consumers' are seen to be motivated by a desire for optimum health rather than dissatisfaction with medicine, and in this regard they need 'quality information' which will 'empower' them as decision-makers. This conflation of 'empowerment' with 'choice' in consumption reflects the pervasiveness of market rationality in healthcare and effectively denies the possibility that many people may be abandoning orthodox medicine through experiences of 'disempowerment' during treatment.

In Britain, the British Medical Association (BMA) has also presented itself as open to the integration of CAMs in healthcare and the medical profession appears to be more receptive than in the past to the inclusion of at least some education on CAMs in medical curricula and to investigating their utility in practice. A 1993 publication of the BMA, *Complementary Medicine: New Approaches to Good Practice*, reflected growing recognition in the 1990s of the challenge posed by CAMs to medical practice. The publication focuses heavily on issues concerning the registration of 'non-conventional therapists' and the regulation and training of practitioners, and proposes a 'risk-assessment model' for assessing different methods. Its Introduction points to 'an increase in the use of non-conventional therapies over recent years', which is 'not a phenomenon unique to the UK', and suggests this may be explained by a range of factors ranging from 'dissatisfaction with conventional forms of treatment to more general theories of diversification of healthcare' (BMA 1993: 1–2). The medical profession's interest in CAMs is portrayed as motivated by altruism and concern for the patient-as-consumer:

> Doctors have a duty to the individual and to the community to safeguard the public health and, to this end, it is important that patients are protected against unskilled or unscrupulous practitioners of healthcare. It is therefore considered helpful for the BMA to consider, as a *public-health* issue, the principles of good practice in non-conventional therapies which would safeguard the individual against possible harm to health and maximize the potential benefits of particular methods.
>
> (BMA 1993: 2; emphasis in original)

More recently, the BMA has adopted a somewhat less defensive position on CAMs, and has produced a host of print resources, audio-visual resources, databases, weblinks, and information on organisations and libraries devoted to CAMs made accessible on its website.[51] The increasing use of the internet to disseminate information on CAMs has arguably been one way in which the medical profession has shown itself to be in tune with 'consumers'' concerns and to be promoting 'patient choice' in healthcare.

The preparedness of 'consumers' to use CAMs is likely to depend on a range of factors, including the nature of the condition for which they are seeking help (for some conditions like musculo-skeletal pain, people sometimes seek help first from CAM practitioners) and available information on alternative treatments. Many, and probably most 'mind–body therapies' are to be found outside the institutions of biomedicine within the private and largely unregulated market. The rise of the internet in recent years has undoubtedly facilitated consumerism in the use of CAMs by allowing 'direct-to-consumer' advertising by producers of CAM goods and services, by creating the impression of ever-increasing choice in the CAM market-place, and by allowing the ready posting of advice and the sharing of information and recommendations among patient groups. Organisations devoted to CAM are of various kinds, with some established and dominated by expert, medically oriented groups who seek to identify that which is 'complementary' or useful to medicine, which is conceived as relatively unproblematic in relation to its knowledge, practices, and history. However, others are more critical of medical knowledge and are more 'alternative' in their philosophy and approach and are more democratic in membership and organisation. Clearly, there exists a broad spectrum of opinion about CAMs and their compatibility with the philosophy and practices of orthodox medicine. Regardless of their particular views on medicine, CAM organisations have come to constitute a significant industry and focal point for new forms of health expertise, with links to a range of related organisations, patient groups, and healthcare decision-makers.

Some groups depict themselves as in battle against medical reductionism, which they seek to erode through various educative, networking, lobbying, and facilitative activities. In their portrayals, the needs of healthcare workers are seen as needing to be addressed along with the needs of those for whom they care. Sometimes they point to the need for broad illness preventive initiatives, and greater scope for 'diversity' and 'creativity' in healthcare practice. Such aspirations are evident, for example, in the statements of aims and values of The British Holistic Medical Association (BHMA). On its website and in its journal, *The Journal of Holistic Healthcare*, first published in 2004, the Association argues for a more 'humane', 'whole person' approach to healthcare and calls for 'humanistic research' and the 'mainstreaming' of 'holistic' practice in services. It claims that its 'core purpose' is 'to promote holistic practice in UK healthcare' which is underpinned by the belief that:

- effective, humane healthcare must take into account people's thoughts and feelings, their relationships and spiritual life
- healthcare cannot be based on the body alone – although the application of technologies to biological faults can be immensely valuable, it is incomplete

- far greater emphasis should be placed on preventing ill-health, deprivation and environmental decay. These issues are now of urgent concern for all communities
- those who work in healthcare must understand their own needs as well as the needs of those they look after
- healthcare (like Nature) should encourage diversity and creativity, recognising that there are many good ways of being and doing.[52]

Its website serves as a kind of 'one stop shop' for CAM customers, with links to various CAM/holistic medicine organisations, condition- and therapy-specific groups, environmental bodies, 'General health information' (e.g. 'cybersurgery', 'Doctor's guide to the Internet', 'Drugs info', 'European Health Forum'), sources of health news, professional journals, medical/official organisations, and 'social' (curiously devoid of any information). Editorials in a number of issues of the Journal announce that biomedicine is 'in crisis' and call for a more 'compassionate' 'mind–body medicine' and for ways of 'mobilising self-healing'. One editorial notes that 'Bio-medicine is locked in a technological arms race against disease', a consequence being 'soaring costs, side-effects and resistant infections'. It goes on to say that medicine is 'losing its authority and respect it once attracted' and that its 'mechanistic vision of healthcare is threatening its once unquestioned benevolent values' (Peters 2005: 2). It proclaims, 'These crises of cure and costs, compassion and commitment, are telling us we need a new way of looking at medicine and new ways of doing it' (Peters 2005: 2). Other issues focus on themes such as 'Doctor's resilience: can doctors heal themselves?', 'Holism, mental health and mental wealth', 'Spirituality and healthcare practice', and 'Squaring the circle: nursing and the future of holism'. The concern here, and in other forums, is not so much issues of medical power and dominance, but rather the implications of dualistic, 'de-personalised' medicine. The group aims to bring a 'whole person approach' into healthcare and, to this end, seeks to 'reach out to decision makers and those working in healthcare to demonstrate the added value that holistic practice brings to patients and practitioners alike'.[53] In these self-representations, there is a tendency to romanticise and idealise the past, when doctors were supposedly more respected and medicine 'more caring', thus denying the history of the power relations of medicine, including the subordination of women healers who were perceived as a challenge to biomedical dominance (Ehrenreich and English 1979). In this depiction, medical reductionism has affected doctors as much as their patients: they are 'de-humanised', 'stressed', and incapable of delivering the 'humanistic care' which medicine is traditionally renowned for.

In Australia, a similar group, the Australasian Integrative Medical Association (AIMA) notes in its mission statement that it 'promotes the safe integration of holistic and complementary medicine with current mainstream medical practice, in pursuit of complete whole person care'.[54]

The Association's website notes that it was 'founded in 1992 by Dr Vicki Kotsirilos and grew out of the realization that medical practitioners were becoming increasingly interested in incorporating complementary medicines into their practice. In order to provide this holistic approach to patient care, they needed representation, support and accurate information'. Like the BHMA, the AIMA publishes its own journal, hosts a regular conference, as well as seminars, meetings and workshops, and offers a website with referral services and links to related organisations. Also like the BHMA, its Board is heavily dominated by medically trained individuals, some of whom are prominent in their profession, and who claim an interest or expertise in CAMs and/or 'integrated healthcare'.

Rethinking approaches to 'the mind–body problem'

Cartesian dualism has had a profound impact on conceptions of health, healing and self-care as well as views on the development and regulation of bodies. As noted, the idea that the mind can be conceptually separated from the body is congruent with broader social arrangements, and in particular the division of labour between mental and physical work. It reflects and reinforces the separation between areas of expertise, such as between the 'psy-knowledges' (psychiatry, psychology, and psychoanalysis), which focus on the mind, and biomedical and paramedical practices, which focus on the body, its treatment, enhancement, or discipline. As has been explained, this separation is arguably implicated in many problems and much suffering. Although much recent writing has contributed to highlighting the 'mind–body problem' and the need to move beyond dualistic thinking to create more 'holistic' approaches to health, healing and living, efforts thus far have not been without shortcomings and unacknowledged consequences. 'Holistic' approaches are not immune to the influence of consumerism and individualism and are not always opposed to biomedical approaches. The field of CAM/holistic medicine displays the significant influence of individualism and consumerism. An emphasis on confessional practices and 'care of the self' while appearing to be self-evidently beneficial for the individual and society may reinforce power relations between experts and lay people and inequalities in healthcare provision and lead to a 'blame-the-victim' approach to problems which have their genesis in physical and social environments. Thus, personal difficulties arising from poor work conditions and management practices and which require organisational change may be explained in terms of individuals' 'weaknesses' and 'inability to cope' and their need to develop 'resilience', 'emotional literacy', better coping skills, and so on. Greater efforts by healthcare workers to 'listen' to patients, although often presented as examples of more empathetic practice, may do little to change the conditions leading to health problems in the first place while bolstering the authority of the expert 'listener'. While one should not deny the personal benefits that may derive from undertaking holistic healthcare and adopting mind–body approaches, the implications of doing this in the absence of broader social change need to be recognised. This calls for some rethinking of the direction of academic work on 'the body', which is the subject of the next and final chapter.

6   The future of 'the body'

In the early years of the twenty-first century, popular and academic fascination with 'the body' shows no signs of abating. In many contemporary
societies, interest in the health and ageing of the body, the interior of the
body, feeding and fasting the body, modifying the body, disciplining the
body, and 'integrating' mind and body have been the subject of extensive
media coverage, expert commentary, and lay discussion. It would be no
exaggeration to say that contemporary culture has become obsessed with
body-related issues, activities, treatments and projects. I suggested in Chapter
1 that such interest is indicative of the *politicisation* of 'the body', a point
that is emphasised by many writers with different approaches and objectives,
including feminist and sexuality scholars, disability scholars, scholars of
'race' and ethnicity, and influential philosophers and social theorists such as
Foucault, Baudrillard and Bourdieu. The question of how we reproduce,
whom we have sex with, how we care for our bodies and how we use and
present them to others is central to the workings of what Foucault (1980)
has described as 'bio-power'. Diverse authorities are concerned with the
health and utility of bodies, while for the individual increasingly the body
provides the basis for personal and group identity as well as for citizen
activism, as can be seen in the development of groups organised around
shared bodily experiences and concerns. With the declining significance
of class as the basis for identification, 'the body' is a key reference for defining the self, establishing difference, and staking citizenship claims (see
Chapter 3).

The previous chapters drew attention to the significance of the processes
of individualisation, medicalization and commodification for prevailing
conceptions of the body and body practices. Individualisation reinforces the
idea of the body as a project that can be worked upon and improved
or 'fixed' through the purchase of a proliferating number of treatments
available in the market-place. The increasing availability of new technologies
of the body allows 'consumers' to imagine the possibility of a reshaped,
enhanced body, while media portrayals of biotechnology 'breakthroughs'
such as stem cell research and neuroscience reflect and arguably reinforce
expectations of new means of body repair, enhancement and control in the

future. The 'normalisation' of the use of such technologies, assisted through the prodigious promotional efforts of the pharmaceutical industry and sections of the body shape industry, has blurred the line between 'treatment' and 'enhancement' and between 'sickness' and 'health' (see Chapters 2 and 4). As noted, 'the body' has become a major 'item' for exchange value and exploitation within late capitalist, consumer-oriented societies. Increasingly, the body is objectified and, as the recent increases in instances of cosmetic surgery show, is seen by a growing number of individuals and the body shape industry as a modifiable, perfectible entity (see Chapter 3). Body modification is premised on the assumption that there is a clear line between the normal and the abnormal and a belief in the ideal of 'the perfect body'. As indicated, this denies the historical and cultural variability of ideas of normality and of perfection and beauty, and the arbitrariness of biomedical classifications which provide a major point of reference in definitions of health, sickness and normality (see Chapter 4). In the previous chapter, it was noted that there is growing dissatisfaction with and resistance to the objectification and commodification of the body within the arena of healthcare, as revealed by efforts to 'reconnect' or 'integrate' mind and body. The considerable popularity of CAMs/holistic medicine and the increasing tendency for 'consumers' to 'shop around' for alternatives to 'body-only' approaches, it was suggested, would seem to be part of a broad response to the perceived limitations and deleterious implications of the mind–body dualism that is a feature of biomedicine. However, as argued, despite some evident benefits for recipients of particular mind–body therapies and practices, efforts to 'integrate' body and mind have not been without shortcomings and unacknowledged consequences. These include the reinforcement of individualism and consumerism, which is evident with CAM/'holistic' medicine. While the use of the language of empowerment suggests a sharing or equalisation of power relations, the field of CAM/'holistic' medicine does not necessarily represent a threat to the dominance of biomedicine, which has accommodated to and exploited 'consumer' demand by incorporating certain 'complementary' therapies within practice.

The trends outlined in the previous chapters raise a number of questions for further consideration. In particular, what issues concerning 'the body' are likely to emerge in the future and what might this imply for political action and policy development? What new approaches and lines of enquiry may scholars of the body and society usefully pursue? As noted in Chapter 1, although contributions to the study of 'the body' have been diverse and insightful, recent work has been limited in a number of respects. Discussions are often overly abstract and often fail to address significant body-related matters, particularly the challenges posed by innovations in biomedicine and biotechnology to established ways of thinking about the body. Many studies in 'the body and society' are often unconcerned with issues of power relations and strategies of social change. Theorists frequently fail to engage with recent thinking about the nature of contemporary politics and the reformulations of political theory accompanying the ascendance of neo-liberal rule (Rose 1999). On the other hand, research on developments affecting the conceptualisation of the body, such as those occurring in biomedicine and biotechnology, often does not benefit to the extent that it could from the insights offered by body theorists working in fields such as cultural studies, sociology, anthropology, and philosophy. An obvious area that could benefit from more explicit theorisation is the study of technologies of the body, their development and implications.

Emergent technologies of the body

It is never easy to predict the future trajectory of technology developments, and this is perhaps especially so with technologies oriented to the repair, regeneration, enhancement, and regulation of the body. As past developments in biotechnology and reproductive medicine show, new technologies often meet strong resistance and opposition, take directions and find applications unforeseen, and have unintended consequences. In popular cultural imagery and as revealed in public surveys and focus groups, genetic and other body technologies are the subject of both utopian and dystopian visions. Some of these visions were explored in the previous chapters. Science groups and policy makers have expressed concern about media coverage of science and technology issues and the potential of negative coverage to lead to a public backlash against useful and profitable applications. As noted in Chapter 1, the media in its diverse forms constitutes a central element of contemporary culture, and the question of how the body and its parts are represented has become crucial to the formation of public expectations and policy responses to body technology developments, as can be seen in recent debates over cloning, genetic testing, stem cell research and the prospect of 'designer babies'. Although many genetic developments are unlikely to deliver the benefits promised for healthcare (Holtzman and Marteau 2000), for example 'personalised' medicine, policies are being developed in the expectation that genetics *will* eventually be 'mainstreamed' into healthcare and deliver significant benefits, which is helping to shape the future even if not in ways imagined by the proponents of genetic technologies (Petersen 2006). Although the public visibility of nanotechnologies is presently low (see Royal Society/Royal Academy Engineering 2004), an array of forthcoming new applications is predicted. These pertain to the fields of medicine (e.g. nanomachines for repairing or regenerating damaged cells, cleaning arteries and delivering drugs, and engineered body parts), engineering and environmental sustainability (e.g. disassembling organic compounds such as wood, oil, and sewerage, and fabricating food, and light, super-hard materials, and creating self-cleaning windows and clothes) (Milburn 2004: 109–110; RS/RAE 2004: Chapters 3, 4; Nanoforum. org 2006; Thacker 2004: 117–123). Again, this is a field ripe with hype and expectation and a sense of inevitability, with a considerable blurring of 'real science' and 'science fiction' in debates in the area (Milburn 2004: 113).

Visions of nanomedicine, like genetic medicine, are predicated upon certain notions of the body and health and disease. The body is viewed as 'open to the intervention of medical design and engineering at the molecular level' (Milburn 2004: 122). Disease is seen as an external threat and medicine is depicted as fighting a battle for health and normality. As already discussed at some length in Chapter 2, neuroscience is another area in development, with expected new applications 'on the horizon', suggesting that the brain has unlimited plasticity (see, e.g. Restak 2003; Rose 2005). According to neuroscientists, neuroscience promises to revolutionise understandings of the mind–body relationship and in the process conceptions of what it means to be human. This work is proceeding on the premise that 'minds are "nothing but" the products of brains' or that 'mind language' is a primitive form of folk psychology that needs to be eliminated from scientific discourse (Rose 2005: 88). According to neuroscience, neural circuits developed through evolutionary processes and thus 'hard-wired' are seen as potentially subject to modification or 're-wiring' and hence manipulation through the use of 'smart drugs', neuroimaging techniques, and new methods of mind control (Rose 2005: Chapters 10, 11). As Rose argues, in his book, *The 21st Century Brain: Explaining, Mending and Manipulating the Mind,*

> The prospective advances in knowledge of the brain . . . point the way to new and ever more powerful physical, chemical and biological modes of control and manipulation. Such neurotechnologies are not yet fully formed. Some are under active research, some merely on the drawing board, others nothing but science fiction.
>
> (Rose 2005: 244)

The converging of some or all of the above technologies, with digital technologies and a variety of new drugs, may lead to applications as yet unimagined and perhaps bring us a step further towards the 'posthuman' or cyborg society of hybrid natural-artificial systems, much discussed among scholars in cultural studies and science and technology studies (see, e.g. Gray 2002; Hayle 1999; Waldby 2000). Many of the 'science fiction' portrayals of yesterday are now 'science reality' or quickly becoming so, and there is no reason to doubt that contemporary popular cultural visions of science developments will be realised at some stage in the future.

In analysing recent developments in body technologies, one needs to avoid the technological determinist assumption that technologies develop according to some inherent logic and inevitably lead in a certain direction. It needs to be recognised that technologies of the body, like any technologies, rely on a certain set of predisposing and supportive conditions. These include political commitment to their development, support by funders of research, expectations by biomedical/biotechnology and body shape industries about ensuing financial benefits, and the existence of receptive consumers. The rise and fall of stock markets, political activism surrounding certain technologies, and media coverage of emergent issues are among factors that may impact on the trajectory of particular developments. Publicity and ensuing debate surrounding, for example, the cloning of Dolly the sheep (Petersen 2002), transplant patients' use of organs from Chinese executed prisoners (Boseley 2006c), and scientific fraud surrounding embryonic stem cell research in Korea (Gottweis and Triendl 2006) are likely to further affect the regulatory climate and investment decisions governing the development of technologies of the body. However, given the increasingly pervasive rationality of the market, supported by the rhetoric of 'consumer choice' and individual 'empowerment', which has infiltrated virtually all spheres of contemporary social life, there is little reason to doubt that many body technologies, particularly enhancement technologies, will in time become routinely used. If we take by 'enhancement' to mean 'interventions designed to improve human performance beyond what is required to sustain or restore good health' (Juengst 1998, citing Miller and Wilsdon 2006: 15) (the question of what constitutes 'good health' is debatable), then a new set of possibilities for enhancement, some existing and some on the way, are opening up, shaped by culture and consumer expectation (Miller and Wilsdon 2006: 15). These include various chemical, surgical, robotic, and genetic manipulations oriented to strengthening mental and physical capacities (2006: 15). The demand for such enhancement technologies is likely to expand among older, more affluent age groups, which are being increasingly targeted as a potentially lucrative market 'niche' for all kinds of consumer goods and services (see Chapter 4). The questions of whether these technologies will substantially improve bodies and lives and whether they should be supported need to be debated with input from many different constituencies, including lay publics, disability groups and patient groups, natural scientists, social scientists, healthcare professionals, educationalists, NGOs, business interests, and policy makers.

Democratising science and technology and culture

Opening up debate in this way implies the democratisation of science and technology and culture. Recently, the UK think tank, Demos, has called for scientists and policy makers to 'engage' with publics at any early stage of research and development so that the technologies that are developed reflect publics' views and priorities (Miller and Wilsdon 2006: 23–24; see also Wilsdon and Willis 2004). Interestingly, the debate about this so-called 'upstream' public engagement, and a number of related UK public engagement 'experiments' (e.g. ScienceWise), emerged during deliberations within the science and policy communities about nanotechnologies, their opportunities and risks in the wake of concerns about a 'GM-style' backlash in this field. This debate itself illustrated how the development of new technologies may be shaped by reactions to other, earlier technology developments. The question of how to most productively 'engage' publics, however, is not straightforward. Demos, and those who share its views, suggest that public engagement and dialogue efforts should address *substantive* questions such as, who owns research, who benefits from particular applications, and should certain technologies be developed at all? If sociological and other social science studies of the body are to be relevant to emergent debates and to usefully contribute to policy and social change, it is important that scholars consider the question of how publics may help shape research and development agenda and deliberate on the substantive questions that affect different communities.

Any meaningful 'engagement' strategy must begin by acknowledging that biomedical technologies, including reproductive technologies, impact on *publics* in different ways. Technologies are developed with particular users and uses in mind, and not all groups have equal access to or are equally predisposed to adopt technologies. Some groups are opposed to certain kinds of research and development for religious, ethical, or other reasons. It needs to be recognised that the routine deployment of technologies by some groups may help 'normalise' particular ideals of body perfection and reinforce inequalities based upon evaluations of bodily health and difference and lead to increased surveillance and control of those who are deemed to be 'unhealthy', 'abnormal' or 'imperfect'. As shown in Chapter 3, the norms of 'ideal' body shape and size, and associated conceptions of the 'normal, 'healthy' self, vary across cultures and through time, a point which is concealed by prevailing discourses of body weight and body modification. Eugenics has its origins in the belief of an 'ideal' 'healthy' body and the perfectibility of the 'race' through 'selective breeding'. As explained in Chapter 4, one of the concerns about the operation of 'choice' in the use of prenatal genetic tests for reproductive decision-making is that the collective impact of individual decisions 'freely' exercised may have unintended eugenic outcomes. Critical scholarship can help expose the actual and potential variable social impacts of the development and use of particular technologies of the body, by making reference, where possible, to other earlier or parallel technology developments. These include newly emergent fields such as neuroscience and nanotechnologies which have barely begun to be explored by social scientists thus far, but urgently need to be, given recent predictions about their development and convergence with other technologies in the future.

Understanding the role of media

Understanding the role and operations of the media is crucial to the effort to democratise science and technology and culture. As noted in earlier chapters, scientists and policy makers increasingly recognise that the question of how media portray science and technology is of crucial significance to the formation of public views and hence receptivity to certain kinds of research and development. Given this, it is surprising that in discussions about public engagement strategies the media's significance is often overlooked or is acknowledged only in terms of its potential educative role. This suggests blindness to the role of the media in contemporary cultural and political life and the lingering influence of the deficit model of 'public understanding of science' (PUS). (For two useful recent accounts of the history and limitations of the deficit model of PUS see Irwin and Michael 2003: 19–40; and Jasanoff 2005: 250–255.) Forty years ago, Marshall McLuhan documented the profound significance of the media in his book, *The Medium is the Massage: An Inventory of Effects*. He noted there how 'the medium, or process, of our time', namely 'electric technology', was 'reshaping and restructuring patterns of social interdependence and every aspect of our personal life' (McLuhan and Fiore 2001: 8).

> All media work us over completely. They are so pervasive in their personal, political, economic, aesthetic, psychological, moral, ethical, and social consequences that they leave no part of us untouched, unaffected, unaltered. The medium is the massage. Any understanding of social and cultural change is impossible without a knowledge of the way media work as environments.
>
> (McLuhan and Fiore 2001: 26)

Some writers contend that McLuhan overplayed the importance of the media in culture and underplayed the active engagement and resistance of readers/audiences. However, if one accepts McLuhan's argument about the significance of the *form* of the medium, then one cannot deny that with the rise of electronic media the flow of information, including advertising, has become instantaneous and pervasive, especially with the emergence of the Internet, the digitalisation of news, the ubiquity of mobile phones and the growing popularity of other 'hand-held' electronic devices such as iPods. Sociological and other social science perspectives on the media, however, are relatively underdeveloped and focus predominantly on (print) media portrayals rather than on processes of media production and audience reception. As argued in Chapter 2, a thoroughgoing analysis of the politics and workings of the media is crucial if one is to understand how certain images of the body and body-related issues (e.g. cloning, stem cell research, neuroscience, pharmacogenetics) come to be portrayed, why some groups are especially influential in shaping news agenda and debate, and how particular 'framings' become established in public discourse.

The political economy of the body

The previous chapters explored the significance of the various industries that have a stake in the body, its health and illness and size and shape.

Body-related services and products, including cosmetic surgery, the provision of body parts, beauty treatments, weight-loss remedies, and fashions in clothing constitute a huge and apparently growing sector of the economy. Given this, there has been surprisingly little work on the political economy of the body. Many problems within civil society are related to the body and its health and functioning, including patterns of consumption within sections of the population, such as obesity, eating disorders, heart disease, and so on, which need to be managed through various regulatory mechanisms. Diverse forms of expertise have emerged to rationally manage problems and to help achieve a balance between maintaining the conditions for the thriving of capitalist enterprise and the promotion of the health and welfare of citizens. The questions of how science and technology developments are to achieve consent and legitimacy within the population and what policies and programmes are needed to regulate the orderly development of innovations that are seen to have potential economic and social benefits is an ongoing problem for policy makers. As Jasanoff points out, science, like politics, must conform to established ways of public knowing – what she calls *civic epistemologies* (2005: 249) – in order to achieve broad-based support and legitimacy. In practice, this has meant the articulation of programmes and policies in terms of their public benefits and employing a language that is most likely to resonate with publics, say, of citizenship responsibilities, as seen in arguments for public participation in biotechnology research (Petersen 2005a). Increasingly, governance is achieved through 'responsibilisation' or *self*-management, as governments embrace a market-driven approach to health and welfare. In the UK, for example, the emphasis on 'choice', 'empowerment' and 'patient expertise' in healthcare reflect this emphasis in policy. Although currently unfashionable within sociology and many other social sciences, political economy can be reinvigorated through analysis of the significance of the body within processes of production and consumption.

While this book has drawn particular attention to commodification of the body and its parts and consumerism in body practices, these processes cannot be dissociated from processes of production. 'Production' encompasses ideas, material objects and services. As noted in Chapter 4, pharmaceutical companies may 'manufacture' diseases for which profitable treatments are then developed. Some interesting research on the dynamics of the production–consumption cycle of the pharmaceutical and beauty industries has been referred to in previous chapters. Sociology and other social sciences can contribute much to deepening this analysis, by exploring the behind-the-scenes dynamics of this 'body industry', including the interlocking networks of industry, political institutions, consumer groups and citizen activist groups. With the emergence of active citizenship, increasingly focused on the recognition of biological characteristics (Petryna 2002) (see Chapter 4), such citizen groups have become a crucial link within the production-consumption cycle. For example, they may lobby for the development of particular technologies or for the banning of certain products or for regulations which affect investment decisions, positively or negatively. Genetic support groups have successfully lobbied for research into particular genetic conditions (see, e.g. Rapp 1999). In the USA, Christian fundamentalist groups opposed to embryonic stem cell research have had a considerable influence on policies affecting funding of this field of research at the Federal level (Jasanoff 2005: 3–4). Patient groups also seem to be becoming more litigious, as seen in a recent US class action taken by a group of mothers against the makers of a genetic testing kit 'promising to predict a baby's gender with 99.9% accuracy' (Goldenberg 2006: 17). With the globalisation of the body shape and biotechnology industries, and improved means of communication enabled by the internet, 'consumers' and activist groups increasingly are overcoming constraints of time and place and forging links with others in their efforts to self-manage their bodies and shape policies governing life.

The implications of active citizenship

As the case of CAM/holistic medicine shows, increasingly, active citizenship is being expressed through 'consumer choice' in the use of therapies (see Chapter 5). Consumers will 'shop around' for the 'best buys' and reject products and services that are seen as not meeting their needs. The growing use of 'direct-to-consumer' advertising through the internet means that individuals are being targeted by industries producing body-related products and services to an unprecedented extent. In the globalised and de-regulated context of consumer capitalism, effective regulation via legislation is increasingly difficult to achieve. More affluent consumers are geographically mobile and may seek treatments in other countries when these are outlawed or difficult to obtain in their own. Some recently publicised cases of people travelling to other countries for fertility treatments, stem cell therapies, cosmetic surgery, and organ transplants show that biomedical tourism is already occurring. For example:

> **Stem cell firm uses Swansea ferry to evade Irish block on controversial treatment**
>
> A company offering controversial 'stem cell' injections to hundreds of people from the UK with multiple sclerosis and other neurological diseases is planning to get around a ban on treatment in Ireland by carrying it out in international waters on an overnight ferry. Advanced Cell Therapeutics (ACT) which has an address in Geneva and a London telephone number, has been supplying stem cells from umbilical cord blood to 12 clinics around the world, of which two are in the Netherlands and one in Spain. Demand from the UK – where the treatment is illegal – has been huge, following tabloid newspaper stories about apparent

remarkable discoveries and an interview with a clinic doctor on television's Richard and Judy programme.

(Bosely 2006a: 3)

Spain becomes the destination of choice for fertility tourists from Britan

Spain has become the destination of choice for childless, infertile British couples driven to seek help abroad by a dramatic fall in the number of people prepared to donate eggs or sperm at home. Fertility clinics in Spain have told the *Guardian* that numbers have increased between 50% and 100% since Britain passed a law in April last year that gave children the right to know the identity of their biological parents. . . .

(Tremlett 2006: 16)

UK transplant patients go to China for organs from executed prisoners

British surgeons yesterday condemned the use of executed prisoners' organs for transplants in China, saying that shortages in the UK were tempting British patients to travel despite the grave ethical issues involved. . . .

(Boseley 2006c: 4)

Recent trends such as these raise significant normative and justice issues in relation to processes of individualisation, medicalisation and commodification. These include questions of commercial profiteering from the production and sale of body tissue and body-related products and services, heightened public expectations of treatments and cures, different publics' access to new technologies, responsibility of users of technologies to those who live in other countries, and the responsibility of the media in reporting issues. Questions such as whose bodies benefit from the use of particular technologies and which groups are disadvantaged in the process should be part of critical studies of 'the body'. There are no easy answers to these questions, however, because they involve deeply held values and judgements about issues of life and death and life chances upon which there is rarely, if ever, consensus. Critical analyses of 'the body' in its various aspects and contexts can help us to make sense of the rapid changes which characterise late modern societies. What I have sought to demonstrate in this book, and I hope convincingly so, is that new questions are urgently needed in this area if we are to better understand what makes us human and the extent to which we are able to shape the conditions which profoundly affect our lives.

Notes

1 <http://en.wikipedia.org/wiki/Intelligent_design> (accessed 24 May 2006).
2 *The Economist*, 30 July 2005, p. 44.
3 <http://www.genewatch.org>.
4 <http://www.greenpeace.org.uk/index.cfm>.
5 <http://www.anat.ox.ac.uk/groups/itracey.htm> (accessed 22 April 2005).
6 <http://donoghue.neuro.brown.edu/motor.php> (accessed 6 May 2005).
7 <http://www.darpa.mil> (accessed 6 May 2005).
8 <http://www.timesonline.co.uk/article/0,,2-1589642,00.html> (accessed 12 May 2005).
9 <http://news.bbc.co.uk/1/hi/health/4033383.stm> (accessed 12 May 2005).
10 <http://news.bbc.co.uk/1/hi/sci/tech/3639126.stm> (accessed 12 May 2005).
11 <http://news.bbc.co.uk/1/hi/health/3926815.stm> (accessed 12 May 2005).
12 <http://tvnz.co.nz/view/news_health_story_skin/477265%3fformat=html> (accessed 12 May 2005).
13 kaisernetwork.org. Available online at <http://www.kaisernetwork.org/daily_reports/rep_index.cfm?DR_ID=29183> (accessed 16 May 2005).
14 *Seattle Post*, 8 April 2005.
15 *Medical News Today*, 13 April 2005.
16 <http://www.medicalnewstoday.com/medicalnews.php?newsid=22757).
17 WHO 2005; 'Obesity and overweight (Global Strategy on diet, physical activity and health)', <http://www.who.int/dietphysicalactivity/publications/facts/obesity/en> (accessed 27 May 2005).
18 *The Guardian*, August 12 2005, p. 14.
19 *The Guardian*, August 12 2005, p. 14.
20 WHO 2005, 'Obesity and overweight (Global Strategy on diet, physical activity and health)', <http://www.who.int/dietphysicalactivity/publications/facts/obesity/en> (accessed 27 May 2005).
21 WHO 2005, 'Obesity and overweight', <http://www.who.int/dietphysicalactivity/publications/facts/obesity/en> (accessed 27 May 2005).
22 WHO 2005, 'Obesity and overweight', <http://www.who.int/dietphysicalactivity/publications/facts/obesity/en> (accessed 27 May 2005).
23 WHO 2005, 'Obesity and overweight', <http://www.who.int/dietphysicalactivity/publications/facts/obesity/en> (accessed 27 May 2005; emphasis added).
24 WHO 2005, 'Obesity and overweight', <http://www.who.int/dietphysical activity/publications/facts/obesity/en>.
25 <http://www.boots-plc.com> (accessed 5 September 2005).
26 *Daily Mail*, May 24 2005, p. 9.
27 *Daily Mail*, May 24 2005, p. 9.
28 <http://www.thehospitalgroup.org/?engine=adwords!2870&keyword=%28the+hospital+group%29&match_type=> (accessed 2 June 2005).

29 <http://news.bbc.co.uk/1/hi/uk/4510115.stm> (accessed 5 September, 2005).
30 <http://www.beautyserve.com/Downloads/Survey/BeautyIndSurveyResults2004.pdf> (accessed 25 August 2005).
31 <http://www.beautyserve.com/Downloads/Survey/BeautyIndSurveyResults2004.pdf> (accessed 25 August 2005).
32 <http://www.harleymedical.co.uk/index.php?id=53> (accessed 7 September 2005).
33 *The Independent*, 9 May 2005, p. 18.
34 <http://www.marketresearch.com/product/display.asp?productid=1093139&xs=r> (accessed 8 September 2005).
35 <http://www.dove.com/real_beauty/challenging_beauty.pdf> (acccessed 7 September 2005).
36 <http://www.who.int/classifications/icd/en/HistoryOfICD.pdf> (accessed 14 October, 2005).
37 <http://en.wikipedia.org/wiki/Diagnostic_and_Statistical_Manual_of_Mental_Disorders> (accessed 14 October 2005).
38 <http://www.who.int/classifications/icd/en> (accessed 14 October 2005).
39 <http://www.who.int/classifications/icd/en> (accessed 14 October 2005).
40 <http://www.allaboutdepression.com/dia_01.html> (accessed 16 March 2006).
41 <http://www.nsti.org/news/item.html?id=39> (accessed 14 February 2006); Royal Society and Royal Academy of Engineering 2004: 20.
42 <http://www.nsti.org/news/item.html?id=43> (accessed 27 February 2006).
43 *The Australian*, 22 December 2005: 20).
44 <http://www.natcen.ac.uk/elsa/docs/ELSA_04UPDATE2.pdf>; Hill and McKie, 2005.
45 <http://www.publications.parliament.uk/pa/ld200506/ldselect/ldsctech/20/2002.htm> (accessed 20 March 2006).
46 House of Lords Select Committee on Science and Technology 2005: Chapter 6, paragraph 6.3.
47 <http://www.fondazionericci.it/flex/files/D.1e0ca72fef1b866acb72/Complementary_and_Alternative_Medicine_the_consumer_perspective.pdf> (accessed 8 May 2006).
48 See, for example, the definition of CAMs offered by the National Centre for Complementary and Alternative Medicine (NCCAM). Available online at <http://nccam.nih.gov/health/whatiscam> (accessed 6 April 2006).
49 <http://www.leadingauthorities.com/3221/Ken_Dychtwald.htm> (accessed 9 April 2006).
50 <http://www.aima.net.au/documents/media/RACGP-AIMA%20Position%20Statement%20on%20CM%20May%202005.pdf> (accessed 6 April 2006).
51 <http://www.bma.org.uk/ap.nsf/Content/LIBAlternativeMedicine#dab> (accessed 7 April 2006).
52 <http://www.bhma.org/modules.php?op=modload&name=PagEd&file=index&topic_id=0&page_id=50> (accessed 6 April 2006).
53 <http://www.bhma.org/modules.php?op=modload&name=PagEd&file=index&topic_id=0&page_id=23> (accessed 9 April 2006).
54 <http://www.aima.net.au/page.jsp?p_id=3> (accessed 6 April 2006).

References

Abbott, A. (2006) '"Ethical" stem-cell paper under attack', news@nature.com (http://www.nature.com/news/2006/060904/full/443012a.html) (Accessed 12 September 2006).

Abraham, S. and Llewellyn-Jones, D. (2001) *Eating Disorders: The Facts*, 5th edn, Oxford: Oxford University Press.

Adam, D. (2004) 'Computerising the body: Microsoft wins patent to exploit network potential of skin', *The Guardian*, 6 July, p. 3.

Agamben, G. (1998) *Homo Sacer: Sovereign Power and Bare Life*, Stanford, CA: Stanford University Press.

Ahmad, W. and Jones, L. (1998) 'Ethnicity, health and healthcare in Britain', in A. Petersen and C. Waddell (eds) *Health Matters: A Sociology of Illness Prevention and Care*, Crows Nest: Allen & Unwin.

Alison, A. *et al.* (2005) 'The framing of nanotechnologies in the British newspaper press', *Science Communication*, 27, 2: 200–220.

Allan, A. and Hollander, E. (2002) 'Psychopharmacological treatments for body image disturbances', in T. F. Cash and T. Pruzinsky (eds) *Body Image: A Handbook of Theory, Research, and Clinical Practice*, New York and London: Guilford Press.

Armstrong, D. (1989) *An Outline of Sociology as Applied to Medicine*, 3rd edn, London: Wright.

Armstrong, D. (2003) 'Social theorizing about health and illness' in G. Albrecht, R. Fitzpatrick and S. C. Scrimshaw (eds) *The Handbook of Social Studies in Health and Medicine*, London: Sage.

Bailey, R. (1996) 'Prenatal testing and the prevention of impairment: a woman's right to choose?', in J. Morris (ed.) *Encounters With Strangers: Feminism and Disability*, London: The Women's Press Ltd.

Balsamo, A. (1996) *Technologies of the Gendered Body: Reading Cyborg Women*, Durham, NC and London: Duke University Press.

Barnett, A. (2006) 'Dispute led clone expert to quit UK', *The Observer*, 29 January, p. 13.

Baudrillard, J. (1998; orig. 1970) *The Consumer Society: Myths and Structures*, London: Sage.

Beck, U. (1992) *Risk Society: Towards a New Modernity*, London: Sage.

Bendelow, G. and Williams, S. (1995) 'Pain and the mind–body dualism', *Body & Society*, 1, 2: 83–103.

Bendelow, G. and Williams, S. (eds) (1998) *Emotions in Social Life: Critical Themes and Contemporary Issues*, London and New York: Routledge.

Benton, T. (1991) 'Biology and social science: why the return of the repressed should be given a (cautious) welcome', *Sociology*, 25, 1: 1–29.

Black, P. (2004) *The Beauty Industry: Gender, Culture, Pleasure*, London: Routledge.

Bland, L. and Doan, L. (1998a) *Sexology Uncensored: The Documents of Sexual Science*, Cambridge: Polity Press.

Bland, L. and Doan, L. (1998b) *Sexology in Culture: Labelling Bodies and Desires*, Cambridge: Polity Press.

Blood, S. (2005) *Body Work: The Social Construction of Women's Body Image*, London and New York: Routledge.

Bloomfield, S. (2005a) 'Ops for obesity double as epidemic grows', *The Independent on Sunday* (Home section), 20 February, p. 12.

Bloomfield, S. (2005b) 'This girl is fresh-face and 16, so why might she buy anti-wrinkle cream?', *The Independent on Sunday* (Home section), 20 February, p. 5.

Bloomfield (2005c) 'Facelifts in Delhi, tummy tucks in Cape Town: UK's cosmetic tourists go worldwide', *The Independent on Sunday*, 28 August, p. 3.

Body & Society (1999) Special Issue on: Body Modification, 5: 2–3.

Bogard, W. (1996) *The Simulation of Surveillance: Hypercontrol in Telematic Societies*, Cambridge: Cambridge University Press.

Bordo, S. (1993) *Unbearable Weight: Feminism, Western Culture, and the Body*, Berkeley and Los Angeles, CA: University of California Press.

Boseley, S. (2005) 'Childhood obesity study alarms doctors', *The Guardian*, 30 April. Available online at <http://www.ghchealth.com/forum/childhood-obesity-study-alarms-doctors-discussion-597.php> (accessed 15 June 2006).

Boseley, S. (2006a) 'Doctors' concern over MS clinic', *The Guardian*, 20 March, p. 3.

Boseley, S. (2006b) 'Stem cell firm uses Swansea ferry to evade Irish block on controversial treatment', *The Guardian*, 1 May, p. 3.

Boseley, S. (2006c) 'UK transplant patients go to China for organs from executed prisoners', *The Guardian*, 20 April, p. 4.

Bourdieu, P. (1986) *Distinction: A Social Critique of the Judgement of Taste*, London: Routledge and Kegan Paul.

Bourke, J. (1996) *Dismembering the Male: Men's Bodies, Britain and the Great War*, London: Reaktion Books.

Bourke, J. (1999) *An Intimate History of Killing: Face-to-Face Killing in Twentieth Century Warfare*, London: Granta Books.

Bowker, G. C. and Star, S. L. (2000) *Sorting Things Out: Classification and Its Consequences*, Cambridge, MA, and London: The MIT Press.

Bradshaw, V. (1996) *Alternative Medicine Definitions*, BMA website <http://www.whale.to/y/alt.html> (accessed 6 April 2006).

Braithwaite, J. (1984) *Corporate Crime in the Pharmaceutical Industry*, London: Routledge and Kegan Paul.

British Broadcasting Corporation (2005) 'Child TV hours obesity risk link', 13 September. Available online at <http://news.bbc.co.uk/1/hi/health/4238386.stm> (accessed 14 June 2006).

British Medical Association (1993) *Complementary Medicine: New Approaches to Good Practice*, Oxford and New York: Oxford University Press.

British Nutrition Foundation (1999) *Obesity*, The Report of the British Nutrition Foundation Task Force, Oxford: Blackwell Science Ltd.

Broom, B. (1997) *Somatic Illness and the Patient's Other Story*, London and New York: Free Association Books.

Bryant-Waugh, R. and Lask, B. (2004) *Eating Disorders: A Parent's Guide*, revd edn, New York: Routledge.

Bury, M. (2003) 'A commentary', Paper from the Royal Pharmacy Society Expert Patient Conference, May. Available online at <http://www.rpsgb.org.uk/pdfs/exptpatsem1.pdf> (accessed 9 November 2005).

Butler, J. (1993) *Bodies that Matter: On the Discursive Limits of 'Sex'*, New York and London: Routledge.

Campbell, D. and McKie, R. (2004) 'Top athletes seek gene therapy boost', *The Observer*, 11 July, p. 5.

Canguilhem, G. (1989) *The Normal and the Pathological*, New York: Zone Books.

Capra, F. (1983) *The Turning Point: Science, Society and the Rising Culture*, London: Flamingo.

Cash, T. F. and Pruzinsky, T. (2002) *Body Image: A Handbook of Theory, Research, and Clinical Practice*, New York and London: Guilford Press.

Cash, T. F. and Strachan, M. D. (2002) 'Cognitive-behavioural approaches to changing body image' in T. F. Cash and T. Pruzinsky (eds) *Body Image: A Handbook of Theory, Research, and Clinical Practice*, New York and London: Guilford Press.

Castle, D. J. and Phillips, K. A. (2002) 'Disordered body image in psychiatric disorders' disorder' in D. J. Castle and K. A. Phillips (eds) *Disorders of Body Image*, Petersfield, UK and Philadelphia, USA: Wrightson Biomedical Publishing Ltd.

Castle, D. J. and Phillips, K. A. (2002) *Disorders of Body Image*, Petersfield, UK and Philadelphia, USA: Wrightson Biomedical Publishing Ltd.

Celio, A. A., Zabinski, M. F. and Wilfley, D. E. (2002) 'African American body images' in T. F. Cash and T. Pruzinsky (eds) *Body Image: A Handbook of Theory, Research, and Clinical Practice*, New York and London: Guilford Press.

Cohen, C. (1993) 'Wars, wimps and women: talking gender and thinking war', in M. Cooke and A. Woollacott (eds) *Gendering War Talk*, Princeton, NJ: Princeton University Press.

Colapinto, J. (2000) *As Nature Made Him: The Boy Who Was Raised as a Girl*, New York: Harper Collins.

Collyer, F. (2004) 'The corporatisation and commercialisation of CAM', in P. Tovey, G. Easthope and J. Adams (eds) *The Mainstreaming of Complementary and Alternative Medicine: Studies in Social Context*, London and New York: Routledge.

Condit, C. (1999) *The Meanings of the Gene: Public Debates About Human Heredity*, Madison, WI: University of Wisconsin Press.

Connell, R. W. (1995) *Masculinities*, Crows Nest: Allen & Unwin.

Conrad, P. (1999) 'Uses of expertise: sources, quotes, and voice in the reporting of genetics in the news', *Public Understanding of Science*, 8: 285–302.

Conrad, P. and Schneider, J. W. (1992) *Deviance and Medicalization: From Badness to Sickness*, expanded edn, Philadelphia, PA: Temple University Press.

Cooter, R. (1988) *Studies in the History of Alternative Medicine*, Houndmills and London: Macmillan Press in Association with St Antony's College, Oxford.

Corea, G. (1985) *The Mother Machine: Reproductive Technologies from Artificial Insemination to Artificial Wombs*, New York: Harper and Row.

Corrigan, O. (2003) 'Empty ethics: the problem with informed consent', *Sociology of Health and Illness*, 25, 7: 768–792.

Corson, P. W. and Anderson, A. E. (2002) 'Body image issues among boys and men', in T. F. Cash and T. Pruzinsky (eds) *Body Image: A Handbook of Theory, Research, and Clinical Practice*, New York and London: Guilford Press.

Coulter, I. (2004) 'Integration and paradigm clash: the practical difficulties of integrative medicine, in P. Tovey, G. Easthope and J. Adams (eds) *The Mainstreaming of Complementary and Alternative Medicine: Studies in Social Context*, London and New York: Routledge.

Crawford, R. (1994) 'The boundaries of the self and the unhealthy other: reflections on health, culture and AIDS', *Social Science and Medicine*, 38, 10: 1347–1365.

Crossley, M. A. (1996) 'Choice, conscience and context', *Hastings Law Journal*, 47, 4: 1223–1239.

Crossley, N. (2001) *The Social Body: Habit, Identity and Desire*, London: Sage.

Culf, A. (2005) 'Flintoff joins big hitters but is not in Beckham's league', *The Guardian*, 3 September, p. 12.

Curtis, P. (2006) 'Alzheimer's drug could make everyone brainier', *The Guardian*, 27 January, p. 5.

Curtis, P. and Branigan, T. (2006) 'Young women told to raise their sights on pay', *The Guardian*, 28 February.

Cyranoski, D. (2005) 'Japan jumps towards personalized medicine', *Nature*, 437 (6 October): 796.

Daniel, E. V. (1991) 'The pulse as an icon in Siddha medicine', in D. Howes (ed.) *The Varieties of Sensory Experience: A Sourcebook in the Anthropology of the Senses*, Toronto: University of Toronto Press.

Datamonitor (2005) *The Future of Personal Care Occasions*, 25 March. Available online at <http://www.marketresearch.com/product/display.asp?productid=109 3139&xs=r> (accessed 30 June 2005).

Davetian, B. (2005) 'Towards an emotionally conscious social theory', *Sociological Research Online*, 10, 2. Available online at <http://www.socresonline.org.uk/10/2/davetian.html>.

Davies, D. (2003) *The Discourse of Weight Control and the Self*, Ph.D. thesis, Murdoch University, Murdoch, Western Australia. Available online at <http://wwwlib.murdoch.edu.au/adt/browse/view/adt-MU20040303.153523> (accessed June 21 2006).

Davis, K. (1995) *Reshaping the Female Body: The Dilemma of Cosmetic Surgery*, New York and London: Routledge.

Davis, K. (2002) '"A dubious equality": men, women and cosmetic surgery', *Body & Society*, 8, 1: 49–65.

Dean, M. (1999) *Governmentality: Power and Rule in Modern Society*, New York: Sage.

Department of Health (2003) *Our Inheritance, Our Future: Realising the Potential of Genetic in the NHS*, Norwich: HMSO.

Descartes, R. (1973) *The Philosophical Works of Descartes*, vol. 1, trans. E. Haldane and G. R. T. Ross, Cambridge: Cambridge University Press.

Descartes, R. (1993) *Meditations on First Philosophy*, ed. S. Tweyman, London and New York: Routledge.

Dobson, R. (2004) 'GPs offer patients complementary medicine', in C. Donnellan (ed.) *Alternative Therapies*, Issues, vol. 81, Cambridge: Independence Educational Publishers.

Donnellan, C. (ed.) (2003) *Obesity and Eating Disorders*, Issues, vol. 72, Cambridge: Independence Educational Publishers.

Donnellan, C. (ed.) (2004) *Alternative Therapies*, Issues, vol. 81, Cambridge: Independence Educational Publishers.

Dove Report: Challenging Beauty (2004) Available online at <http://www.dove.com/real_beauty/article.asp?id=430> (accessed 7 September 2005).

Dreger, A. M. (2004) *One of Us: Conjoined Twins and the Future of the Normal*, Cambridge, MA: Harvard University Press.

Duncombe, J. and Marsden, D. (1993) 'Love and intimacy: the gender division of emotion and "emotion work": a neglected aspect of sociological discussion of heterosexual relationships', *Sociology*, 27, 2: 221–241.

Duncombe, J. and Marsden, D. (1996) '"Workaholics" and "wingeing women": theorising intimacy and emotion work: the last frontier of gender inequality?', *The Sociological Review*, 43, 1: 150–169.

Duncombe, J. and Marsden, D. (1998) '"Stepford wives" and "hollow men"?: Doing emotion work, doing gender and "authenticity" in intimate heterosexual relationships', in G. Bendelow and S. J. Williams (eds) *Emotions in Social Life: Critical Themes and Contemporary Issues*, London and New York: Routledge.

Duncombe, J. and Marsden, D. (2002) 'Whose organism is it anyway?: "Sex work" in long-term heterosexual couple relationships', in S. Jackson and S. Scott (eds) *Gender: A Sociological Reader*, London and New York: Routledge.

Dupré, J. (2003) *Darwin's Legacy: What Evolution Means Today*, Oxford: Oxford University Press.

Duster, T. (1990) *Backdoor to Eugenics*, London and New York: Routledge.

Duster, T. (2003) 'The hidden eugenic potential of germ-line interventions', in A. R. Chapman and M. S. Frankel (eds) *Designing Our Descendents: The Promises and Perils and Genetic Modifications*. Baltimore and London: John Hopkins University Press.

Dychtwald, K. (1986; orig. 1977) *BodyMind*, Taos, NM: Redwing Book Co.

Edwards, T. (1990) 'Beyond sex and gender: masculinity, homosexuality and social theory', in J. Hearn and D. Morgan (eds) *Men, Masculinities and Social Theory*, London: Unwin Hyman.

Ehrenreich, B. and English, D. (1979) *For Her Own Good: 150 Years of the Experts' Advice to Women*, New York: Anchor Books.

Ehrenreich, B. and Hochschild, A. R. (2002) *Global Woman: Nannies, Maids and Sex Workers in the New Economy*, London: Granta Books.

Elias, N. (1978) *The Civilizing Process: The History of Manners*, New York: Urizon Books.

Elliott, C. (2003) *Better Than Well: American Medicine Meets the American Dream*, New York: WW Norton.

Engel, G. L. (1977) 'The need for a new medical model: a challenge for biomedicine', *Science*, 196: 129–134.

Ettorre, E. (2002) *Reproductive Genetics, Gender and the Body*, London and New York: Routledge.

Euromonitor International (2004) *Beiersdorf AG*, July 2004. Available online at <http://www.euromonitor.com/Cosmeticsandtoiletries> (accessed 30 June 2005).

Evans, J. (2002) *Playing God? Human Genetic Engineering and the Rationalization of Public Bioethical Debate*, Chicago, IL and London: University of Chicago Press.

Faircloth, C. A. (ed.) (2003) *Aging Bodies: Images and Everyday Experience*, Walnut Creek, CA: AltaMira Press.

Falk, P. (1994) *The Consuming Body*, London: Sage.

Faludi, S. (1992) *Backlash: The Undeclared War Against Women*, London: Vintage.

Fausto-Stirling, A. (1992) *Myths of Gender: Biological Theories About Women and Men*, 2nd edn, New York: Basic Books.

Featherstone, M. and Hepworth, M. (1991) 'The mask of ageing and the post-modern life course', in M. Featherstone, M. Hepworth and B. Turner (eds) *The Body: Social Process and Cultural Theory*, London: Sage.

Featherstone, M., Hepworth, M. and Turner, B. S. (1991) *The Body: Social Process and Cultural Theory*, London: Sage.

Fisher, G. A. and Chon, K. K. (1989) 'Durkheim and the social construction of emotions', *Social Psychology Quarterly*, 52, 1: 1–9.

Fleming, N. (2006) 'Women buying creams made of tiny particles "used as guinea pigs"', *The Daily Telegraph*, 5 May, p. 6.

Ford, R. and Charter, D. (2006) 'ID fraud figures "inflated to play on public fears"', *The Times*, 3 February, pp. 16–17.

Foster, G. D. and Matz, P. E. (2002) 'Weight loss and changes in body image', in T. F. Cash and T. Pruzinsky (eds) *Body Image: A Handbook of Theory, Research, and Clinical Practice*, New York and London: Guilford Press.

Foster, M. W. and Sharp, R. R. (2005) 'Will investment in biobanks, prospective cohorts, and markers of common patterns of variation benefit other populations for drug response and gene susceptibility gene discovery?', *The Pharmacogenomics Journal* (2005): 1–6. Available online at <http://www.ou.edu/casr/publications/MF_Biobanks.pdf> (accessed 24 May 2006).

Foucault, M. (1975) *The Birth of the Clinic: An Archaeology of Medical Perception*, New York: Vintage Books.

Foucault, M. (1977) *Discipline and Punish: The Birth of the Prison*, Harmondsworth, Middlesex and New York: Penguin.

Foucault, M. (1980) *The History of Sexuality*, vol. 1, *An Introduction*, New York: Vintage Books.

Foucault, M. (1985) *The Use of Pleasure*, trans. R. Hurley, Harmondsworth: Penguin.

Foucault, M. (1986) *The Care of the Self*, trans. R. Hurley, Harmondsworth: Penguin.

Francis, M. and Jackson, C. (2005) 'Try this for thighs: could you banish cellulite? Six REAL women test the latest treatments . . . ', *Daily Mail*, 30 June, pp. 48–49.

Frank, A. (1995) *The Wounded Storyteller: Body, Illness, and Ethics*, Chicago, IL: University of Chicago Press.

Frank, A. (2001) 'Can we research suffering?', *Qualitative Health Research*, 11, 3: 353–362.

Freund, P. (1990) 'The expressive body: a common ground for the sociology of emotions and health and illness', *Sociology of Health and Illness*, 12, 4: 452–477.

Freund, P. E. S. (1998) 'Social performances and their discontents: the biopsycho-social aspects of dramaturgical stress', in G. Bendelow and S. J. Williams (eds) *Emotions in Social Life: Critical Themes and Contemporary Issues*, London and New York: Routledge.

Fulder, S. (1996) *The Handbook of Alternative and Complementary Medicine*, Oxford: Oxford University Press.

Gard, M. and Wright, J. (2005) *The Obesity Epidemic: Science, Morality and Ideology*, London and New York: Routledge.

Garland, D. (1997) 'Governmentality and the problem of crime: Foucault, criminology, sociology', *Theoretical Criminology*, 1, 2: 173–214.

Gibson, O. (2005) 'L'Oréal pulls TV ads after ruling', *The Guardian*, 17 August, p. 9.

Giddens, A. (1991) *Modernity and Self-Identity: Self and Society in the Late Modern Age*, Cambridge: Polity Press.

Giddens, A. (1992) *The Consequences of Modernity*, Cambridge: Polity Press.

Gilleard C and Higgs P. (2005) *Contexts of Ageing: Class, Cohort and Community*, Cambridge: Polity Press.

Gillman, S. (1988) *Disease and Representation: Images of Illness from Madness to AIDS*, Ithaca, NY and London: Cornell University Press.

Gimlin, D. L. (2002) *Body Work: Beauty and Self-Image in American Culture*, Berkeley, CA: University of California Press.

Goffman, E. (1959) *The Presentation of Self in Everyday Life*, New York: Doubleday.

Goldenberg., S. (2006) 'Mothers sue over gender test that promised 99.9% accuracy', *The Guardian*, 18 March, p. 17.

Goldner, M. (2004) 'Consumption as activism: an examination of CAM as part of the consumer movement in health', in P. Tovey, G. Easthope and J. Adams (eds) *The Mainstreaming of Complementary and Alternative Medicine: Studies in Social Context*, London and New York: Routledge.

Gottweis, H. and Petersen, A. (in press) *Biobanks: Governance in Comparative Perspective*, London and New York: Routledge.

Gottweis, H. and Triendl, R. (2006) 'South Korean policy failure and the Hwang debacle', *Nature Biotechnology*, 24, 2: 141–143.

Grant, J. (1993) *Fundamental Feminism: Contesting the Core Concepts of Feminist Theory*, London: Routledge.

Gray, C. H. (2002) *Cyborg Citizen: Politics in the Posthuman Age*, New York and London: Routledge.

Grogan, S. (1999) *Body Image: Understanding Body Dissatisfaction in Men, Women and Children*, London and New York: Routledge.

Grogan, S. and Richards, H. (2002) 'Body image: focus groups with boys and men', *Men and Masculinities*, 4, 3: 219–232.

Grosz, E. (1994) *Volatile Bodies: Toward a Corporeal Feminism*, Crows Nest: Allen & Unwin.

Hacking, I. (1986) 'Making up people', in T. C. Heller, M. Sosna and D. E. Wellberg (eds) *Reconstructing Individualism: Autonomy, Individuality and the Self in Western Thought*, Stanford, CA: Stanford University Press.

Hacking, I. (1990) *The Taming of Chance*, Cambridge and New York: Cambridge University Press.

Hacking, I. (1999) *The Social Construction of What?*, Cambridge, MA: Harvard University Press.

Hahn, R. and Kleinman, A. (1981) 'Belief as pathogen, belief as medicine: "voodoo death" and the "placebo phenomenon" in anthropological perspective', Paper presented at the conference on 'Symbols, Meaning and Efficacy in the Healing Process' at the Meeting of the Society for Applied Anthropology, Edinburgh.

Cited in D. Howes (ed.) *The Varieties of Sensory Experience: A Sourcebook in the Anthropology of the Senses*, Toronto: University of Toronto Press.

Haraway, D. (1991) *Simians, Cyborgs, and Women: The Reinvention of Nature*, New York: Routledge.

Hayle, N. K. (1999) *How We Became Posthuman: Virtual Bodies in Cybernetics, Literature, and Informatics*, Chicago, IL and London: University of Chicago Press.

Hedgecoe, A. (2004) *The Politics of Personalised Medicine: Pharmacogenetics in the Clinic*, Cambridge: Cambridge University Press.

Henderson, S. and Petersen, A. (2002) *Consuming Health: the Commodification of Healthcare*, London and New York: Routledge.

Hill, A. (2005) 'Why beauty spas thank heaven for little girls', *The Observer*, 1 May, p. 9.

Hill, A. and McKie, R. (2006) 'We're having too much fun to act our age', *The Observer*, 5 March, p. 13.

Hochschild, A. R. (1983) *The Managed Heart: The Commercialization of Human Feeling*, Berkeley, CA: University of California Press.

Hochschild, A. R. (2003) *The Commercialization of Intimate Life: Notes from Home and Work*, Berkeley, CA: University of California Press.

Holtzman, N. A. and Marteau, T. (2000) 'Will genetics revolutionize medicine?', *New England Journal of Medicine*, 343, 2: 141–144.

House of Commons Health Committee (2004) *Obesity*, Third Report of Session 2003–04, vol. 1, Report, together with formal minutes, London: House of Commons Stationery Office.

House of Lords Science and Technology Committee (2005) First Report: *Ageing: Scientific Aspects*. Available online at <http://www.publications.parliament.uk/pa/ld200506/ldselect/ldsctech/20/2002.htm> (accessed 20 March 2006).

Hughes, K. (2004) 'Health as individual responsibility: possibilities and personal struggle', in P. Tovey, G. Easthope and J. Adams (eds) *The Mainstreaming of Complementary and Alternative Medicine: Studies in Social Context*, London and New York: Routledge.

Irwin, A. and Michael, M. (2003) *Science, Social Theory and Public Knowledge*, Maidenhead and Philadelphia: Open University Press.

James, N. (1989) 'Emotional labour: skill and work in the social regulation of feeling', *The Sociological Review*, 37, 1: 15–42.

Jasanoff, S. (2005) *Designs on Nature: Science and Democracy in Europe and the United States*, Princeton, NJ and Oxford: Princeton University Press.

Jeffreys, S. (2005) *Beauty and Misogyny: Harmful Cultural Practices*, New York: Routledge.

Jha, A. (2006) 'The future of old age', *The Guardian* (G2), 8 March, pp 6–9.

Juengst, E. (1998) 'What does "enhancement" mean?, in E. Parens (ed.) *Enhancing Human Traits: Ethical and Social Implications*, Washington, DC: Georgetown University Press.

Kallianes, V. and Rubenfeld, P. (1997) 'Disabled women and reproductive rights', *Disability and Society*, 12, 2: 203–21.

Karpf, A. (1988) *Doctoring the Media: The Reporting of Health and Medicine*, London and New York: Routledge.

Kawamura, K. Y. (2002) 'Asian American body images', in T. F. Cash and T. Pruzinsky (eds) *Body Image: A Handbook of Theory, Research, and Clinical Practice*, New York and London: Guilford Press.

Kelly, S. (2005) '"New" genetics meets the old underclass: findings from a study of genetic outreach services in rural Kentucky', in R. Bunton and A. Petersen (eds) *Genetic Governance: Health, Risk and Ethics in the Biotech Era*, London and New York: Routledge.

Kennedy, O. (2004) 'Hands-on-healing or a con? what do scientists think about "alternative" therapies?', in C. Donnellan (ed.) *Alternative Therapies*, Issues, vol. 81, Cambridge: Independence Educational Publishers.

Khamsi, R. (2005) 'Slim chance', *The Economist*, Summer 2005: 102–104.

King, D. (1995) 'The state of eugenics', *New Statesman and Society*, 25 August: 25–6.

Kingsbury, K. B. and Williams, M. E. (2003) *Weight Wisdom: Affirmations to Free you from Food and Body Concerns*, New York: Brunner-Routledge.

Kleinman, A. (1980) *Patients and Healers in the Context of Culture*, Berkeley, CA: University of California Press.

Kleinman, A. (1986) *Social Origins of Disease and Distress: Neurasthenia, Pain and Depression in Modern China*, New Haven, CT: Yale University Press.

Kleinman, A. (1988) *The Illness Narratives: Suffering, Healing and the Human Condition*, New York: Basic Books.

Krueger, D. W. (2002) 'Psychodynamic approaches to changing body image', in T. F. Cash and T. Pruzinsky (eds) *Body Image: A Handbook of Theory, Research, and Clinical Practice*, New York and London: Guilford Press.

Laqueur, T. (1990) *Making Sex: Body and Gender from the Greeks to Freud*, Cambridge, MA: Harvard University Press.

Larsen, R. and Pleck, J. (1998) 'Hidden feelings: emotionality in boys and men', in D. Bernstein (ed.) *Gender and Motivation*. vol. 45 of the Nebraska Symposium on Motivation, Lincoln, NB: University of Nebraska Press.

Latour, B. (1987) *Science in Action*, Milton-Keynes: Open University Press.

Latour, B. (2004) *The Politics of Nature: How to Bring the Sciences Into Democracy*, Cambridge, MA: Harvard University Press and London.

Latour, B. and Woolgar, S. (1986) *Laboratory Life*, 2nd edn, Princeton, NJ: Princeton University Press.

Law, J. (2005) *Big Pharma: How the World's Biggest Drug Companies Control Illness*, London: Constable.

Leder, D. (1990) *The Absent Body*, Chicago, IL and London: University of Chicago Press.

Leland, J., Murr, A., Kalb, C., Wingert, P., Hager, M. and Gegax, T. T. (1997) 'A pill for impotence?', *Newsweek* 17 November: 62–68.

LeVay, S. (1996) *Queer Science: The Use and Abuse of Research into Homosexuality*, Cambridge, MA: MIT Press.

Levine, M. P. and Smolak, L. (2002) 'Body image development in adolescence', in T. F. Cash and T. Pruzinsky (eds) *Body Image: A Handbook of Theory, Research, and Clinical Practice*, New York and London: Guilford Press.

Levitt, J. L., Sansone, R. A. and Cohn, L. (2004) *Self-harm Behaviour and Eating Disorders: Dynamics, Assessment and Treatment*, New York: Brunner-Routledge.

Lloyd, G. (1984) *The Man of Reason: 'Male' and 'Female' in Western Philosophy*, London: Methuen.

Loe, M. (2004) *The Rise of Viagra; How the Little Blue Pill Changed Sex in America*, New York and London: New York University Press.

Logan, R.A. (1991) 'Popularization versus secularization: media coverage of health', in L.Wilkins and P. Patterson (eds) *Risky Business: Communicating Issues of Science, Risk and Public Policy*, New York: Greenwood.

Lois, J. (2005) 'Gender and emotion management in the stages of edgework', in S. Lyng (ed.) *Edgework: The Sociology of Risk-Taking*, New York and London: Routledge.

Lopez, J. (2004) 'How sociology can save bioethics . . . maybe', *Sociology of Health and Illness*, 26, 7: 875–896.

Luscombe, R. (2005) 'US gets fatter – and faster than ever', *The Guardian*, August, p. 13.

Maason, S. and Weingart, P. (2000) *Metaphors and the Dynamics of Knowledge*, London and New York: Routledge.

McCartney, M. (2005) 'Take with a pinch of sodium chloride', *The Guardian* (G2), 18 August, pp. 2–3.

McCurry, J. (2006) 'Video games for the elderly: an answer to dementia or a marketing tool?', *The Guardian*, 7 March, p. 23.

McKie, R. (2005) 'Scans that read mind fuel ethical worries', *The Observer*, 20 March, p. 13.

MacLennan, A. H., Wilson, D. H., Taylor, A. W. (2002) 'The escalating cost and prevalence of alternative medicine', *Preventive Medicine*, 35: 166–173.

McLuhan, M. and Fiore, Q. (2001; orig. 1967) *The Medium is the Massage: An Inventory of Effects*, Corte Madera, CA: Ginko Press.

MacSween, M. (1993) *Anorexic Bodies: A Feminist and Sociological Perspective on Anorexia Nervosa*, London and New York: Routledge.

Malcolm, N. (1972) *Problems of Mind: Descartes to Wittgenstein*, London: Allen & Unwin.

Mamo, L. and Fishman, J. R. (2001) 'Potency in all the right places: Viagra as a technology of the gendered body', *Body & Society*, 7, 4: 13–35.

Marks, D. J. B., Harbord, M. W. N., MacAllister, R., Rahman, F. Z., Young J., Al-Lazikani, B., Lees, W., Novelli, M., Bloom, S. and Segal, A. W. (2006) 'Defective acute inflammation in Crohn's disease: a clinical investigation', *The Lancet*, 367, 9511 (25 February): 668–678.

Martin, K. A. and Lichtenberger, C. M (2002) 'Fitness enhancement and changes in body image', in T. F. Cash and T. Pruzinsky (eds) *Body Image: A Handbook of Theory, Research, and Clinical Practice*, New York and London: Guilford Press.

Marx, K. (1972) *The Economic and Philosophic Manuscripts of 1844*, ed. D. J. Struik, New York: International Publishers.

Matz, J. and Frankel, E. (2004) *Beyond a Shadow of a Diet: the Therapist's Guide to Treating Compulsive Eating*, New York: Brunner-Routledge.

Mauss, M. (1973) 'Techniques of the body', *Economy and Society*, 2, 1: 70–88.

May, C. (1992) 'Nursing work, nurses' knowledge, and the subjectification of the patient', *Sociology of Health and Illness*, 14, 4: 473–87.

Medical News Today (8 December 2004) Available online at <http://www.medical newstoday.com/medicalnews.php?newsid=17472> (accessed 12 May 2005).

Meikle, J. (2005) 'Public health bodies issue warning over the growing number of cases of diabetes', *The Guardian*, 16 May. Available online at <http://society. guardian.co.uk/publichealth/story/0,,1484784,00.html> (accessed 16 June 2006).

Mellor, P. A. and Shilling, C. (1997) *Reforming the Body: Religion, Community and Modernity*, London: Sage.

Miah, A. (2004) *Genetically Modified Athletes: Biomedical Ethics, Gene Doping and Sport*, London and New York: Routledge.

Milburn, C. (2004) 'Nanotechnology in the age of posthuman engineering: science fiction as science', in N. K. Hayles (ed.) *Nanoculture: Implications of the New Technoscience*, Bristol: Intellect Books.

Miller, F. A., Ahern, C., Smith, C. A. and Harvey, E. H. (2005) 'Understanding the new human genetics: a review of scientific editorials', *Social Science and Medicine*, 62, 10: 2373–2385.

Miller, P. and Wilsdon, J. (2006) *Better Humans?: The Politics of Human Enhancement and Life Extension*, London: Demos. Available online at <http://www.demos.co.uk/catalogue/betterhumanscollection> (accessed 19 May 2006).

Minton, H. L. (1996) 'Community empowerment and the medicalization of homosexuality: constructing sexual identities in the 1930s', *Journal of the History of Sexuality*, 6, 3: 435–458.

Mitchell, J. E. and Peterson, C. B. (2005) *Assessment of Eating Disorders*, New York: Guildford Publications.

Monaghan, L. F. (2005) 'Big handsome men, bears and others: virtual constructions of "fat male embodiment"', *Body and Society*, 11, 2: 81–111.

Morgan, K. P. (1991) 'Women and the knife: cosmetic surgery and the colonization of women's bodies', *Hypatia*, 6: 25–53.

Morris, B. (1994) *Anthropology of the Self: The Individual in Cultural Perspective*, London: Pluto Press.

Morris, D. B. (1998) *Illness and Culture in the Postmodern Age*, Berkeley, CA: University of California Press.

Moynihan, R. (2003) 'The making of a disease: female sexual dysfunction', *British Medical Journal*, 326: 45–47.

Moynihan, R. and Cassels, A. (2005) *Selling Sickness: How Drug Companies Are Turning Us All Into Patients*, Crows Nest: Allen & Unwin.

Moynihan, R., Heath, I. and Henry, D. (2002) 'Selling sickness: the pharmaceutical industry and disease mongering', *British Medical Journal*, 324: 886–891.

Nanoforum.org (2006) *Nanotechnology in Agriculture and Food*, April 2006. Available online at <http://www.nanoforum.org>.

Nasser, M. (1997) *Culture and Weight Consciousness*, London and New York: Routledge.

Nasser, M. Katzman, M. A. and Gordon, R. A. (2002) *Eating Disorders and Cultures in Transition*, New York: Brunner-Routledge.

National Audit Office (2001) *Tackling Obesity in England*, Report by the Comptroller and Auditor General, London: Stationery Office.

Negrin, L. (2002) 'Cosmetic surgery and the eclipse of identity', *Body & Society*, 8, 4: 21–42.

Nelkin, D. (1985) 'Managing biomedical news', *Social Research*, 52, 3: 625–646.

Nelkin, D. (1987) *Selling Science: How the Press Covers Science and Technology*, New York: W. H. Freeman and Co.

Nelkin, D. and Andrews, L. (1999) 'DNA identification and surveillance creep', in P. Conrad and J. Gabe (eds) *Sociological Perspectives on the New Genetics*, Oxford: Blackwell.

Neumark-Sztainer, D. (2005) *'I'm, Like, SO fat!': Helping your Teen Make Healthy Choices about Eating and Exercise in a Weight-Obsessed World*, New York: Guildford Press.

Nowotny, H., Scott, P. and Gibbons, M. (2001) *Re-thinking Science: Knowledge and the Public in an Age of Uncertainty*, Cambridge: Polity Press.

O'Malley, P. (1996) 'Indigenous governance', *Economy and Society*, 25, 3: 310–326.

O'Malley, P. (2004) *Risk, Uncertainty and Government*, London: Glasshouse Press.

Öberg, P. (2003) 'Images versus experience of the ageing body', in C. A. Faircloth (ed.) *Aging Bodies: Images and Everyday Experience*, Walnut Creek, CA: Alta Mira Press.

Olshansky, S. J., Perry, D., Miller, R. A., and Butler, R. N. (2006) 'In pursuit of the longevity dividend: what should we be doing to prepare for the unprecedented aging of humanity?', *The Scientist*, 20, 3: 28. Available online at <http://www. the-scientist.com/toc/2006/3/> (accessed 9 March 2006).

Ong, C-K and Banks, B. (2003) *Complementary and Alternative Medicine: The Consumer Perspective*, The Prince of Wales Foundation for Integrated Health, p. 13. Available online at <http://www.fondazionericci.it/flex/files/D.1e0ca72fef1 b866acb72/Complementary_and_Alternative_Medicine_the_consumer_perspect ive.pdf> (accessed 21 April 2006).

Oudshoorn, N. (1994) *Beyond the Natural Body: An Archeology of Sex Hormones*, London: Routledge.

Orbach, S. (1989; orig. 1978) *Fat is a Feminist Issue: How to Lose Weight Permanently – Without Dieting*, London: Arrow.

Orbach, S. (1993) *Hunger Strike: The Anorectic's Struggle as a Metaphor for Our Age*, London: Penguin Books.

Parfitt, T. (2005) 'Beauty salons fuel trade in aborted babies', *The Observer*, World, 17 April, p. 24.

Paul, D. (1998) *The Politics of Heredity: Essays on Eugenics, Biomedicine and the Nature–Nurture Debate*, New York: State University of New York Press.

Peiss, K. (1998) *Hope in a Jar: The Making of America's Beauty Culture*, New York: Metropolitan Books.

Peters, D. (2005) 'Editorial: Bio-medicine in crisis: cost, cure, compassion and commitment', *Journal of Holistic Healthcare*, 2, 1: 2–3.

Petersen, A. R. (1996) 'Risk and the regulated self: the discourse of health promotion as politics of uncertainty', *Australian and New Zealand Journal of Sociology*, 32, 1: 44–57.

Petersen, A. (1998a) *Unmasking the Masculine: 'Men' and 'Identity' in a Sceptical Age*, London: Sage.

Petersen, A. (1998b) 'Sexing the body: representations of sex differences in Gray's Anatomy, 1858 to the present', *Body & Society*, 4, 1: 1–15.

Petersen, A. (1999) 'The portrayal of research into genetic-based differences of sex and sexual orientation: a study of "popular" science journals, 1980–1997', *Journal of Communication Inquiry*, 23, 2: 163–182.

Petersen, A. (2000) 'Homosexuality, pathologization of', in L. Code (ed.), *Routledge Encyclopedia of Feminist Theories*, London: Routledge.

Petersen, A. (2001) 'Biofantasies: genetics and medicine in the print news media', *Social Science and Medicine*, 52: 1255–1268.

Petersen, A. (2002) 'Replicating our bodies, losing our selves: news media portrayals of human cloning in the wake of Dolly', *Body & Society*, 8, 4: 71–90.

Petersen, A. (2004) *Engendering Emotions*, Houndmills: Palgrave Macmillan.

Petersen, A. (2005a) 'Securing our genetic health: engendering trust in UK Biobank', *Sociology of Health and Illness*, 27, 2: 271–292.

Petersen, A. (2005b) 'The metaphors of risk: biotechnology in the news' (Editorial) *Health, Risk and Society*, 7, 3: 203–208.

Petersen, A. (2006) 'The genetic conception of health: is it as radical as claimed?, *Health*, 10th Anniversary Issue on 'Conceptions of Health', 10, 4: 481–500.

Petersen, A. (In press) 'Is the new genetics eugenic? Interpreting the past, envisioning the future', *New Formations*.

Petersen, A. and Bunton, R. (2002) *The New Genetics and the Public's Health*, London and New York: Routledge.

Petersen, A. and Bunton, R. (eds) (1997) *Foucault, Health and Medicine*, London and New York: Routledge.

Petersen, A. and Lupton, D. (1996) *The New Public Health: Health and Self in the Age of Risk*, London: Sage.

Petersen, A. and Regan de Bere, S. (2006) 'Dissecting medicine: gender biases in the discourses and practices of medical anatomy', in D. Rosenfeld and C. A. Faircloth (eds) *Medicalized Masculinities*, Philadelphia, PA: Temple University Press.

Petersen, A. and Winkler, A. (1992) 'The contribution of the social sciences to nurse education in Australia', *Annual Review of Health Social Science*, 2: 21–33.

Petersen, A. R. and Davies, D. (1997) 'Psychology and the social construction of sex differences in theories of aggression', *Journal of Gender Studies*, 6, 3: 309–320.

Petersen, A., Anderson, A. and Allan, S. (2005) 'Science fiction/science fact: medical genetics in news stories', *New Genetics and Society*, 24, 3: 337–353.

Petryna, A. (2002) *Life Exposed: Biological Citizens After Chernobyl*, Princeton, NJ and Oxford: Princeton University Press.

Phillips, K. A. and Castle, D. J. (2002) 'Body dysmorphic disorder' in D. J. Castle and K. A. Phillips (eds) *Disorders of Body Image*, Petersfield and Philadelphia, PA: Wrightson Biomedical Publishing Ltd.

Pitts, V. (2003) *In the Flesh: The Cultural Politics of Body Modification*, New York and Basingstoke: Palgrave.

Popenoe, R. (2004) *Feeding Desire: Fatness, Beauty, and Sexuality among a Saharan People*, London: Routledge.

Porter, R. (2003) *Flesh in the Age of Reason*, London: Allen Lane.

Rabinor, J. R. and Bilich, M. A. (2002) 'Experiential approaches to changing body image', in T. F. Cash and T. Pruzinsky (eds) *Body Image: A Handbook of Theory, Research, and Clinical Practice*, New York and London: Guilford Press.

Rabinow, P. (1992) 'Artificiality and enlightenment: from sociobiology to bio-sociality', in J. Crary and S. Kwinter (eds) *Incorporations*, New York: Urzone.

Ramazanoglu, C. (ed.) (1993) *Up Against Foucault: Explorations of Some Tensions Between Foucault and Feminism*, New York: Routledge.

Rapp, R. (1999) *Testing Women, Testing the Fetus: The Social Impact of Amniocentesis in America*, New York and London: Routledge.

Reddy, W. M. (2001) *The Navigation of Feeling: A Framework for the History of Emotions*, Cambridge: Cambridge University Press.

Restak, R. (2003) *The New Brain: How the Modern Age is Rewiring Your Mind*, London: Rodale.

Revill, J. (2002) 'Transplant surgeons look the future in the face', *The Observer*, 24 November, p. 1.

Rheinberger, H.–J. (1995) 'Beyond nature and culture: a note on medicine in the age of molecular biology', *Science in Context*, 8, 1: 249–263.

Richardson, R. (2001) *Death, Dissection and the Destitute*, London: Phoenix Press.

Rock, P. J. (1996) 'Eugenics and euthanasia: a cause for concern for disabled people, particularly disabled women', *Disability and Society*, 11, 1: 121–127.

Rojek, C. (2001) *Celebrity*, London: Reaktion Books.

Rose, N. (1990) *Governing the Soul: The Shaping of the Private Self*, London: Routledge.

Rose, N. (1999) *Powers of Freedom: Reframing Political Thought*, Cambridge: Cambridge University Press.

Rose, S. (2005) *The 21st Century Brain: Explaining, Mending and Manipulating the Mind*, London: Jonathan Cape.

Royal Society (2005) *Personalised Medicine: Hopes and Realities*, London: Royal Society. Available online at <http://www.royalsoc.ac.uk/displaypagedoc.asp?id=17570> (accessed 17 March 2006).

Royal Society and Royal Academy of Engineering (2004) *Nanoscience and Nanotechnologies: Opportunities and Uncertainties*, London: RS/RAE.

Rozemond, M. (1998) *Descartes' Dualism*, Cambridge, MA: Harvard University Press and London.

Sabo, D. F. and Gordon, D. (1995) *Men's Health and Illness: Gender, Power and the Body*, London: Sage.

Saks, M. (1995) *Professions and the Public Interest: Medical Power, Altruism and Alternative Medicine*, London and New York: Routledge.

Saks, M. (1996) 'From quackery to complementary medicine', in S. Cant and U. Sharma (eds) *Complementary and Alternative Medicines: Knowledge in Practice*, London and New York: Free Association Books.

Sample, I. (2005) 'Overweight who diet risk dying earlier, says study', *The Guardian*, 27 June, p. 1.

Sample, I. (2005a) 'Chip reads mind of paralysed man', *The Guardian*, 31 March, p. 1.

Sample, I. (2005b) 'Read the book, seen the movie? Now smell it too', *The Guardian*, 7 April. Available online at <http://www.guardian.co.uk/life/news/story/0,12976,1453921,00.html> (accessed 24 May 2006).

Sappol, M. (2002) *A Traffic in Dead Bodies: Anatomy and Embodied Social Identity in Nineteenth-Century America*, Princeton, NJ and Oxford: Princeton University Press.

Sapsted, D. (2006) 'Uproar over IVF woman expecting a baby at 63', *The Daily Telegraph*, 5 May, p. 1.

Sarwer, D. B. (2002) 'Cosmetic surgery and changes in body image', in T. F. Cash and T. Pruzinsky (eds) *Body Image: A Handbook of Theory, Research, and Clinical Practice*, New York and London: Guilford Press.

Sarwer, D. B. and Didie, E. R. (2002) 'Body image in cosmetic surgical and dermatological practice', in D. J. Castle and K. A. Phillips (eds) *Disorders of Body Image*, Petersfield and Philadelphia, PA: Wrightson Biomedical Publishing Ltd.

Sawicki, J. (1991) *Disciplining Foucault: Feminism, Power and the Body*, New York: Routledge.

Schiebinger, L. (1989) *The Mind Has No Sex?: Women in the Origins of Modern Science*, Cambridge, MA: Harvard University Press.

Schiebinger, L. (1993) *Nature's Body: Gender in the Making of Modern Science*, Boston: Beacon Press.

Sedgwick, E. K. (1994) *Epistemology of the Closet*, London: Penguin.

Seed, J., Allin, L. J., Olivier, S. C., Szabo, C. P., Nxumalo, S. (undated) *Socio-cultural Factors and Perceptions of Attractiveness in Black South African Female University Students: The Role of Men*, Project summary document, Newcastle: Northumbria University.

Shakespeare, T. (1998) 'Choices and rights: eugenics, genetics and disability equality', *Disability and Society*, 13, 5: 665–681.

Sharma, U. (1995) *Complementary Medicine Today: Practitioners and Patients*, London and New York: Routledge.

Shell, E. R. (2003) *Fat Wars: The Inside Story of the Obesity Industry*, London: Atlantic Books.

Shilling, C. (1993) *The Body and Social Theory*, London: Sage.

Smith, D. (1987) *The Everyday World as Problematic: A Feminist Sociology*, Toronto: University of Toronto Press.

Smith, D. (1999) *Reading the Social: Critique, Theory and Investigations*, Toronto: University of Toronto Press.

Soper, K. (1995) *What is Nature?: Culture, Politics and the Non-Human*, Oxford: Blackwell.

Spivak, G. C. (1993) *Outside the Teaching Machine*, New York: Routledge.

Stafford, N. (2005) 'EU won't up stem cell funding', *The Scientist*, 19 April.

Steinberg, D. (1997) *Bodies in Glass: Genetics, Eugenics, Embryo Ethics*, Manchester and New York: Manchester University Press.

Stenson, J. (1998) 'Beyond histories of the present', *Economy and Society*, 27, 4: 333–352.

Stock, G. and Campbell, J. (eds) (2000) *Engineering the Human Germline: An Exploration of the Science and Ethics of Altering the Genes We Pass to Our Children*, New York and Oxford: Oxford University Press.

Striegel-Moore, R. H. and Franko, D. L. (2002) 'Body image issues among girls and women', in T. F. Cash and T. Pruzinsky (eds) *Body Image: A Handbook of Theory, Research, and Clinical Practice*, New York and London: Guilford Press.

Synnott, A. (1991) 'Puzzling over the senses: from Plato to Marx', in D. Howes (ed.) *The Varieties of Sensory Experience: A Sourcebook in the Anthropology of the Senses*, Toronto: University of Toronto Press.

Szaz, T. S. (1974) *The Myth of Mental Illness: Foundations of a Theory of Personal Conduct*, New York: Harper and Row.

Terry, J. (1995) 'Anxious slippages between "us" and "them": a brief history of the sexual search for homosexual bodies', in J. Terry and J. Urla (eds) *Deviant Bodies: Critical Perspectives on Science and Popular Culture*, Bloomington, IN: Indiana University Press.

Thacker, E. (2004) *Biomedia*, Minnesota, MN and London: University of Minnesota Press and Minneapolis Press.

Thornhill, R. and Palmer, C. T. (2000) *A Natural History of Rape: Biological Bases of Sexual Coercion*, Cambridge, MA and London: MIT Press.

Tomlinson, H. and Adam, D. (2005) 'China surges ahead in stem cell science', *The Guardian*, 24 January. Available online at <http://www.guardian.co.uk/genes/article/0,2763,1396905,00.html> (accessed 16 May 2005).

Tonkinson, R. (1974) *The Jigalong Mob: Aboriginal Victors of the Desert Crusade*, Menlo Park: Cummings Publishing.

Tovey, P., Easthope, G. and Adams, J. (2004) 'Introduction', in P. Tovey, G. Easthope and J. Adams (eds) *The Mainstreaming of Complementary and*

Alternative Medicine: Studies in Social Context, London and New York: Routledge.

Tremlett, G. (2006) 'Spain becomes the destination of choice for fertility tourists from Britain', *The Guardian*, 12 May, p. 16.

Turner, B. (1992) *Regulating Bodies: Essays in Medical Sociology*, London and New York: Routledge.

Turner, B. (1996) *The Body and Society: Explorations in Social Theory*, 2nd edn, London: Sage.

Turner, B. S. (1991) *Religion and Social Theory*, London: Sage.

Twine, R. (2002) 'Physiognomy, phrenology and the temporality of the body', *Body & Society*, 8, 1: 67–88.

van der Meer, T. (1994) 'Sodomy and the pursuit of the third sex in the early modern period', in G. Herdt (ed.) *Third Sex, Third Gender: Beyond Sexual Dimorphism in Culture and History*, New York: Zone Books.

Vincent, J. (2003) *Old Age*, London and New York: Routledge.

Waldby, C. (2000) *The Visible Human Project: Informatic Bodies and Posthuman Medicine*, London and New York: Routledge.

Warren, K. (ed.) (1994) *Ecological Feminism*, London: Routledge.

Weeks, J. (1977) *Coming Out: Homosexual Politics in Britain from the Nineteenth Century to the Present*, London: Quartet Books.

Weeks, J. (2003) *Sexuality*, 2nd edn, London and New York: Routledge.

Wertz, D. C. (1999) 'Patients' and professionals views on autonomy, disability and "discrimination": results of a 36-nationl survey', in T. A. Caulfield and B. Williams-Jones (eds) *The Commercialization of Genetic Research: Ethical, Legal and Policy Issues*, Dordrecht: Kluwer Academic/Plenum Publishers.

West, C. and Zimmerman, D. H. (1991) 'Doing gender', in J. Lorber and S. A. Farrell (eds) *The Social Construction of Gender*, Newbury Park, CA: Sage.

Wilkinson, I. (2005) *Suffering: A Sociological Introduction*, Cambridge: Polity Press.

Wilkinson, R. G. (1996) *Unhealthy Societies: The Afflictions of Inequality*, London and New York: Routledge.

Williams, S. J. (2006) 'Medical sociology and the biological body: where are we now and where do we go from here?', *Health*, 10, 1: 5–30.

Williams, S. J. and Bendelow, G. (1998) *The Lived Body: Sociological Themes, Embodied Issues*, London: Routledge.

Williams, S. J., Birke, L. and Bendelow, G. A. (eds) (2003) *Debating Biology: Sociological Reflections on Health, Medicine and Society*, London and New York: Routledge.

Willis, E. (1989) *Medical Dominance*, revd edn, Crows Nest: Allen & Unwin.

Willis, E. and White, K. (2004) 'Evidence-based medicine and CAM', in P. Tovey, G. Easthope and J. Adams (eds) *The Mainstreaming of Complementary and Alternative Medicine: Studies in Social Context*, London and New York: Routledge.

Wilsdon, J. and Willis, R. (2004) *See-through-Science: Why Public Engagement Needs to Move Upstream*, London: Demos.

Wintour, P. (2006) 'Radical moves to tackle obesity crisis', *The Guardian*, 16 June, p. 1.

Winzelberg, A. J., Abascal, L. and Taylor, C. B. (2002) 'Psychoeducational approaches to the prevention and change of negative body image', in T. F. Cash and T. Pruzinsky (eds) *Body Image: A Handbook of Theory, Research, and Clinical Practice*, New York and London: Guilford Press.

Wolf, N. (1990) *The Beauty Myth: How Images of Beauty Are Used Against Women*, New York: Vintage.

Wouters, C. (1991) 'On status competition and emotion management', *Journal of Social History*, 24, 4: 699–717.

Wouters, C. (1998) 'Changes in the "lust balance" of sex and love since the sexual revolution', in G. Bendelow and S. J. Williams (eds) *Emotions in Social Life: Critical Themes and Contemporary Issues*, London and New York: Routledge.

Young, R. J. C. (1995) *Colonial Desire: Hybridity in Theory, Culture and Race*, London: Routledge.

Zuckerman, D. (2003) 'Hype in health reporting: "check book" buys distortion of medical news', *International Journal of Health Services*, 33, 2: 383–389.

Index

Contradictory
Cultural
impulses